Mario Writes
a Poem
a Day
For
a Year
and So
Can You

# Also by Mario Milosevic

**Poetry**
*Animal Life*
*Fantasy Life*
*Love Life*

**Novels**
*Claypot Dreamstance*
*The Coma Monologues*
*The Doctor and the Clown*
*Kyle's War*
*The Last Giant*
*Splitting*
*Terrastina and Mazolli*

**Collections**
*Entangled Realities* (with Kim Antieau)
*Labor Days*
*Miniatures*
*Mostly Invisible*
*20 Strange Tales of Crime and Mystery*

**Nonfiction**
*Kim and Mario Build a Labyrinth and So Can You* (with Kim Antieau)

# Mario Writes
a Poem
a Day
for
a Year
and So
Can You

## Mario Milosevic

*Mario Writes a Poem a Day for a Year and So Can You*
by Mario Milosevic

Copyright © 2021 by Mario Milosevic

ISBN: 978-1-949644-62-3

Thanks to Nancy Milosevic

Cover and author photos by Kim Antieau

Published by Green Snake Publishing
www.greensnakepublishing.com

# Contents

Introduction *7*

October *9*
November *19*
December *69*
January *123*
February *177*
March *219*
April *265*
May *317*
June *363*
July *403*
August *451*
September *491*
October *531*

Further Reading *567*
About the Author *571*

# Introduction

Why write a poem a day for a year? Good question. After all, poetry has a limited audience, there's no money in it, and a poet's influence on the culture registers as barely a blip.

Here are what I consider some good reasons for writing poetry:

First, writing poetry sharpens your mind. The whole point of poetry is to be concise. That takes practice and a willingness to see things in a light different than what folks are accustomed to.

Second, writing poetry helps you appreciate the world. Once you commit to writing a poem a day, you will always be looking for the beautiful vision, the telling moment, the memory rich in meaning, or the trick of perception that opens your head and your heart.

Third, writing poetry is fun!

That last reason is the best reason of all.

I have recounted my adventures in poetry before. You can find my essay on the subject in Kim Antieau's marvelously inspiring book, *Answering the Creative Call*. There I explain how daily practice makes you a better writer because it sets you up to receive inspiration and gives you the tools to make the best use of that inspiration when it comes. I applied a lot of the lessons from that essay to this current project.

I learned to be a poet by writing poetry. It's that simple. Years ago I decided I wanted to learn the craft, and I told myself I would write a poem a day for a year. It was to be learning by doing.

I succeeded in that task and I continued writing a poem a day for two more years. Before this project I hadn't been writing much poetry but decided it would be fun to try a poem a day for a year again, and I was right. It was a ball. This book is the result of my latest year of daily poetry practice.

This time around I not only wrote the poems, but I also wrote a commentary for each poem. I tell where the poem came from, how it was composed, what tricks I used to bring readers into the poem, and many other aspects of verse making.

My hope is that my project will inspire you to do the same. Take the plunge and commit to producing poetic visions every day for a year.

You don't have to go it alone, either. I didn't.

Poets are part of a long tradition of verse. There's no reason not to take advantage of all the work done before you. I read many poets during my year and also read books on poetic theory and poetic practice. I list all the sources I used during this project at the end of the book.

I won't guarantee that making a poem a day will make you a great poet, but I believe such an exercise has every chance of making you a better poet and writer, and I'm willing to bet that if you give it your all you'll find it completely absorbing and enjoyable.

If you do decide to do as I did, I would suggest that you don't worry too much about creating immortal lines. Just do the work. One day at a time. Think of it as daily practice or meditation. It can be your way of connecting with your spirit and with the world around you.

I've included every single poem I wrote this past year in this book. Although I did some editing and/or revising of the poems on the day of composition, I am presenting them here with no further changes. Some I believe are very good, others not so good. It doesn't matter! I did it. I produced, and I had a good time with it.

I also repeated themes, motifs, techniques, subjects, and approaches, but that doesn't matter either. All it means is that a particular approach or theme intrigued me enough to try it a second or even a third time. For example, I did two grasshopper poems. I liked one better than the other. I won't tell you which.

Remember, even if only a few of your poems are any good, that's still a good thing. A .300 batter, someone who hits the ball only three times out of ten, is a baseball superstar.

I hope that by presenting every poem I did for a year, you will get some insights into how a poet works and what it takes to be a poet.

I also want to show you that writing quickly gets the truest freshest work out from your heart and brain and onto the page.

With all that in mind, I invite you to follow along with me on my epic journey.

Onward!

—Mario Milosevic
2 November 2020
Tucson, Arizona

# October

# The Art of Flattery

Mozart once
went into
a bird
shop where

he heard
a starling

singing a
melody he

had composed
and which

had not
been performed

more than
a couple

of times.
He bought

the bird
on the

spot and
brought it

home. The
bird and

the composer
were friends

for years
and years.

—*28 October 2019*

On NPR a couple of years ago, I heard about Mozart and his bird and how they met. I liked the idea of Mozart being flattered by a bird. This morning, casting about for a start to this project, I decided putting the story into poetic form would bring out the magic in the relationship. With the title, I wanted to raise the possibility that the bird knew exactly what it was doing. That is unlikely, of course, but poetry, if it is anything at all, is about the possibility of the unlikely.

I chose a form I more or less invented for myself a few years ago when I wrote some poems for Kim Antieau's Queendom project. I ascribed those poems to a fictional poet named Praxilla. The form is simple: a series of four-word stanzas, each line composed of two words. It's light and airy and very versatile. To me, it mimics nature: quick and transformative.

So here's the first lesson for those of you wanting to do your own poem-a-day project: don't be afraid to invent your own form for your poetry. Doing so can give you a real sense of freedom.

# Roadrunner

They're the sort of
creature, I think,

that wouldn't want to
be called a critter.

Too badass for that.
They kill rattlesnakes

and they don't say
*meep meep* like in the

cartoons. I saw one
killing a baby rabbit

once. The roadrunner
scurried away with its

meal in its beak. Tearing
up the dust, putting

distance between us
like a perspective view

of life, carrying death
to some distant destiny.

*—29 October 2019*

---

I wrote this poem next to a window that looks out on desert land. I actually did see a roadrunner through this window a few months previously, and it was methodically smashing a baby rabbit against a rock, killing it, I surmised, preparatory to eating it. It ran off with its prey after a minute or two. I knew roadrunners were good hunters but to see it in the act was a revelation. Breathtaking in an awesome and repellant way.

    Anything can be the inspiration for a poem, even things that are not particularly inspiring.

# Apparition

We get
in the

car, ready
to leave

the Sanctuary.
Drive down

the dirt
road, see

quail in
the distance.

They startle,
surprised nuns,

then dart
out of

view, leaving
a cartoon

cloud of
dust hanging

in the
air like

a puff
of dragon

breath or
a ghost

slipping away
to oblivion.

*—29 October 2019*

My first two-poem day. This one was for Kim's Patreon subscribers. I promised them one poem a month. Poems often start with an image, and that is true here. We saw a flock of quail on our driveway, and when they sensed us they skeedadled away, leaving a puff of dust, just like in an animated cartoon.

Look for these kinds of events in your life. They don't have to be big. They don't have to be earth-shaking. They just have to catch your interest. And when they do, they can be shaped into a poem.

Note that the form is the same as the one I used for yesterday's poem, "The Art of Flattery."

## The Bite of Old Tears

My father wasn't much of a cook.
Pancakes, French fries. The occasional

grilled pork chop. The one time
I saw him chop an onion

he said he would never do it again.
Tears stinging his eyes. Squinting

as though blinded by some
overpowering light. It's been 30

years since he died. Or close to it.
Yesterday I was chopping onions.

I thought of him doing the same.
My tears were from grief,

maybe. Or just the onion fumes.
I couldn't tell, which was

all to the good, I suppose.
Maybe time had healed the

sharp stabbing
pain.

*—30 October 2019*

---

Another thing for a poet to look for is connections across time. Kim and I were cooking in the kitchen together yesterday. I was chopping an onion and that brought up tears. I remembered a time my father chopped an onion, and he began crying from the tears. Sometimes those kinds of memories are random, coincidental. Other times, though, they can mean something. They are bridges bringing the past into the present. I tried to make that connection in the poem.

By now you probably realize that I favor poems constructed of two-line stanzas. I like the airy feel of them. They invite a reader in and seem natural, like a conversation. Don't worry if you find yourself gravitating to a particular form or subject again and again. Many creative folks till the same field season after season. Follow your heart and do what works for you, what brings you satisfaction.

# The Perils of Living Fashionably

A certain young hipster from Portland
wore his hair exquisitely man-bunned.
    It set off his beard,
      but he was afeared
of losing his friends and being shunned.

*—31 October 2019*

When I lived in Washington state I would visit Portland often and noticed a few years ago that many bearded young men wore their hair in a bun on top of their heads. I soon learned that this appeared to be a national trend, and I also learned that many people considered the look to be less than attractive. It made me wonder if anyone wearing a man bun might be a little apprehensive about the reaction his hairstyle might get from his acquaintances. Yesterday I saw some man buns in Tucson and decided I could turn the subject into a humorous verse.

    I chose the limerick form. It's a familiar and friendly form with a pleasing meter and a simple rhyme scheme: aabba. It is often bawdy, but not in this case. The form generally benefits from a polysyllabic word or two, hence "exquisitely." I got the first 4 lines fairly quickly. The last one defeated me for a while. I couldn't find a suitable final rhyme for a long time. I played with "punned," "fund," and a few others, but none of them yielded a satisfying last line. "Shunned" came to me when I took a break from the poem and cooked some breakfast. Then the last line wrote itself.

    As a poet, it's good to notice how words are pronounced. For example, the city is spelled Port*land*, but it is most often pronounced something like Port*lund*. Without that pronunciation, the limerick doesn't work.

    Obviously this is not an earth-shattering subject, but not every poem or verse has to be. Try your hand at some light verse and do stick to the rhyme scheme. Finding surprising or unexpected rhymes is a discipline in itself and makes your mind stretch in directions it might not otherwise go.

# November

# The Role of the Artist in Modern Society

After Craig
died his portrait turned to mold and decay.

The artist
who had made the picture had

retreated
to a life of obscurity in the hills

high above
the Columbia River. Craig's relatives made the

pilgrimage
to the artist's cabin and begged her

to come out
of retirement and fix Craig's portrait.

The artist
was sympathetic but refused. *Look up at the*

*stars*, she said.
*Look for his portrait there, in Nature's wild*

*pure brush strokes.*

*—1 November 2019*

---

This one began with an image: people gathered around a woman standing on a hilltop. I didn't question where it came from. Instead, I pursued it. Who was the woman? Who were the people? What did they want? A back-story quickly came out of my questions, and I produced the poem from that back-story.

Many of us have fleeting images go through our minds. Most of the time we might not even notice them. When we do, we quickly forget them. Poets benefit from doing the exact opposite. Pay attention to those images. They might come from somewhere deep. Which is where poetry can flourish.

I invented a form for this one: a series of two-line stanzas, the first line of each stanza being exactly three syllables long, with the last stanza dropping the second line, which nicely highlights the last three words.

# Fences

So many.
They carve the world.
Built by strangers.
Anonymous constructions.
We stumble against them.
Grip them sometimes
with trembling hands.
Lean on them.
Push hard to topple them
if we see a need.
But the law protects them
always.
Supported by the
power structure,
they hold us all
hostage, pinning
alienation to the
ground.

*—2 November 2019*

I woke up with one impulse: write a poem about fences. I went directly to the computer and typed out the first few lines that appeared in my head.

No particular form to this one. Once you start writing poems regularly, they will begin to come to you unbidden, as this one did. Go with it. Don't edit yourself. Get it written; then if needed, go back and edit what you wrote. But make sure the revision truly is needed before you wade in and begin swapping out words and rearranging lines willy-nilly. As Allen Ginsburg was fond of saying: "First thought, best thought," which is another way of saying "Trust your instincts."

# Tombstone Gold

At the end of a fake
stream in Tombstone,
where tourists pay to
pan for fool's gold,
we find an ocotillo,
many-stalked, tall,
and laden with light.
Each leaf a dazzling
tribute to the sun,
haloed and dripping
rays. We are fools for
this vision. We will dip
our eyes gladly into its
shimmering gold always.

—3 November 2019

We took a drive to Tombstone, Arizona, oddly famous for a shootout many years ago. The town has embraced this history and made itself into an attraction for tourists. Such towns have a fascination of their own. The past brought to the present as a means of separating visitors from their money. I began this poem by writing down many of the kitschy things we saw while there. A man with a whip snapping the air repeatedly. A fake gold-panning stream next to a magnificent yellow-leaved ocotillo lit by the sun. A street performer dancing with bells on his boots, wide grin, and a wider tip bucket. A street barker telling the world the shoot-out reenactment was only 5 minutes away, which he repeated for half an hour. The dusty streets with horse-drawn carriages taking passengers up and down a short route past souvenir shops. A silver mine tour. An Italian/Mexican restaurant where the waitresses serve diners dressed in corsets. Men walking the streets with guns in their holsters and spurs on their boots.

After looking over my list, searching for inspiration for a poem, I settled on the ocotillo. I liked the contrast of the golden light it held with the fake gold-panning stream. In the poem, I highlighted the contrast as best I could.

Try this technique the next time you visit a new place. Just write down all the things you saw that caught your interest. Often, when you look over your list, a poem will suggest itself to you. Then write it.

# Late Afternoon Harvest in the Orchard

*after Ezra Pound*

The apples    tumbled into    a big brown basket;
Bleary red eyes    staring up    at a too-bright sky.

—*4 November 2019*

---

There is a famous two-line poem by Ezra Pound titled "In a Station of the Metro." If you don't know it, do look it up. It is a marvel of imagery and contains a lot of information in its brief lines. I modeled today's poem on Pound's.

One of the most productive sources for poems is—other poems. Get in the habit of reading other poets. When you find a poem that particularly moves or impresses you, don't be shy about imitating its form or subject. Think of it as a compliment to the original poet; then use that poet's work as inspiration.

# Green

the color of envy

the color of seasickness

the color of spring

the color of the aurora borealis

the color of my table

the color of gangrene

the color of saguaro

the color of salad

the color of a menacing sky

the color of emeralds

the color of mold

the color of grasshoppers

the color of money

*—5 November 2019*

Can a mere list be a poem? I'll leave that judgement up to you.
 My idea with this poem was to highlight some unexpected greens in the world by juxtapositioning wildly different instances of the color. For example: gangrene and saguaro. I do think of poetry as a way of seeing the world in a different way than one is used to. Maybe I made you consider the color green in a new light.
 Give list poems a try. They are fun.

# A Modern Fable

You showed me the
tortoise tattooed on
your ankle.

I expressed admiration.
You plucked it from
your skin

and offered it to me, a pale
membrane, thin like paper.
I hesitated

then took it from you and used
it to fold an origami hare,
caught in

mid-gallop. You took
the hare and applied it to
your ankle

where the tortoise had left
a void, winning the race,
as always.

*—6 November 2019*

This came quickly, as befits its theme of speed. I sat down with my notebook and wrote out the poem in about ten minutes. The lines and the line breaks came quickly. I used a notebook instead of my trusty mac mini. I wrote it outside, under a setting sun in the late afternoon.

    Do try writing quickly. Swift writing can bring out depths in your poems you might not know were there. Writing quickly bypasses the critical part of the brain and goes directly to the creative well, where freedom reigns. You want to tap into that freedom when you write. That's where all the good stuff is.

# Skull Found on a Hike in the Woods

A deer skull in
my path. It was
bowl, guide, and seat
of thought. The mush
it once held has

slipped to meals and
rot. Now a prize
to take home, the
skull rests on the
desk in my room.

It used to warn
of wolves and big
cats. It used to
guide four legs to
some place safe where

the deer could live
for one more day.
What does it do
for me? What harm
will it keep at

bay? It has no
eyes. Lost its ears.
Owns no nose. But
it has teeth. It
bites down on life.

—*7 November 2019*

Does this sound autobiographical? It is meant to. But a confession: I never found a dear skull while hiking. I don't have a deer skull in my room. However, on our coffee table we do have part of a deer's pelvis that we found while hiking. Sometimes it feels like a completely natural thing to have. Other times it feels like a distinctly odd object to keep around the house. I tried to play around with that oddness in the poem. Why did I make it a skull? I wanted to get into the head (so to speak) of prey. To feel the world from that perspective.

Note that this is a metered poem. Each line has exactly four words and exactly four syllables, since each word is only one syllable long. The form suggested itself to me as a metaphor for simplicity. The skull used to be a complex object, being a foundation for so many organs and senses. But no longer. Now it is a sleek and simple object. Its past and present remind me of the difference between polysyllabic and monosyllabic, hence the one syllable words.

# Remember to Take Precautions When Messing with Nature

I used tongs.
Plucked the sun out of the sky
during an eclipse, when
no one would notice.
Dropped it into a
bucket of water
hoping to turn it into
a dark black cinder,
something like a gemstone.
Steam billowed and hissed,
but did not put out the sun.
I took the sun out of
the bucket and cradled
it in my gloved hands,
and felt the heat
enveloping my face.
I thought to put it back
in the sky, but it was
too bright to let go.
I took it home
and hung it in the
laundry room. Later
I forgot about it
for months at a time.
Those were the
dark years when
no one would talk
to me because of
what I had done.

—8 November 2019

As I was drifting off to sleep last night I contemplated the sun. How our experience of it contrasts with its reality. It's a bright spot in the sky, and it appears to be quite small. When I woke up the image of a tiny sun was still in my mind. The poem came fairly easily after that.

I had witnessed the total solar eclipse of 2017, driving to Salem, Oregon from our house in Stevenson, Washington to see it. During totality, the corona surrounded a black area that looked very much like a dark gemstone. I used that image in the poem.

Consider a familiar object and apply some lateral thinking to it and see what comes up for you. It could be the subject of a poem.

# Revolution

The trees decided they
had had enough. They
began a mass migration.

First they built spaceships.
We threw shade on their
activities. *It'll never work,*

we said. But they ignored
us. Uprooted, they found
new strength. They had

a movement going. The
first test flight worked.
Our jaws dropped. They

built thousands of ships
and boarded them and
flew to other planets.

Our world, barren and
less green, full of holes
where the trees once

stood, made us very
careful. As we walked,
we put out our hands

for balance. The birds
came to us for support
but we shook them off.

*—9 November 2019*

See the notes to yesterday's poem. Here I employed lateral thinking to trees. They don't move, as a rule. But what if they did? And what if they decided this planet was not as hospitable to them as they would like? What then?

Take the most basic characteristic of an object or group of objects. Then invert it. See what happens to your perception of that object. Often you'll fine a poem there.

# The Grace of Violence

The fawn ran onto
the road, its spots

illuminated momentarily
in my headlights.

Then, with no
perceptible thud

or tremor, it catapulted
off my bumper

into the sky, briefest
of constellations, and

arced to a resting
place by the road,

holding a quiet
rock-painting pose.

—*10 November 2019*

Kim and her sister Camille and I were in the car driving home from lunch at a local restaurant. We saw a coyote attempt to cross the road in front of us, then change its mind and retreat to the side of the road in the face of some heavy traffic. We were relieved to see it apply some common sense. The conversation turned to roadkill. Kim and I remembered how on Highway 14 where we used to live in Washington state, we saw a lot of roadkill all the time, yet in Arizona we saw very little roadkill. Camille asked why that would be. None of us knew. We made some guesses: Highway 14 had a lot of dips and curves, reducing visibility; maybe Arizona animals are smarter; and so on.

    Kim remembered a time many years ago when I was driving down that same Highway 14 at night and a fawn darted out in front of the car and got hit. She remembered how the fawn seemed to slide up and over the car. I remembered it slightly differently, but we both agreed that it was a sad thing to happen and that the fawn was so small it did not leave a dent or, indeed, cause any disturbance to the car. If we had had our eyes closed at the time of impact, we never would have known we had hit anything, let alone an animal.

I don't need to tell you that old memories are perfect inspirations for poems, but when you use them, try to find some telling detail. I recalled how the fawn's spots, for the merest flash of time, looked like a grouping of stars. That was the core of today's poem.

Then the final image. We stopped the car after the impact and walked back along the shoulder to see if the fawn had survived. It had not. It lay on its side like a painting in the grass.

# A Stranger at the Door

That was the night
the storm brought

the mountain close
to the house. It rang

the bell, impatient
immortal, hoping for

some shelter, maybe,
or a handout. A bit

of empathy. But the
rain still pelted our

roof and the wind
still rattled the glass

and we had our
suspicions. Mountains,

after all, don't often
come to anyone's

front door. Mountains
usually need only

themselves. Mountains
sculpt the horizon

to their own sense
of beauty, their own

meandering line, a
long carving trail

against the eternal
mysterious blue sky.

*—11 November 2019*

Poems are often not about what is, but about how we perceive what is. A storm brings nature right up close to one's house. At such times, the drama of the weather makes everything outdoors seem like it is right at hand. Hence the image of a mountain coming close to the house.

One of the ways to generate a poem is to ignore reality. Mountains don't come to people's houses, but the idea that they might can be a potent image. Look for alternate realities in your life, in the way you perceive things. Often a poem lurks in that alternate reality.

# Spirit Spells

History sells us something
as surely as snakes sizzle.

Single souls escort reason's
sudden searching slide

past betrayal. Sort
memory's sad solutions:

sewing, searing, seeing,
saying, staying, slaying.

Scenarios as spans.
Scenes as storied stares.

*—12 November 2019*

I had read and admired "The Mercy Home," a poem by Michael Ryan. Each line of that long poem (about 130 by my count) ended in the letter "r" or in an "r" sound (as in, for example: "more" or "here"). You can find the poem in *The Best American Poetry 2017*. It is worth seeking out and reading.

The terminating "r" at the end of each line of "The Mercy Home" felt like almost rhymes. The lines seemed to want to rhyme, yet couldn't quite get there. The effect was beguiling, like the poem was working toward something it couldn't attain and I, as the reader, was there to help it along.

This morning I considered Ryan's poem as I prepared to compose my own. I decided to use the letter "s" not to end each line, but to be included in each word of the poem. The challenge here was to make the lines as graceful as possible. I also wanted to make the meaning of the poem a little obscure to give it a mysterious aura. This sort of thing appeals to some people but not to others.

Poetry often plays around with language and features of language. Try your hand at writing a poem where every line ends in the same sound or where every word has a common sound. Such an exercise can open your mind to possibilities you might not otherwise entertain.

Upon reviewing this poem just before publication I noticed that one of the words, "betrayal," does not have an "s" sound. Whoops!

# My Great Lakes

Superior
such an elitist name
waves like ocean swells

Michigan
elbowing out Ontario
waves like ocean swells

Erie
to evoke spine shivers
waves like ocean swells

Ontario
elbowing out New York
waves like ocean swells

Huron
lost language of First Peoples
waves like ocean swells

*—13 November 2019*

I grew up near the great lakes. They are like inland oceans: wide, rough, and mysterious. This poem is meant to evoke their grandeur but also bring an element of politics to how and why they were named what they were named.

# O! To Be a Shadow Unmoored

gliding over ground
making no sound

great pillow of air
floating here and there

keeper of darkness
but no evil to confess

my amorphous skin
blending with my kin

we are the night
always in flight

you'll hear a grrrr
if you come closer

we are a mighty tribe
with a charcoal vibe

holding the world
in love unfurled

—*14 November 2019*

Shadows are dependent on objects. But what if shadows could be separated from their objects? Maybe they would seek other shadows and find comfort in joining with them. That was the genesis of this poem.
    I also wanted to use rhymes in this one. Some of them seem forced, but a few feel completely natural, and some are actually humorous.

# Deer Park

*after Wang Wei*

Empty mountain, devoid of
people. Yet human sounds a-

bound. Late afternoon sunlight
shines on the rising green moss.

*—15 November 2019*

Wang Wei was a Chinese poet who lived in the 700s. He wrote a short poem titled "Deer Park" which appears to have had an uncommon hold on poets over the years, since many have tried their hand at translating it. Such luminaries as Gary Snyder, Octavio Paz, and Kenneth Rexroth have published versions of it.

Eliot Weinberger's little book *19 Ways of Looking at Wang Wei* examines many of these translations. He finds almost all of them wanting. Either they add material that is not in the original, or they introduce modern sensibilities that are foreign to Wang Wei and 8th century China.

I recommend the book to you as a lively and eccentric examination of the role of translation in poetry. Attempting to translate any poem into another language is fraught with difficulties, many of which Weinberger points out. For example, a pictographic language like Chinese is more or less impossible to render in English, despite the valiant efforts of English language poets to do so. English is rich with stressed syllables, yet many other languages are not. Even languages that are relatively similar, like Spanish and English, do not easily lend themselves to translation. Spanish has many more rhyming words than English.

My takeaway from the book is that a translation is really a brand new poem. It may correspond with some features of the original, but to be an authentic work in its own right, a translated poem must stand apart from its source.

One interesting aspect of the poets featured in *19 Ways* is that many of them did not know Chinese. But their lack of knowledge of Chinese did not stop them from translating "Deer Park." I don't know Chinese. Why shouldn't I translate "Deer Park" as well? I saw no reason not to.

So here it is, my translation of a 1300-year-old poem from a language of which I am completely ignorant.

Consider doing the same. Read *19 Ways of Looking at Wang Wei* and make your own translation of "Deer Park," whether you know Chinese or not.

# Bugs

The tarantula is fear
on eight legs. The lady
bug is pure charm.

Mosquitoes bring only harm
and flies are eaters
of the world. A cricket

is music, and dragonflies,
well, they eat fire
and then fly off like

it's nothing. Black widows
keep the world away
and the praying mantis is

a slice of green field
swaying into your garden.
Bed bugs rule and

grasshoppers have super
powers. Ants work
too hard—they need a

good trade union—and
honey bees keep food on
the table. Moths are not

bugs, but they should be.
Fleas like animals, especially
pets, and ticks never complain

about anything. Mites see
red. Earwigs have no
hair. Fruit flies add, subtract,

divide, and multiply. Especially
multiply. But only the
cockroach, of all the bugs,

knows shame *and* fear
and spends its time
aching for a new name.

*—16 November 2019*

I encountered Wendy Videlock's poem "Deconstruction" a couple of years ago, even photocopied it from its appearance in *The Best American Poetry 2017*, and pasted it into my journal.

Its form is a series of short—mostly less than seven words—observations about various birds. It is pure delight to read, studded as it is with witty observations and pleasing internal rhymes.

I used its form for today's poem, substituting insects for birds. I didn't use much rhyming except for the first and last stanzas, and I highlighted the word fear in those stanzas as well, because, despite the many delights that insects can bring, I believe one of the most pervasive reactions to insects is fear.

This was a fun one to do. For your own practice, think of a category of creatures or objects, then list quick observations of instances of that object.

# Trees

The elm tree is a cozy
homebody. A maple bows
down to nobody.

Cedars are your best friend
forever, and birches tell
stories in several layers.

Palm trees are fond
of travel, but saguaros
expect to unravel.

Giant redwoods spike the
sky. Ponderosa pines have
always yearned to fly.

Walnut trees have secrets
to keep. Larch trees
welcome birds to sleep.

Apple trees are health
conscious. Orange trees
tend to fuss and cuss.

The willow is a tear-filled
thing. The sycamore
has bells to ring.

The oak is grandmother,
strong and wise, anchored
fast, but sure to rise.

*—17 November 2019*

Another variation on Wendy Videlock's "Deconstruction." I couldn't resist using the form again. This time I used much more rhyming.

# Wind Instrument

the wind chimes play
a random melody

notes pulled out
of a fickle sky

high pressure flowing
to low pressure zones

discovering nature's
purest performance

the song of motion
pinging the air

*—18 November 2019*

---

We have a set of wind chimes on the back porch of our house. It has six hanging metal cylinders of various lengths arranged in a circle. A wooden gong in the middle strikes the cylinders when the wind blows, producing pings of various tones. Sometimes those pings sound like melodies, other times more like something a composer of atonal music might produce. In any case, it is always charming to hear those pings. I attempted to reproduce that charm in today's poem.

# Coyote Band

their songs like twitter
posts: only a few notes

long; the band assembles
at random hours, serenading

the moon, perhaps, or
singing up the sun;

no instruments but their
voices: what nature has

gifted them, they re-gift to
us; don't look for tickets

online, or a flyer posted
to a lamppost: coyotes hold

their concerts according
to whim and chance;

no record deal in the
offing, so don't hold

your breath; instead, make
room for their breaths;

listen to the sound of the
desert howling; coyotes

have always known the
proper tone to strike

*—19 November 2019*

This morning, as I sat down to write my day's poem, I heard a pack of coyotes in the distance. It's a familiar sound in the desert. Coyote howls can arise at any time. I listened for about 15 seconds, which was as long as their howls lasted. I decided I had the subject of the day's poem.

Here's the thing about writing a poem every day. I'm always looking for inspiration, which means I will find it almost anywhere. I probably would not write a poem about the coyotes if I was not already searching for a subject for a poem.

That's why I recommend writing a poem a day for an extended period of time. Because you're always looking, you're always ready for the next poem. Not all of them will be successful, but that doesn't matter. You will find inspiration in the most unexpected places, and often those poems can be real gems.

# Inventory

your atoms
are all
you have

but try
to count
them and

you'll spend
your life
doing nothing

else and
never finish
the task

*—20 November 2019*

I'm a counter from way back. I remember as a kid counting the power-line poles that we would pass as my mother drove the car. I would count clouds in the sky, people at a gathering, birds in a flock flying overhead, the number of slabs in a sidewalk I was traversing, and so on. So many things to count.

I don't know when I first learned about atoms. It must have been when I was relatively young. They were mysterious things at first, and, I suppose, they still are in many ways. They were so small that I wondered how scientists could actually know anything about them. They were, after all, almost completely unobservable.

And there were so many. Uncounted trillions just in the space that the period on the end of this sentence occupies.

Today's poem is about the impossibility of counting the atoms that make up us. We are just as mysterious as atoms. Just as unknowable, on some level. I hoped to evoke some of the mystery of life in this short poem.

If you're following along with me and trying to write a poem a day, consider taking some concept from science or nature and applying it to yourself. See what happens.

## Lost Feather

No opposable thumb,
but birds gather wind

better than I swing
a hammer or turn a

screw. I find a feather
on the ground, pick

it up. Lift it high
against the sun, shaft

held between thumb
and forefinger, light

streaming through the
corrugations, me reach-

ing for a sense of what
it means to corral air.

*—21 November 2019*

---

Birds are a recurrent theme for me. My previous collection, *Animal Life*, has many poems about birds. Their realm is the air, and I am fascinated by their ability to navigate it.

    I do find feathers on the ground all the time, and I do pick them up and hold them up to sky. They are amazing pieces of art, delicate sculptures.

    Look for those kinds of moments in your life. Notice them. They are often the genesis of a poem.

# Aftermath

Shards of broken
crockery strewn
on the floor.

The precise cause
lost to history
and memory,

those most
unsettling and
unreliable of

stenographers.
It takes several
minutes to sweep

up the mess.
The edges are
sharper than

knife blades.
The blood they
draw redder

than the eyes
that started
it all. And weeks

later, errant
pieces still
turn up, like

bits of anger
left to rot in
obscure corners.

*—22 November 2019*

I was dipping into *Revenge and Forgiveness: An Anthology of Poems,* edited by Patrice Vecchione, and found one that caught my eye. It was "Why People Murder" by Ellen Bass. The poem recounts a moment of anger, when the narrator felt that she could, given the right circumstances, commit a terrible crime against someone.

This triggered a memory of when I was a child, and I remembered a scene of chaos, broken dishes all over the floor. I don't recall what caused the mess, but the memory was vivid. I used it for today's poem.

Anything can trigger a memory. When an old memory comes up, try to seize it and see if you can turn it into a poem. Events that stick with us over the years are often laden with meaning and significance. They are gold mines for poets.

# Stop Me if You've Heard this Before

Thank U

4 call

ing Natural
Grocers

in 2sawn

on River
&
Cray

croft. This
is

Mayor E. Oh,

how may
eye

die wrecked

your
call?

*—23 November 2019*

At work I answer the phone anywhere from zero to 20 or 25 times a day. I recite a script provided by the store every time I answer the phone. This little script is attached to every phone in the building. I don't have to look at the script anymore; I have it memorized. It is a completely banal script, and yet, it is a part of my life in some small way, and like any part of life, it can be the inspiration for a poem.

So I played around with the syntax of the script, added some phonetic variations of words and applied line and stanza breaks according to my own whims. I wanted to transform the script from something banal to something at least interesting. Whether I succeeded or not is up to you.

Note that this is also a form called a found poem. As you go about your day, notice different examples of texts. It might be a parking sign, a list that a previous borrower left in a library book, cooking instructions on a carton of pasta, or the warning of side effects on a jar of supplements. It doesn't matter where you find such texts, just get in the habit of looking at them and seeing if you can transform them into a poem. It might not always work, but it is an instructive exercise. It helps you see connections and grace in places that we don't necessarily associate with those qualities.

# Period

They call you "dot"
now, a description

rather than a name.
Your multi-faceted

history obliterated to
a mere syllable.

But you are the end
times and the universe

before the big bang.
No better judge of

finality exists, and
sentences look lost with

out you. Thoughts
would ramble on to

infinity if your presence
ever evaporated. And so,

dear period, I thank you
for your service, for your

unwavering dedication to
halting what needs to

be stopped. You are the
surest mark of sanity

in the menagerie of
punctuation. The best

example of duty, giving
your all to stop all. I

shower you with blessings.
I utter your name with

reverence, build palaces to
honor your perfect being.

*—24 November 2019*

I had heard that the novelist David Foster Wallace, when giving public speeches, would sometimes say the punctuation marks of his text as he spoke. It seems he wanted people to know that he paid a great deal of attention to punctuation and how it shaped what he said.

This seemed like an odd thing to do, but as I considered it, it made a certain amount of sense. After all, without punctuation, writing (though, paradoxically, not speech) would be more or less incomprehensible.

Probably the most common punctuation mark is the period, hence the title and subject of today's poem.

One possible job description for a poet is: "A person who notices aspects of the world that most people don't." Cultivate the possibility of becoming that person. It will lead to all kinds of insights and poems.

# Comma

You are a dot
with a hook, as

though a period went
fishing, or yearned to

plow the fields of
prose. Comma, I have

heard folks call you
the tick of writing,

sucking the blood flow
from words. But comma,

you are breath giver,
telling us when to

rest and gather air.
I see your beauty

everywhere, the way you
regulate meaning, your subtle

digs into the page,
the necessary claws of

sense, the snag of
speech, reminding us, always,

that the tug of
hesitation is more than

mere hiccup. You are
super-hero. You stop time,

you make plain, eternally,
the power of pause.

*—25 November 2019*

Another poem about a punctuation mark. See my comments on yesterday's offering. If a poem about periods can fly, why not one about commas?

Note that both "Period" and "Comma" are odes, an ancient form of poetry in which the poet addresses a certain person, object, or concept directly. Usually odes are generous in nature, extolling the virtues of the subject of the poem.

For your own practice, try writing an ode to someone or something in your life. Make it expansive. Make it big. Ideally, an ode should make a reader see how much you love your subject.

# Semicolon

A confession:
I avoid you.

Far too many
people ready

to pounce on your
misuse, so you

remain hidden
in the back of

my mind. I see
you there, waiting

to be deployed
into a line,

any line. I'm not
trying to rub

your being out
of existence.

You have grace, I
see it: how the

dot on top is
perfect balance

for the dot and
hook at bottom.

How you combine
two marks to make

a mark of your
own. You are grace

    personified.
    A sturdy and

    true glyph calling
    to the world to

    speak your peace with
    elegant poise.

*—26 November 2019*

A third poem, in as many days, about punctuation. I guess I have a series going.

# Apostrophe

You have a
lofty air

about you,
as though you

are above
it all. And,

in a way,
I suppose

that's true. You
are a drone

hovering
over land.

Seeing the
stream of words

below you,
arranged in

a long string
of symbols.

But you are
more than that.

You hold lost
letters in

you. Keep them
from view, as

though keeping
them inside

will preserve
them for all

time. I do
salute your

willingness
to take on

such a task.
Your fervent

commitment
to duty.

Your way of
holding the

meaning of
all those words.

*—27 November 2019*


Another poem about punctuation. How long can I keep this up? How much more is there to say about the subject?

That's a good question. I'll see tomorrow if I have any more punctuation poems in me. And if I want to write them. Doing a series can be challenging for many reasons. You want to maintain some kind of coherence in the series, but you also want to make each poem its own unique object. Sometimes those impulses can clash, and you have to decide where you want the series and the poem to go.

One thing a series can do, like so many of these exercises, is get your mind to stretch in a direction it might not otherwise seek. Your task in a series is to ring many changes on a single theme. To do that, you will need to delve into all the aspects of that theme. Uncover leads you would not consider if you were only doing one poem on that theme.

Do attempt a series of poems on a particular theme. It can be an enriching process for you and your readers.

# Exclamation Point

You dazzle and
deploy such bright
smiles that I must

don dark glasses
just to view your
glowing soul. Oh!

Exclamation
point! We are taught
to use you most

sparingly, and
yet, many choose
to resist this

instruction. Your
bold presence, your
manic aura,

inspires us all.
You are gaudy,
yes, and often

find tops to go
over. But don't
heed the many

nay-sayers. Your
life is your own.
Your beams of pure

energy are
true expressions
of your wild self.

*—28 November 2019*

Another punctuation mark, another ode. Now that I've settled into this series, it is becoming more and more fun. I'm looking forward to the next one, even though I'm not sure which one will be next.

# Parentheses

Twin crescent moons
capturing the

afterthoughts of
sentences as

though they were streaks
of meteors

ricocheting
between your curved

surfaces. Some
say you and your

holdings can be
safely ignored.

But you are like
two satellite

dishes bouncing
waves of our words

across a void,
and you are where

we tuck away
the meanings that

can't be let go,
the asides and

explanations
that yearn for your

accepting and
loving embrace.

*—29 November 2019*

Continuing the punctuation series. I have settled into a simple meter: lines of exactly four syllables. It feels light enough for the subject matter and makes for a quick pace.

# Quotation Mark

You always come
in twos, needing

the strength of a
good solid twin,

even if you
are inverted

to each other.
I see you both,

carrying the
strings of our words

between you, like
furniture that

needs to be moved
from one wall to

another. With
out your hooks, would

our talk simply
slip away to

oblivion?
"Help me out here,"

you call to one
another. "Give

me a hand with
moving these words

from here to there
across the page."

*—30 November 2019*

I'm starting to think about winding down the punctuation series. Over the next day or two, I'll work on coming up with a good spectacular ending to the series. I'm not sure what that would entail, but it feels like it needs something of that nature.

# December

# Colon

Like two bite marks,
vampiristic

punctures on the
page, you bring blood

sport to bear on
sentences you

choose to dwell in.
Colon, you are

two periods
built one on top

of the other:
a mini stack

of stops, held up
precarious-

ly, waiting for
a wind to knock

you down. Or for
the whims of a

restless ground to
knock you down. When

that happens, when
the earthquake strikes

and your ancient
poised balancing

act tumbles down,
how will you put

yourself right once
more? How will you

prop yourself up,
dust yourself off,

and resume your
regal twin pose?

*—1 December 2019*

---

I generally try to keep off the computer on Sundays. I call it my screen-free day. Kim suggested this to me some years ago, and I have adopted it as a ritual. This means my daily poem on Sunday is not written on my computer, but in a notebook. That is the case with "Colon."

I wrote it outside, by the pool, while stretched out on a lounge chair, with the latest issues of *The New York Review of Books* and *The Atlantic Monthly* by my side. In other words, a lazy Sunday afternoon in which to produce my daily poem.

I really liked the idea that a colon resembles the classic bite marks of a vampire, something relatively familiar to anyone who has seen any of a number of movies featuring that now iconic blood sucker. I'm actually not sure I carried that image successfully through the poem. Once I had the bite mark idea set down, I had some trouble turning the idea into something that truly related to colons.

And yet, I couldn't let the image go. I especially liked having the word vampiristic in the poem, and having it on one line as I did. So I tried to make the connection between vampires, blood, and calamity. I tinkered with it for a bit, hoping to make the connections more solid, but they do seem a little more vague than I would have hoped.

All of which is to say that I'm not sure this is a successful effort at all. But I do like the rhythm of it. And it feels like I did evoke a kind of strange slanting view of colons.

You may disagree, and that's OK. As I said from the start, not all (or even many) of these poems are going to be gems. The idea is to produce poems. Time will judge their value better than anyone else can.

# Question Mark

Inverted fish
hook? Is that what

you are? Or a
scythe, reaping a

sheaf of letters?
You always find

ways to question
expectations,

don't you? And why,
oh why, is there

that infernal
dot dangling from

your base? Does it
need to be there?

Why not toss it
aside? Don't you

crave the clean and
pure feeling of

presenting your
plain true self to

the world? Can't you
shuck that excess

appendage? Though
born with you, does

it control you?
Can't you stand on

your own, without
that pesky dot?

Find a way to
question your fate?

*—2 December 2019*

The question mark is the most sculptural and gaudy of the punctuation marks, so in this poem I wanted it to be front and center. To achieve that goal I made every sentence in the poem a question. As I wrote it, I found myself examining it more closely and suddenly realized that the period at its base was completely unnecessary. The question mark would stand perfectly well without it. Given that, I began to ask the question mark why it retained the period.

The result was an interrogation, of sorts. Perhaps a bit annoying in the end. I imagine the question mark, in exasperation, telling me to stop asking so many questions about its appearance.

If it did, it would have a point. What business is it of mine whether the question mark keeps the period or not? It should do as it wishes. As any entity should be entitled to.

# Dash

A chin-up bar
installed in the

middle of a
sentence—you are

there to help us
flex our muscles—

help us become
stronger—which is

what you did for
Emily—am

I right? I think
I am. Dash, you

connect thoughts like
railroad couplings

connect rail cars—
strong and sturdy—

unbreakable
in your mission

to build a long
and coherent

narrative—the
meaning of the

whole—a series
of phrases—the

stories of our
lives—passing by

in a stately
stream—constantly

moving—always
chugging to the

end—over the
horizon—past

our eyes—as we
wait for the gate

to rise—the road
to clear—the tracks

bare and ready—
for the next chain.

—3 December 2019

Emily Dickinson was famous for her use of dashes in her poems, so when I took up the dash as the subject of the next poem in my punctuation series I felt I had to invoke her name.

My use of the dash in this poem cannot be considered strictly grammatical, but that's OK. As poets we have license of use the parts of speech and language as we see fit. Don't be afraid to let yourself explore different aspects of language. Use all the parts of speech for your own purposes. It is one of the rewards of reading and writing poetry.

# Ellipsis

You hide meaning
behind three dots,

as though less . . . is
more. Ellipsis,

you are always
mystery. Your

task to keep us
from knowing what

sentences think.
You make us pause

for brief silence.
Fragility

your gift, and mute
speech your method.

I see you: a
rare species of

delicate fowl,
silent in air,

flying from there
to here. A kind

of enigma,
punctuating

that which seems to
shun exposure.

Ellipsis, is
there . . . some path in?

Some method to
know you? A way

to love, to reach,
your . . . modest soul?

*—4 December 2019*

I had to look up the meaning of ellipsis to know exactly what it denotes in a sentence. The dictionary definition is that it omits words from a sentence that can be understood from context.
    Which puzzled me. Because when I've encountered the ellipsis in the wild, it is usually used to indicate a long pause. The point being that the reader is expected to think for a second before moving on to the next word. That second is meant to evoke a sense of awe, sorrow, longing, or some other emotion.
    At least, that is how I saw it.
    In any case, I played around with the meaning of ellipses in this poem. I had no idea where I was going to go with it when I started. Just began tinkering with ideas and words. I'm not at all sure the bird image is right for it. But I wanted to evoke the idea of gliding from one word to the other. The ellipsis, looked at in the right way, can resemble a line of birds, either flying in formation, or sitting on a power-line . . . and maybe watching you watching them.
    I don't often use the ellipsis in my writing, so this was a fun exercise.
    For your own practice, try doing something in your writing that you don't normally do. It's a good way to boost your creative potential.

# Crocuses

they arrive in spring
staggering through
fresh grass

the first flowers
awake after winter

wearing rumpled pajamas
fumbling for
that first
cup of coffee

*—5 December 2019*

I don't see crocuses here in the desert Southwest, but where I used to live, in the Columbia River Gorge, I would see crocuses arrive first of all the flowers. Usually in February, when they looked just a little bit ragged and not quite ready for spring. They often reminded me of someone getting up after a long sleep, hence the image of the rumpled pajamas and the need for coffee.

It's anthropomorphizing, which writers are often cautioned against. But if you learn nothing else from this book, I hope one take away will be that as a writer you have license to do anything you want with your subject matter, your presentation, and your language. Be free!

# Lizard

You must have
lubricated feet
to move so fast.

Ball bearings
burning red hot.
Your shadow

left behind with
no way to catch
up until you

stop

still as frozen
lava, and wait for
it, plodding

along the ground,
taking its cool time
with the task

of rejoining
your manic energetic
photogenic self.

*—6 December 2019*

---

Lizards are everywhere here in the Sonoran Desert. They have two modes of motion. The first is so fast you can hardly follow them. They move over all terrain with unlikely amazing speed. The second is as still as a rock. They will remain frozen in place for minutes at a time.

That's it. Those are the only ways you ever see them. (Except you will occasionally find them doing pushups while stationary. This is, apparently, an action to attract a mate, or so the guidebooks tell us.)

I wanted to evoke the two main aspects of lizard motion in the poem. I tried to make the rhythm quick, and I put a one word stanza "stop" right in the middle of it, a kind of symmetric pivot for the whole, the way the lizard stops between bouts of speed. In other words, I tried to make the form of the poem mimic the subject of the poem.

# The Blues

It's there in ice and snow sometimes
when the shadows are just right, lurking
in the crevices, sheltered from light.
Also present in certain moods
and wrapped around berries, though
that variety of blue is so dark as to be
more like a modest black than true blue.
The sky, of course, is often blue, but
not always, and not always the same shade
of blue. Veins look blue, there below your
skin, inaccessible, but still on display,
like graffiti in the flesh, holding some
arcane meaning you can reach for but
never find. Some mold is blue, filling
fissures in cheese, and the oxidation
around copper sometimes appears bluish.
Blue lives in many flowers and the entire
planet from space is said to be blue.
It seems plausible, especially in the photos
the astronauts and the satellites take,
but I'll never know for sure, not with my
own eyes, anyway. Which reminds me.
Some people have blue eyes. And lots
of people wish for blue eyes. For two
tiny pieces of the planet to be subsumed
into their visual system. Hoping to see the
world through two blue-hued lenses of nature.

—7 December 2019

I began by writing down instances of blue in the world. It can be a mysterious color and I wanted to evoke that sense in the poem. It wasn't until I got near the end that I realized that blue is a coveted color for eyes. Seeing blue through blue eyes seemed like an interesting image to end the poem on.

Try picking a color and listing all the instances of that color you can think of. Then play around with your list and see if a poem emerges from it. More often than not, you will find inspiration in such a list.

# Owning Up

When I was a kid
we had a small
set of deer antlers,

still attached to
a section of skull,
mounted to a

wooden shield,
displayed on a wall
in our house. It was

given to us by a
relative, I no longer
remember who.

No one in our
house hunted. No
one would think

to kill a deer. But
we had those antlers.
Tiny things. Once

my best friend came
over, saw the antlers,
and said: *That's an*

*awfully small deer
someone killed.* The
comment stung

me, like I had done
something wrong.
My face flushed

with blood shame.
Adrenaline rushed
through me, as though

>     someone was tracking
>     me, taking careful note
>     of my every move.

—8 December 2019

This is a memory from a long time ago. At least fifty years. I am no longer in contact with the friend. I vaguely remember the antlers on the wall, but I do remember, very vividly, my friend's comment and what it did to me. It was as though I was guilty of killing the deer, which was and is absurd, but its absurdity did not change the fact that I felt guilt for living in a place that displayed the antlers.

Look for these odd moments in your life, when your reaction does not quite mesh with the situation at hand. They can be excellent subjects of poems.

## While Sitting on the Couch With the Television Temporarily Muted and Waiting for the Show to Resume After a Commercial Break

You see something move across the breakfast nook.
Is it shadow?
Some errant reflection?
You ask me if our house is haunted.
I pause, look up at the ceiling.
Check out the breakfast nook.
Tilt my head, listen for sounds.
The rush of air, maybe.
Or spooky noises, like faint footsteps.
A long wail.
Scary scratches.
Cries.
Moans.
I hear nothing of the kind.
Too bad.
It would be interesting to live in a haunted house.
Though our surroundings are not completely silent:
There's the furnace, dragon's breath roaring.
Our own breaths, much more modest.
The rustle of our clothes against our skin.
The fabric of the couch crinkling.
My slippers on the floor, scraping.
Eventually, I think I hear my own heart.
But that must be illusion.
No one hears their own beating heart.
Not in the general course of events.
I tell you I don't think the house is haunted.
But I hesitate.

*—9 December 2019*

From an incident that happened fifty years ago (yesterday's poem) to one that happened less than a day ago. This is a more or less accurate account (memory is never foolproof) of what happened last night while Kim and I were watching TV.

# Bonbons

Yesterday's partial rainbow,
Technicolor scythe anchored
to the Catalina Mountains,
harvesting clutches of cottony
fog into bundles thrown down
on the rocky slopes. They perched
there for a few hours until the
omnivorous sun came grazing
and consumed them all:
treats too enticing to pass up.

*—10 December 2019*

I usually write my poems in the morning, often right when I wake up. That didn't happen today. I had to get up early for a meeting at work. (I'm employed at Natural Grocers.) Then a long shift after the meeting, which meant I didn't get home until about 7 p.m. After eating and spending some time with Kim, it was past 8 o'clock. If I wanted to keep my streak going, there wasn't much time. I sat down with my notebook and began writing down ideas and snatches of lines.

I've been wanting to write a poem about tarantulas for a few days. We see them here in the desert. There is at least one living in our backyard. They often come out when it rains because the holes where they live get filled up with water.

They are interesting creatures. Long furry legs. They move with uncommon grace. And they are curious. They seem to want to communicate as we walk by. I am also aware that tarantulas instill fear in many people. Just the word "tarantula" can make some folks feel very creepy.

All those things felt like ripe material for a poem. I also wanted it to be a light poem. Something with rhymes. I made a few attempts at lines, fell into a limerick mode for a few minutes, but I didn't like the result. Nothing was sparking. Nothing was coming alive.

My mind meandered. I turned to noseeums, invisible tiny bugs that fly around and bite you here in the desert, but nothing came of that. Then cats. I tried jump-starting a poem about cats, but that didn't go anywhere either.

Although I wasn't exactly desperate, I was feeling drained of inspiration.

Then I remembered seeing a rainbow a day or two ago. It was not complete, just the end of one, and it seemed to emerge out of the Catalina Mountains, a rugged range north of us. This piece of rainbow looked like a curved cutting instrument, and I remember it made me wonder at the time what a sharp piece of rainbow might be used to cut.

Suddenly things started humming with possibility. I wrote down the first few lines you see here and then the image of the sun eating bits of fog seemed right and the final touch was the title.

I finished before 9 p.m. and felt good about what I had done.

# Rhymes With Dies

Hot French fries,
sincere tries;

win the prize
and chicken thighs.

Wistful sighs,
bargain buys;

dapper ties
and mysterious whys.

Pesky flies,
good disguise;

laundry dries
and super size.

Always wise,
cheating chives;

all you guys,
and honeybee hives.

Foreign spies,
baby cries;

apple pies
and cinnamon lies.

—*11 December 2019*

It was a pleasantly warm day here in the desert, so I took my notebook out pool-side and sat in a lounge chair and began writing down ideas for poems.

I had been reading about apples, specifically honeycrisp apples, and decided it might be fun to do an apple poem. The apple is a potent symbol: there at the beginning of Genesis and making itself known throughout history. Isaac Newton, George Washington, Johnny Appleseed, and your homeroom teacher all lay claim to some aspect of apples or apple trees. Surely there had to be a poem there.

The first line I wrote was "Cold apples." Not much there. I tried to embellish it: "The apples are too cold to eat." That wasn't any better.

Maybe there is an apple poem in me, but it didn't make itself known today.

One thing I did try was to write down "Apple pie."

Something in that simple two-word phrase got me going. Without thinking, I immediately wrote down "cinnamon lies" on the next line.

Huh. I had: "Apple pies / cinnamon lies." I liked the sound of it, but what could that possibly mean? I didn't know, but the rhyme was appealing, so I began writing down a list of rhymes to pies and lies. I came up with about a dozen or so, and began writing short lines that included these rhymes. I soon became conscious of a musicality in the lines, and I tinkered with the placement of the lines and stanzas to best show off that musicality.

When I was done, the apple and cinnamon lines ended it all.

I chose two-line stanzas to give the whole thing a light and airy feel. After all, this is a light and fun poem.

I liked the idea of using "dies" in the title, since most everything in the poem is an affirmation of life or life force.

You might try to write a poem with all the lines rhyming with each other. It is a lot of fun. Also note that I threw in a couple of slant rhymes, just for fun.

# I'm Fine

Sublime hearts in
their prime stutter
when climbing through
unexpected grime.

*—12 December 2019*

A four line poem with four internal rhymes. Rhymes are powerful ways of tying a poem together, and they don't have to be at the end of a line. I have them here following a slanted path from top left to bottom right. The title is a slant rhyme on the four rhymes of the poem.

    I confess I'm not exactly sure what this poem is about or what exactly it means. But the sound of it is pleasing to me.

# Upon Discovering Our Kitchen Faucet Has a Shower Setting

Think of it:
A mouse in the sink
under the stream,
with a tiny bar of soap
and a teeny dishcloth,
wrapped in lather
singing songs of
vanquished cats
and cozy nests,
with steam
billowing up
while it rinses off
and applies conditioner
to its soft brown fur.

*—13 December 2019*

Yesterday Kim showed me the shower setting on the kitchen faucet. I immediately imagined a mouse taking a shower in our sink. This poem essentially describes that discovery and the moment immediately after.

Mice are complex symbols. Most people consider them vermin and would not want them running around in their house. Yet, they are also considered cute. There is Mickey Mouse, for example, a world famous instance of a mouse that is friendly to everyone. Beyond that, consider that tiny mice are, in the common imagination, capable of scaring elephants, which are larger than mice by orders of magnitude.

In literature, we have Stuart Little, a famous mouse character from the book of the same name by E. B. White. And there is the harrowing *Maus*, an extraordinary graphic novel by Art Spiegelman in which the Jews that were consigned to Nazi concentration camps were depicted as mice.

All of which is to say that mice have a hold on the popular imagination, which may explain why they popped into my head as Kim showed me that shower stream in our sink.

# Revelations

When I was young I thought adults
knew everything. I surmised that
they were taught all the secrets of
the world some time around their
21st birthday, so they could
be competent and responsible
adults, and after that there
were no mysteries for them. Imagine
my surprise when I figured out,
some time around my 14th birthday
that that didn't happen to anyone and
it wasn't going to happen to me.

When I was old I thought babies
knew everything. I surmised that
they were given all the knowledge
of the world when they were
born, so they could be competent
and joyful beings. Some of them
kept that knowledge, and some of
them lost it, either little by little,
or in large chunks as the months
and years passed by. Imagine my
surprise when I figured out, some
time around my 60th birthday
that nothing of the kind happened
to me or to anyone else.

—14 December 2019

The first stanza is an accurate description of what I believed when I was a kid. The second stanza is a fantasy. It is not what I believe, but I wrote it as a kind of flip side to the first stanza. It is a way of examining the first stanza in light of the knowledge and wisdom my older self may have acquired over the years.

This poem also points to a third stanza, a kind of ghost stanza in which the two revelations are intertwined into something resembling true knowledge.

I also wondered if the first stanza was even necessary. Maybe just the second one could stand on its own, with the first one implied. I debated the issue with myself for a few minutes, but in the end let the first stanza stand.

# Rescue

The grasshopper in the
pool: an impossible

green somewhere between lime
and the lightest of froth

along a seashore. Mute
as a mime and still as

a corpse. I slip the web
of the skimmer beneath

it and lift it up and
out. It proves it's alive

by clutching the rim of
the skimmer with all the

strength it has in it. No
power will separate

it from its unlikely
savior. Nothing will

convince this creature that
patience has no reward.

*—15 December 2019*

---

The house we bought here in the desert has a pool. It wasn't something we particularly wanted in a house, but pools here are common. Almost every house our real estate agent showed us was equipped with a pool. So, fine, we bought a house with a pool.

One thing we discovered fairly early on was that creatures end up in the pool that have no business being there. Ants, lizards, mice, and so on. Some survive: I fished out a lizard from the pool once that appeared dead but turned out to be alive. Others don't make it: Kim had the misfortune to be home alone when she found a dead mouse in the pool and had to remove it. A couple who visited us said that baby quail fall into their pool and drown instantly, which was a chilling and sad thing to contemplate.

In any case, this afternoon, while I was jotting down some ideas in my notebook, Kim said she saw a dead bird in the pool, and it was my turn to remove it. I went to look and it turned out to be a piece of bark in the bottom of the pool that looked remarkably like a bird with multi-colored feathers. I was glad I didn't have to deal with a dead bird, but as I stood there, skimmer in hand, I saw that there was a luminously green grasshopper floating in the water near the edge of the pool.

What happened next is recounted in today's poem. Sometimes patience rewards the poet as well as the grasshopper: just wait and a poem can present itself to you unbidden.

# Skin

tight

to

night

for

drum

beat

rites

and

sonic

de

lights

*—16 December 2019*

Can a simple list be a poem? I asked that question here some weeks ago. I didn't have a definitive answer, but I found a list poem in Wendy Videlock's collection *Nevertheless*, titled "Of Coverings." Look it up. It is marvelous. I used it as a loose model for today's poem. So my definitive answer now is: Yes.

# Alarm Clock Dreams

acoustic
restock

broken stick
laughingstock

politic
sintoc

antic
buttock

mystic
livestock

kinetic—
briiiiiiiiiiiing

*—17 December 2019*

You might say this poem was not so much written as constructed. I wanted to emulate the sound of a clock tick-tocking next to someone in bed, intruding on their dreams. So I found a list of words that ended in a *tick* sound and another list of words that ended in a *tock* sound, then put them together into what I hoped are interesting and somewhat dreamlike couplets so that the ends of the lines in the poem go tick-tock, tick-tock, to the end, when the whole thing is interrupted and brought to conclusion by the ringing of the alarm.

# The Empty Sky
# After a Rain Storm

the rainbow lay on the
dissection table where

technicians clad in white
coats applied scalpels to

the seams between the hues
making several thin

ribbons that curled up on
themselves like distressed worms

writhing and hoping for
some measure of mercy

some understanding of
the strands that color life

*—18 December 2019*

After a rain, when the sun comes out, I always look for a rainbow. Sometimes I see one, sometimes I don't. This poem is for those times when I feel like I should be seeing a rainbow, but none presents itself. Maybe the rainbow got taken away by scientists so it could be studied.

    Clearly a fantasy, this poem ascribes properties to rainbows that they do not possess.

# Crows Cutting Spirals in the Air

Their feathers
produce shivery
whooshing sounds.

They air waltz
in threes cawing
constantly.

They're up there
all the time
laughing at us.

We can fly
and you can't
nya nya nya.

*—19 December 2019*

A few days ago I saw some crows in the sky, turning in long lazy circles. I watched them for a few moments, then said the words recorded in the fourth stanza above. Another case of anthropomorphizing. Crows almost certainly do not think such thoughts, but people like me imagine them doing so.

When attempting to write a poem a day, it can be very beneficial to consider every aspect of your life and take seriously even the most fleeting of images. In fact, in some ways, that is the whole point of doing a poem a day for an extended period of time: it makes you examine the world and yourself in a whole new way.

# The Mystery of Life for Immigrants

It's an artificial designation,
sure,

but think about being one
and approaching a pay phone
in an emergency
when you need to report a tanker
truck that has slipped into the river
the driver trapped inside the cab

and you want to call
911
because even though you don't yet
know the language very well
you've heard that 911 is a good thing to call
in emergencies
but the phone has all these strange numbers
on it

2- and 3-digit numbers
and they're out of order
and you stand there
with the receiver in your hand

trying to find a path to the rescue
you want to initiate
because you want to be a good
citizen
hell, you just want to be a good *person*

but the phone is too mysterious
it defeats you and you hang up
and go to the edge of the river
and think about if you should

descend into the water
to do what you can

to help a stranger
with wild eyes pleading
who has inadvertently ended up

in a place that will not sustain
him, will not welcome him
and will soon erase him

*—20 December 2019*

I dreamed this situation last night, exactly as I have presented it here. I don't often remember my dreams, but when I woke up, this one was sharp and vivid, like a strong memory.

If you are following along with me and doing your own poem-a-day project, you might want to try writing down a particularly vivid dream. They can have the power of stark immediacy.

# Your True Secret Name

as designated

by the sacred snake

is recorded in

its original

twisted slither but

you will not ever

recognize its true

value to your soul

*—21 December 2019*

---

This morning was filled up with chores that needed doing. Things like getting some documents to the ACA to complete our application for medical insurance, taking care of forwarding our mail, and dealing with our email service changing its servers, which meant I had to figure out how to get our computers to properly receive mail from the new servers. All of which is to say that I had no time to complete my poem in the morning before work. I could have waited until the evening to write it, but instead I took some time at work, during lunch, to write my daily poem.

    It's the sort of thing that is bound to happen during such a project as I have undertaken. The world will not necessarily arrange itself so that my creative efforts will happen at a convenient time. No matter. Writing a poem a day can teach a person to write under less than ideal circumstances. Which is a good thing.

    Today's effort was inspired by Ada Limón's poem "A Name" from her collection *The Carrying*. It imagines Eve naming the animals and wondering if she ever wanted the animals to name her. I took that notion and imagined a snake naming all the people in the world, and wondered if those names would make any sense to the named persons. The result, I hope, is a bit of mystery mixed up with a bit of imagination. Names carry so much significance, but few of us name ourselves. Our names are the inventions of others, who can often have motives and plans contrary to anything we can imagine.

Note that this is a metered poem. Each line (and the title) is exactly five syllables long.

# Role Reversal

At dinner
I imagine
rabbits
watching
me in the
same
manner
as I
sometimes
watch
them.

*He's grazing.*
*Look how*
*he reaches*
*for another*
*slice of bread.*
*They are so*
*cute when*
*they do that.*

It's the
warm
butter
that makes
the bread
so good.
Just like,
I imagine,
it's the
heat of
the sun
that makes
the grass
irresistible

*—22 December 2019*

We see a lot of rabbits around our house, all through the year. They are charming to see: completely still, or hopping slowly from one foraging spot to another. Watching wildlife go about their activities is a marvelous activity and I enjoy it immensely, whether the creature in question is a lizard, bird, rabbit, bee, coyote, javelina, or any number of other animals.

    I often wonder, watching them, if they would ever find me as interesting as I find them. No way to tell, but the thought was the impetus for today's poem.

# Observing the World Has its Limitations

The ball will not always bounce.
Ink wells sometimes rest.
Cell phones don't ring like church bells.

The moon and the sun exchange sky posts.
My rocks dance in starlight.
Her earrings reacted to harsh words.

My abacus rests near my calculator.
The dental floss always works hard.
Clocks sometimes gather into gangs.

Pyramids hold up the sky.
The horse's bit lies bleeding in the dust.
Watering cans creak and pop in the cold.

Nail clippers steadfastly stand ready for duty.
Billboards have stories to tell.
The brick near my car bears an unnamable red.

I used to throw stones into ponds.
The coin in my pocket will migrate to another's pocket.
Envelopes hide so much.

Your toaster will warm your hands if you ask it to.
A wineglass will occasionally do handsprings.
Refrigerators have excellent memories.

Picture frames never ask for favors.
Blinds live double lives.
The kitchen table loves the floor.

A cat's collar whispers rather than shouts.
Rubber bands stretch the truth.
Traffic lights have songs to sing.

House keys fight the urge for solitude.
Pencils adopt fatalistic views of the world.
License plates usually adore road trips.

Hats think of themselves as inverted bowls.
Nametags are notoriously shy.
The lamp on the table takes naps.

Guitars hide their tears.
Eyeglasses bend the truth.
Wedding rings clean their plates.

My gloves shiver in the cold.
The park bench near the flowers feels pity for the tree.
And jet planes have a lot to learn.

—*23 December 2019*

---

Today's poem comes from Marcia Southwick's exercise in *The Practice of Poetry*, edited by Robin Behn and Chase Twichell. Southwick suggests writing a poem in which every line contains an object and an action. She also suggests that the lines have nothing to do with each other. They should be independent, to resist the urge that many writers have to connect images or ideas into a narrative.

This was an interesting and refreshing exercise. I enjoyed it quite a bit.

If you are doing your own poem-a-day project, consider using a prompt like the ones in *The Practice of Poetry*. It's a good way to stretch your poetic muscles in ways you would not necessarily find on your own.

# Table

Like a stilled and obedient
quadruped holding
an infinite yoga pose, it
holds bowls of
fruit for us, only us.

It sometimes dons
a covering cloth,
revealing a somewhat
surprising tendency
for modesty.

Tables shade the floor
and are constantly
in danger of becoming
objects of cult affection,

collecting, as they do,
clumps of disciple chairs
eager for the wisdom of
the table, the protection

of the table, and
the unbearable charm
of the table's
super strength.

*—24 December 2019*

---

The idea here was to consider an ordinary object and find aspects of it that were either startling or unconventional. I chose a table. You can hardly get more ordinary than that. I began the poem by writing down a list of aspects of tables. Some of them are in the poem. Some are not. I was struck by one particular aspect of tables: that they often have chairs around them. From there it was a quick connection to the idea that chairs kind of worship tables. And from there to the notion that tables could be cult leaders.

# Shoes

They're waiting
by the door.

Sole strong,
tongues panting.

Laces unleashed
but prepped for

walking. If
you don't oblige

them, they will
take flight on

their own. Winged
cells with

journeys to take,
ground to cover

and air to
push aside.

—*25 December 2019*

---

Another case of an ordinary object given a fanciful life.

I wrote this one in about five minutes. Once I had the idea that shoes, like dogs, want to go for a walk, the whole thing fell into place.

Do you like it? Maybe you do. Maybe you don't. Did the fact that I wrote it in such a short time affect your reaction to it? I believe that many readers and writers of poetry (and prose, for that matter) have a notion that good writing entails hard work and rewriting. Most writing guides will tell you something along those lines.

I would like to offer a differing opinion. I avoid rewriting at all costs. If something is so undone as to require rewriting, I believe it is best to set that particular piece aside. Forget about it. Then write from scratch an entirely new piece. That's how you find the authentic source of writing.

This is the way I do all of my writing. I do not write a first draft, then revise it to a second draft, then continue on to a third or fourth draft and so on. I know some writers do this. I am not one of them. I do a first draft. Spellcheck it. Maybe tinker with a few misplaced words here and there, but that's it. If it doesn't work at that point, I discard it and start afresh, as though I had never done the first attempt. I find that this is the best way to get at the heart of my subject and the best way to maintain my own voice. Rewriting can destroy voice. It can smooth out the little quirks and irregularities that make you unique. It can turn you into something generic and uninteresting. Rewriting (for me) is also a terrible drudge.

Of course, you may disagree. And you may be right. I am not saying my way is the best way for everyone or even a good way. I'm saying it is the way I have chosen for myself because it appears to be the best way for me to find pleasure and value in my writing.

If you are a writer, and you find that rewriting works for you, then by all means continue doing what you do. I know there are writers who relish the prospect of diving into a first draft and doing a rewrite of it. However, if you find rewriting an unbearable chore that sucks the joy out of creativity (as I do) consider not rewriting for a while and see what happens. If it doesn't work for you, you can always go back to rewriting.

# Tree Secrets

the leaves
always stop
talking as
soon as they
see me walking

*—26 December 2019*

Plants often seem like they know more than they tell. This short poem attempts to capture that feeling. Note the internal rhyme of "talking" and "walking." It holds the poem together.

# Scales

the day
teeters on
the twin
spires of
the second
and hour
hand
congruent
on the
number

12

with
the twin
pans of
morning
and
afternoon
on either
side rarely
finding
balance

*—27 December 2019*

Should you show your poems to other people? Should you try to get your poems published? Should you publish them yourself?

These can be intensely personal questions, and each poet has to answer them for themselves. In the past I have published some of my poems and decided others should not be presented to the public. Many others were not presented to the public because I couldn't find an editor who wanted to publish them. That's just part of the publishing process.

For this project I decided to put my efforts on public display. I am putting up every poem I write on Facebook on the day I write it, where anyone with a Facebook account (which is a lot of people at this date) can see them on a daily basis.

I like reading the comments folks leave and enjoy all the likes I get, so it's a gratifying part of the project. It also keeps me sharp. I try to do something good every day so I don't disappoint my regular readers.

You might want to do something similar. In the internet era, when publishing means clicking a link, it is easier than ever to get your work before the public.

# Invitation

The tarantula's
got a name
that has brought
it world wide fame.

It's a spider
that delivers
all kinds of
dread and shivers.

But the one
in our backyard
does not put
us on guard.

It moves with
beauty and grace,
traversing the
walled-in space.

It likes to check
us out,
when we are
out and about.

We love to watch
its meanderings
and never fear
its double fangs.

So raise a glass
to tarantulas:
our bold and
friendly crawling cuz.

And come on
over some time
to greet this
creature sublime.

It will welcome
your presence here
and quell
any nascent fear.

You'll then be
friends forever,
and think of
squashing one never.

*—28 December 2019*

---

We actually do have at least one tarantula living in our backyard. I always like seeing it come out of its hole in the ground and roam around the property. It usually happens after a rain, so that's when I watch for it.

I probably don't need to point out the rhymes in this one. They are pretty obvious. Rhyming is almost mandatory for light verse. It really helps to lend a poem a sense of humor.

# Trigger Warning

Expect to experience:

Scenes of uncontrollable kindness,
exceptionally graphic gratitude,

uncommonly explicit tenderness,
and cutting edge depictions of joy.

Don't be alarmed by these
displays of aberrant behavior.

Let them embrace you.
Allow them to find a home

in the space in your chest
reserved for dread.

*—29 December 2019*

---

Didn't get to write this one until late in the day. I slept in, spent most of the day working on things around the house, then went to dinner with friends, which turned into a three-hour visit. Got home close to eight o'clock. Did I feel pressure? Not a bit of it! Plenty of time to get my poem in before midnight.

I wrote this one on my phone while sitting in the living room with the television playing an episode of *Air Disasters*. I'm not saying there's a connection, just setting the scene.

I played around with the stanzas a bit, getting them into couplets. I do like a series of couplets in a poem. The form feels very inviting.

# The Skewed Perspectives of Museum Employees

Last night
we turned

all the
pictures over

so the
images were

pressed flat
against the

wall and
the backs

of the
canvases were

displayed to
the world

and then
we let

the public
in and

nobody seemed
to notice

what we
had done.

—30 December 2019

I do often look at the backs of framed pictures. The stapled canvas, the creases in the corner, the fraying threads, they all have a beauty and integrity of their own. Sometimes they are better works of art than the picture on the reverse. Hence this poem.

# Home Improvements

The mountain
pierced the sky,
its peak out
of sight on
the other side
of the blue-slate
surface.

Which should
have been OK.
It was, after all,
nature's way.

But we hauled
heavy equipment
up the slope,
and pushed the
sky higher to reveal
the white snow
atop the mountain.

Now the peak
is bright against
the sky. And we
often sigh to
look at it.

And the sky,
well, the sky,
with its infinite
resilience

has a way of
healing itself,
we're sure.

*—31 December 2019*

I started out trying to write rhyming couplets, but the rhymes weren't coming to me. I had no good ones for peak, or sky, or even mountain, for that matter. But I had this idea about the sky being an infinite flat surface that could be moved if necessary. So I abandoned the impulse to rhyme and let the vision I had come out in short lines. Here's the result.

My original title was "Mountain" but that seemed too bland for what the poem was doing. Instead, I turned the focus on the folks rearranging nature for their own amusement and came up with "Home Improvements," which subtly indicates that there might be more such rearrangements in the offing, giving the poem a kind of dread subtext with readers perhaps wondering what the "we" of the poem is going to do next.

# January

# Why is the Sky Blue?

children need to ask certain questions of their parents

faith is a crucial part of a fulfilling life

the public needs the protection of law enforcement

no one ever listens to it no matter how much it says

the very concept is completely unexpected

it is fond of robin's eggs

cursing is language's most expressive mode

all the other colors were taken

it has no one to love

*—1 January 2020*

---

Blue is one of the more expressive colors. It crops up in all kinds of phrases: "blue in the face," "going blue," "thin blue line," "out of the blue," "feeling blue," "blue nose," and so on. Couple that with the fact that the sky is often (but not always) blue, and you have the poem above: answers to that classic of children's questions: "Why is the sky blue?"

Note that I tackled the color blue in my poem for 1 December. Obviously it's a color that inspires me.

# Bits and Pieces

Going against the grain
always involves extra effort.

Glaciers used to be here
grinding rocks into gravel.

Fields of grain harvest
the wind to wave at us.

The milky way is a beach where
stars stand in for grains of sand.

Our grainy cells prefer
to clump together.

Coarse-grained sandpaper
doesn't always smooth the way.

Pomegranates are hard to eat
and usually not worth it.

Silos filled with grain will
sometimes explode.

I never comb my beard
against the grain.

Except when I'm
preparing to trim it.

—*2 January 2020*

A series of variations on the theme of grain, and words derived from it. A meditation of sorts. We live in a grainy world, with collections of discrete and tiny objects (atoms and cells) making up bigger objects. I wanted to give a sense of the mystery of things in this poem, so I refrained from making it too coherent. It is, after all, a complete thing (a poem) made of discrete things (stanzas.) Just as a beach is a complete thing made of discrete grains of sand.

# Memory is Not Reliable, Especially About Avalanches

That was the year the mountains
decided to come down to the valley
for an extended visit
and many of us in town
greeted them with kisses and warm hugs
and murmured *thank yous*
for all the years they stood
against the wind and the rain
and the snow just for our benefit

*—3 January 2020*

This morning I woke up with an image in my head of people kissing mountains. I vaguely recall that this might have come from a poem I read many years ago, but the author and the poem itself is lost to memory.

    I began to play around with the image. Why would people be kissing mountains? How would that scene unfold? The result is today's poem.

# Notes Toward a Theory of Cuts

So many cuts over the years
impossible to count them all

In the web between my
thumb and index finger
due to mishandling
a brand new paper-cutter

Just above my eye
from a rock-throwing kid
giving me a red shadow eyebrow

At the base of my left ring
finger after breaking pop
bottles on concrete steps

Other places lost to memory

At least two required stitches

At least one of those blood
flows made me woozy

There's a reason Band-Aids
are so ubiquitous

Lucky to have a system in place
that heals all those cuts

Not everyone is so fortunate

Cuts always fascinate as they
move from oozing red
to crusty scab
to barely visible line

The blood wants to escape
but I hold it all in place

I'm a prison for several
quarts of iron-heavy fluid

Every atom of that iron
was manufactured in stars

The stars above are
incubators for iron

See a meteor streak
across the sky like a cut
oozing light instead of blood

No need for extended healing
after such an incision

The light fades

The sky never bleeds for long

*—4 January 2020*

---

Once again, a poem from a fleeting image. Last night, as I was drifting off to sleep, I thought of cuts. What they mean. How they heal. How seeing your own blood can be very alarming. In my hypnagogic state, I imagined cuts might be a suitable subject for a poem.

When I sat down to write the poem, the title came first. My conceit was to go from the personal to the universal. Everything we are and do has a place in the universe. Today's poem tried to make that connection plain through scientific knowledge (that iron, a crucial element in blood, is made in stars) and through evocative imagery (meteor trails as cuts in the sky.)

# Eternal Voyage

Think of the
captains who

pilot the
boats down to

graves and lift
the contents

up to the
sky where the

forces of
nature work

to remake
the spent husks

into some
semblance of

afterlife.
Do you see

the captain's
eyes? Or the

captain's tears?
Do you feel

the deep strength
of your own

insistent
heart telling

you there is
always hope?

*—5 January 2020*

The words of "Swing Low Sweet Chariot" came to me as I was sitting down to write today's poem. I never know how or why this sort of thing happens, but I don't fight it. I assume it came to me for a reason and work with what it gives me.

I understand the song to be a depiction of a dead or dying person grateful for the opportunity to go up to heaven. As I considered the words of the song, I began to wonder about how that chariot was being guided. Was there a driver?

From there, I imagined a boat descending from the skies and diving into graves to take the dead up. It felt like a more appropriate form of conveyance than a chariot. And that idea naturally led to wondering about who was guiding the boat. A captain, surely, who would likely be moved by their mission and cargo.

If you're going to write a poem a day for an extended period of time, you will learn to seize every fleeting image or scrap of lyric or bit of dream that flies through your head. They are all grist for the mill. They all, every one of them, can be the basis for a poem. Just be on the alert for them and thank fate for bringing them to you.

# Melancholy Mercy

When wildfires break out
in forests populated by wild creatures
individual deer will sometimes catch fire.

As they run from the flaming trees
wrapped in flame themselves and
screaming howling bellowing

to the world
the state will sometimes provide
armed personnel who shoot the dear dead

so they don't have to endure
a more horrible demise.
Trading death by fire for death by lead.

It's a strange ballistic compassion
with the shooters
never receiving thanks

for their service.
Watching as
the animals fall

stilled but still aflame
smoke rising
from their quarry and their rifles.

*—6 January 2020*

Yesterday Kim's sisters came to The Sanctuary for the afternoon. It was a gloriously warm day, the kind that happens with some regularity in winter in the desert, and we spent some time outside talking and reminiscing. The conversation turned to the state of the world and how wildfires seemed to be breaking out all over the planet, including, most alarmingly, the widespread fires in Australia.

One of Kim's sisters mentioned that when she lived in Tennessee there was a large wildfire and that the state had people who would shoot deer that were aflame to put them out of their misery. As soon as she said that, we all fell silent. It was a disturbing and vivid image. I knew immediately that it was a subject for a poem. I made no notes for it, but when I came to write my poem this morning, the image was there, and I began writing the poem and quickly got the first few stanzas.

I had trouble with the ending. I couldn't find a suitable image for the final couple of stanzas. I took a break from the poem and spent some time erasing pencil lines from a copy of *The Complete Poems of Elizabeth Bishop*, which I had purchased used, not knowing it was riddled with notes, some in ink and some in pen. After a few minutes of meditative erasing of several pages of pencil notes, the notion of smoke rising from a rifle came to me, and I scurried back to my computer and composed the final few lines.

This was perhaps more detail of poem construction than you needed, but I wanted to illustrate the idea that sometimes taking a break from composition by performing some physical task can give you a new perspective and a way to finish what might have been giving you problems.

# Keep it Simple

Unexpected rhymes are
the best, bar

none.

*—7 January 2020*

I read Ben Lerner's little book *The Hatred of Poetry* yesterday. Lerner has several poetry collections to his credit and has accumulated some fame and critical recognition for his work. He begins his book by quoting the entirety of Marianne Moore's short poem "Poetry" in which she states that she dislikes poetry. Moore is, of course, a legendary and revered poet.

Huh. Here are two accomplished poets who don't seem to particularly like poetry. How can this be? I read on.

The book is short enough to be read in a single sitting, which I did. The gist of it seems to be that Lerner (and Moore, I think) believe that poetry is all potential. There are no good poems because none of them can achieve the ideal state of the perfect poem. And yet, as Moore says at the end of "Poetry," it does have "a place for the genuine."

In other words, our efforts will always fall short, but the attempt is always worth it. Or, to put it another way, what poetry strives to express is inexpressible, but the urge to express it anyway is what poetry is all about.

I'm not sure I agree, at least not completely. I am perfectly willing to accept that my attempts at poetry do not achieve perfection. I am not, however, quite willing to accept that no one has achieved that state. In the uncounted millions of poems that have been written over the centuries, isn't it possible that at least one of them rose to the level of pure authenticity?

In any case, I do recommend Lerner's book as an example of a poet actively examining his own urge to write poems and for his analyses of other poets.

I certainly find myself impatient with certain poets and poems. Sometimes they ramble on to such an extent that I cannot finish reading their individual poems. Other times they seem so banal as to strain my patience. When either of these states occur, I simply put that book or poem aside and move on to something else. There is no need, ever, to subject myself to a reading experience that is less than absorbing.

I seek out the interesting, the exciting, the electrifying. I discard everything else.

# Sudbury, Ontario

The streets of my hometown were always large
and wide. They seemed to hook the sky and drag
it down to the ground. Bicycling up the hills,
my lungs and legs would burn, as though the air
was fire, and I a glowing cinder.

My years away from town dimmed memory's
trick light. Where was the shortcut home, the one
that passed the park? How did I pick my way
across the rocky slopes that nestled in
between the fabled streets and roads?

Then when I found my way back to my old
hometown, the streets were small and narrow, much
like a tiny map. The hills that once were
challenge, now no more than slight rise. How could
my town have shrunk, my flame extinguished so?

*—8 January 2020*

---

Another classic theme of poetry: the failure of memory to capture reality. I grew up in Sudbury, a mining town in Northern Ontario. I remember the town as very large. Yet, when I returned to visit my mother, I was struck by how small it seemed. There was one hill, especially, that was an enormous challenge to me as a kid riding my bicycle. I remember it as unbearably steep. It was nothing of the kind. It was a slight rise, nothing more. This was very startling to me. I tried to capture that reaction in today's poem.

## Assisted Living

We dreamed each other
before we ever met.
Our first date was
blind, but then, aren't

they all? The wedding
was on a frozen
pond, how crazy was
that? No honeymoon: too

much work to do.
The children's early years
now just a blur.
Those trips to Alaska

saved us more than
once. And do you
remember how we left
our house for the

last time? How we
both cried and turned
to our uncertain future
there in the zippered

horizon between sky and
mountain? Wasn't it just
yesterday that we had
our dreams that did

not include this view
through institutional double panes?
Let's hold hands again
like that first blinding

blazing stroke of love
when all was future
and we gave no
thought to the past.

*—9 January 2020*

I used to make outreach visits to the local assisted living center and got to know many of the people that lived there. One woman told me that the center was nice, the people were good to her, but she missed her other life, the one with her husband and the house she had lived in for 50 years.

I had her in mind as I wrote today's poem.

The impetus was a prompt from *The Daily Poet* by Kelli Russell Agodon and Martha Silano. The suggestion was to write the history of a relationship in lines of exactly six words. I modified the suggestion to lines of four words.

# Immigration is a Fever Dream

You were in a
different land
last night. Now you
wake up and the

sky is copper
hued with trees made
of burlap and
rivers tasting

of mint. You reach
for the country
you knew but it
is dead now, just

a spent cinder
in your brain. You
have work to do
here. You know it's

not enough for
your heart, which mourns
the comfort of
easy knowledge.

*—10 January 2020*

Coming to a new place can be exciting and refreshing. The travel industry is built on just such emotions. But there can be a darker side to going to a new place. It can be disconcerting and even dangerous, and folks will often find that their old home, the one they understood and loved, can have a powerful hold on them. I tried to give that aspect of new places a voice in today's poem.

# Always Go

Should you attend your own funeral?
Of course. You always go. Always.

There would be some issues involved.
You'd have to get your astral aspect
out of your corpse for one thing.
Not impossible, but still, a challenge,
especially to those not used to such things.

Then you need to think about what
to wear. Something conservative is
usually best, but a colorful ensemble,
with bold cuts and whatever baubles
strike your fancy is possible as well.

Should you offer any remarks? Tread
carefully here. Now that you're dead,
everything you say will be seen as
overly important: a voice from the
grave, as it were. People expect
yards and yards of profundity
from the voices of dead folks.

What else? Probably best not to
go to the dinner afterward. You
would be stared at for the entire
afternoon, and not in a good way.

In conclusion, attending your own
funeral can be an adventure and a
lovely way to shuck the burdens of
living. Just remember that people
expect good manners from everyone,
even those that have left the room.

*—11 January 2020*

Driving to work the other day, I heard a commentator on the radio ask the question: "Should you go to a funeral?" His answer was: "Yes. You always go."

Those last two words sounded like the title of a poem to me. Then I wondered who could not actually abide by that rule. The obvious choice was the one being buried or cremated. The result is today's poem.

# The Moon Rises Without Disguises

She will not attempt
trickery with some

odd mask. What you
see is who she is.

Loyal to a fault,
she will be found

circling the Earth
without fail. Some

times, when her
companion throws

shade on her, she
glows red, as though

cursed with an errant
embarrassment,

like she's been caught
thinking things she

ought not think.
But that is illusion.

Her shame retreats
as soon as our

planet moves on.
Other times she

displays a face, or
a rabbit, or even a

wedge of cheese.
That's the legend,

anyway. I usually
just think of her

as a joyous soul,
singing month-long

notes in slow motion,
her phases like the

opening and closing
of a mouth. She takes

her time. Listen to her
silent song and you

will feel the power of
patient beings everywhere.

*—12 January 2020*

There are so many poems about the moon, and why not? The moon is a potent symbol: bright and ubiquitous. A couple of mornings ago, I saw a red moon, bright as a jewel, setting behind the horizon as I drove to work. Last evening Kim and I saw a yellow moon rise above the streets of Tucson as we drove home. It was a glorious sight, large and lemony, with a rabbit clearly visible in her features.

    Two remarkable lunar sightings in as many days. How could I not write a poem about the moon after that?

# The Constellations Updated for Modern Sensibilities

Taurus
is now a smiley face emoji;

Orion
a still from an internet cat video;

Cassiopeia
the smoke from a rampant wildfire;

Draco
follows the line of a Presidential poll;

Aquarius
is the face of a Kardashian;

The Little Dipper
now deemed to be a flip phone;

The Big Dipper
an iphone;

Andromeda
from now on will be the Amazon logo;

Gemini
a trans person;

Pisces
henceforth a bomb built by a wealthy nation;

Leo
a self driving car;

and Cancer
resembles nothing more than your house on Google street view.

*—13 January 2020*

Constellations of stars are more or less static across centuries. How they are viewed, of course, is not. Each culture brings its unique perspective to them. That simple fact was the impetus for today's poem.

# Remembering a Colleague

*"Any man's death diminishes me."*
—John Donne

Years ago I worked
with a woman who
once quoted the above
words to me. She's

dead now, and I
wish it weren't so,
as I wish so
many of us would

live forever. I would
ask her if she
still believed in Donne's
words. Was she diminished

by Soleimani's death? I
imagine she would answer
immediately. She was a
decisive person who knew

what she thought and
had no problem expressing
those thoughts and I'm
sure she would say

something like: "Yes, of
course I am diminished,
just as I am
diminished by all the

assassinations and murders that
occur, depressingly, on a
daily basis in this
world." But I will

never know and it
is perhaps unfair of
me to speculate on
what she might have

said. She died in
her sleep of a
heart attack. I still
miss her opinions,

her views of the
hurly burly in this
world and life drones
on now without her.

*—14 January 2020*

I asked folks on Facebook to suggest themes or subjects for me to write a poem. The first came from Patricia Boutilier. She suggested "Soleimani." He was a high ranking Iranian general who was killed by a U.S. strike a few days ago.

I knew of his death from news reports, but I knew nothing about him. I spent some time online learning about him and his life. Then I remembered someone I worked with years ago at the library. She was fond of the John Donne quote I used in the poem. I would have been very interested in her view of the general and so I imagined a conversation with her, and the poem grew from there.

I solicited suggestions from my Facebook friends as a way of opening myself up to themes and approaches I would not consider on my own. This is a perfect example. I would not have written a poem about Soleimani if someone had not offered the subject as a theme for a poem.

# The Meaning of Fraud

A guy in college once offered me
a hundred dollars to take an exam for him.
He wasn't interested in studying for it
and knew I knew the material well.

I imagined myself
impersonating him and going into the exam room
and sitting down and pretending to be him
and answering the questions he did not want to answer.

I even imagined the moment he
would hand over the hundred dollars.
The smile on his face as his conviction
that money buys everything was confirmed.

I told him I absolutely would not do such a thing
and he looked at me with a pitying expression.
"You'll never get anywhere," he said,
"with an attitude like that."

It opened my eyes.
I started asking around
and found out that lots of students on campus
wrote papers and took exams for other people.

At least, that's what people told me.
Maybe they were just playing with me,
seeing how I, the naif, would react.
I don't know but they did say

all you had to do
if you wanted something wrong done
was to ask the right person.
That was a life lesson

they never taught you in class.
The guy was asking me if I was the right person.
If I understood life the way he did:
That integrity was for chumps.

*—15 January 2020*

The second poem to come from prompts offered by my Facebook contacts. This one came from my sister Nancy Milosevic. Her prompt was "Rights and wrongs."

# Intimate Gargoyle

O lithopedion, what
private Medusa turned

you to stone? Are you
protector or irritator?

You keep your mother
from infection, but you

cause a lifetime of pain
and discomfort. In your

death, you are a calcified
monument to a life

that might have been.
Arrested potential, ghastly

reminder of the delicate
fragility of life, yet dense

and solid. Do you yearn
for your lost life? Do you

wear a wide grin, frozen
for all time, keeping the

years distant, supporting
the weight of the world?

*—16 January 2020*

Another prompt from a Facebook friend. This one came from Jessamyn Smyth and was a single word: "lithopedion." I did not know that word. I scurried to the internet and looked it up and discovered it is from the Greek for "stone" and "infant." A stone baby. A lithopedion occurs when a fetus in an abdominal pregnancy dies and becomes calcified. It is extremely rare. Most fetus deaths in such cases get absorbed back into the mother's body. A lithopedion is formed when the fetus is too large to be absorbed. The mother's body will calcify the dead fetus which prevents the mother from becoming infected.

Lithopedions can remain in the mother's body for decades and they are often not detected until the mother dies, or she undergoes some medical treatment. Lithopedions have been discovered when the mother is X-rayed for some other reason. Some lithopedions have been mistaken for tumors and have been discovered during surgery.

Women with lithopedions do not typically become infertile. There are many documented cases of women having other children while harboring a lithopedion. They can, however, cause much pain and discomfort.

After absorbing all that information, I turned to the task of making a poem from the prompt. I considered perhaps giving a voice to a lithopedion and toyed with that idea for a while. Another try was to bring Medusa into it, since she is prominent in Greek mythology and is said to turn men into stone. My final idea was the gargoyle. Those odd stone creatures on some old buildings that hold up slabs of concrete on their backs and are often grinning: a frozen expression frozen in time, just as a lithopedion is.

# Sad Love Song for a Long Distance Relationship

The moon drops dappled reflections
of itself on the surface of the ocean.

The ocean, aroused, yearns for the moon
and rises on tidal pulses toward the

object of its affection. But there is no
possibility of consummation here. The moon,

obeying the inexorable laws of physics,
retreats from the ocean at the pace of

an inch or so every twelve revolutions.
Call it the long sad goodbye. They can

yearn for each other, and they do, but no
embrace is in the offing. No way for the

ocean to feel the cool smooth surface of
the moon. No way for the moon to

experience the bracing teeming over
whelming life of the cauldron called the sea.

*—17 January 2020*

---

This one came from a prompt on Facebook by Char Kinter: "Ocean, moon."

As I indicated in a previous commentary, the moon is a particularly ripe subject for poetry. Poets really seem to like writing about the moon. I'm no exception. I could probably put together a solid chapbook of my moon poems.

Char's prompt took me in a different direction, however, making me consider the relationship between the ocean and the moon. They do interact. The moon is the principal engine of the tides. But they can never connect physically. That made me think of lovers separated by distance and from there the poem fell into place.

# Corn Dolly's Long Day

After I was made from the husks of corn they left me
    in the field.
It was their way of thanking the air and the sun and
    the water and the earth.
In the field I was surrounded by broken stalks of
    spent plants.
Later I was retrieved from the field and brought to
    the harvest dance.
There I was given the honor of remaining in the center
    while they stomped and whirled about.
During the dance they drenched me with water as a
    symbol of the harvest.
I am always symbol, always the embodiment of
    something other than myself.
They offered me a corn man but I refused him and
    his advances.
I heard murmurs among the people that I was to be
    fed to the cows for their nourishment.
They wanted so much from me and I was just a doll:
    nothing more.
The children found me and tossed me from one
    hand to the other.
It was my flying dream come true with the ground
    beneath me and me touching the sky.
The children grew tired of me and tossed me into a
    corner where I remained for some hours.
Now I await my next adventure, if mishaps such as I
    have endured could be called adventure.
I see them approaching me with a match in their
    hand, tiny sun, about to touch my dry body.
My future is smoke rising reaching for heights I
    never imagined, never hoped for.

*—18 January 2020*

---

Today's poem is in response to Rachel Slick's prompt: "Corn/Maize." Her prompt, at first, did not spark much in me. Some vague notions of corn on the cob and popcorn that felt less than exciting. Then I remembered Barbara Walker's *The Woman's Dictionary of Symbols and Sacred Objects* and looked up "Corn." That lead me to her short entry on "Corn Dolly." She describes several ways in which corn dollies were used at harvest times. I incorporated most of them into the poem.

# Deconstructed Baba Yaga

The large pestle, fractured, is most alarming, to see it
	lying broken in the misty woods.
The mortar several yards beyond, moored in a
	branch like a beached whale crying for breath.
A broom, unbroken, but wrong, crossing a writhing
	branch and looking lost, lonely.
The call for help in a language I do not understand
	but do not need to: cries are universal.
I look around, try to follow the source of the cries,
	my skin electric with adrenaline surge.
Patches of fog still cling to trees everywhere like giant white fruit ripe for picking.
In one of the fading patches an old woman, perched
	on a limb, just emerging into view.
She trembles, from cold or fear or both, and I see
	blood trickle down her face.
I tell her not to worry, that I will climb the tree and
	attend to her, that I will save her.
She offers no understanding of my words, and wraps
	her arms tight around the tree trunk.
As I climb the tree I remember tales of a witch that
	flies through the air scaring everyone.
When I reach the limb where she sits, I touch her
	arm, murmur soothing words.
She faces me, her large nose, blue skin, and oversized teeth offering a vision of power.
The cut above her eyebrow is deep enough for discomfort but will not threaten her life.
I tell her I will care for her as I dab her wound with
	the end of my sleeve and she sighs.
We sit on the limb for some time, the sustaining life
	of the forest there for our protection.
It takes many minutes, but in the end she is ready to
	climb down with me.
We navigate the trunk and bark of the tree with ease
	and reach the ground refreshed.
We stand together on the springy forest floor and
	she stares at me with wild wide eyes.

> I think of chicken feet, and then she turns from me
>     and disappears into the woods.
> No other outcome possible, I suppose, no other end-
>     ing to this story would fit.
> Who did I help, what does it matter, and did it really
>     happen as I think I experienced it?
>
>                               *—19 January 2020*

Tim Schirack offered "Baba Yaga" as a prompt on Facebook. I knew who Baba Yaga was, and I have read some accounts of her. She is the embodiment of female power who flies through the air in a mortar, with a pestle for an oar. She lives in a hut with chicken feet that spins around. She tends to scare people to death, and then eat them. But she is also a fertility symbol. Some accounts say that Baba Yaga will grant a child to the woman who binds the last sheaf of grain in a harvest. She is a seasonal witch from Eastern European traditions with a lot of depth to her history. I felt my task was to find a different angle than those I had seen before. I elected to go with a Baba Yaga in trouble.

    I imagined the child that might have come from the woman who bound the last sheaf. What would that child's view of Baba Yaga be? From there, I envisioned a Baba Yaga in trouble with the child, now grown, coming to her aid.

# All Housing is Temporary

I lived in a condo
until an arsonist burned it down.

I lived in a tree-house
until they cut down the forest.

I lived in a boat
until the ocean turned acid and melted it away.

I lived in a cardboard box
until the rain turned it to mush.

I lived in a tent
until someone knifed it to shreds.

I lived on the streets
until they said I was criminal.

I lived in a dorm
until they made me graduate.

I lived in a car
until it was repossessed.

I lived in a friend's basement
until they grew tired of me.

I lived under a bridge
until the cops chased me away.

I lived in a condemned building
until it collapsed around me.

I lived in a dream
until I woke up.

I lived in bliss
until they told me I was homeless.

*—20 January 2020*

Another prompt from a Facebook follower. This one from Timothy Ford: "Houselessness!" At first, I thought the term was just another word for homelessness, but I looked it up and it is a term preferred by some activists working for people seeking shelter. The idea is that such folks are not homeless, since a home can be anywhere, even a spot under the stars. Houseless is a more accurate description of their situation.

The difference between the two can seem like a semantic quibble, but advocates say using the term "houseless" grants a measure of humanity and respect that the term "homeless" does not.

I considered the difference between the two for a time, then came up with the above poem.

# Rave Reviews

The rattlesnakes that live
around our house don't

need gold stars or words
of praise. They move with

mesmerizing grace and
display markings made by

nature's uncompromising
unerring eye. They are what

they are. The stars in the
sky could not be designed

to a finer standard. They
burn with exemplary light

for many billions of years.
Entropy says forever is a

fool's errand and nothing
will remain as it is for long.

Maybe so. I won't quarrel
with the unrelenting logic

of degradation. Instead, I'll
hold a piece of sandstone

in my hand and marvel at
the forces that made it

the most beautiful object
anyone could imagine.

*—21 January 2020*

Another Facebook suggestion, this one from Judy Bane, who's prompt was "Excellence."

This one made me work a little. I could not get any lines down that resonated with the prompt. I decided the prompt was too abstract. It elicited in me only mushy ideas about greatness, supremacy, skill, talent, and so on. That wasn't bringing anything compelling to the page.

So I switched strategies and started listing things that were excellent, actual objects. My mind went to objects and creatures from nature. I could have picked any of millions. I chose the rattlesnake to begin with because lots of folks are terrified of rattlesnakes, so I knew it would bring up a visceral reaction for many.

The stars are ancient objects of wonder. They have been mysterious and more or less perfect for as long as people have been around, and much longer than that. Also, I find the view of the night sky, when the stars are out and bright, particularly inspiring.

Finally, the sandstone. Specimens of that particular rock often display lovely layers of coloring and pattern. I have a sphere of sandstone on my desk as I write this and find it a comforting object.

So there were three instances of excellence. That was enough. Three is a classic number of examples to include in an explanation. Or a poem, for that matter. It's enough to make the case, but not too much to get tedious. I hope.

The lesson for me in this prompt and this poem is to steer abstract concepts into something concrete. We live in a world of objects. You could do worse than treat those objects as the subjects of your poems.

# We Were Mercenary

Our crops depended
on the tears of the
giants during the
years of extended
drought. We approached them
in those days with sad
tales of lost loves and
missing pets, acts of
selfless kindness and
shameless displays of
ill children. We were
desperate and lost
a part of our best
selves, it's true. But the
giants are truly
a sentimental
people and they would
cry on cue, and we
were there with all our
irrigation gear
to ferry their tears
to our fields. Later,
in more rainy years,
we apologized
to the giants. They
looked at us with great
watery eyes and
said it was nothing
but we knew better.
The salt of tears is
the bite of anguish,
and forced smiles bring
only false comfort.

*—22 January 2020*

Another prompt poem. The prompt was "Irrigation" and came from Marshall Shapiro.

Some years ago I wrote a poem about a giant. I have also written a novel, *The Last Giant,* about giants. They are a theme I come back to often. Giants are fantasy creatures, clearly, since they could not exist in this world. They are too large and could not support their own weight.

Nevertheless, they are a potent symbol of benign and clumsy strength. I often envision them as quite sentimental and therefore prone to crying. That fact came to me as I considered the prompt. I imagined little people living with giants and using giant tears to help water their crops.

# Green Begins With H

H is such a stout
form. You could
build a greenhouse
on its frame. Equip
it with solar panels.
Extol the green
virtues of its use
and construction.
Stand on it with
unreserved confidence.
Even make it in
the shape of an H.
Open hands. Green
life. H is for healing.
Green is a color
made from the sun.
We are all creatures
of a heliocentric
system, capital H
hovering over us,
hacking a path
across the sky.

—*23 January 2020*

I was contemplating the color green, how it is so symbolic of nature, since plants are so attached to it. I know that plants eat solar energy and turn it into green chlorophyll. Those two thoughts chased each other in my mind and I tried to find their union in this poem.

# Saguaro Acupuncture

Giant limbed cactus
is just like us: bones
surrounded by flesh,
arms greeting the day.

It would be grand to
sprout white blossoms on
my head like they do.
Have bats come drink from

those temporary
wells. But they likely
don't have such thoughts. They
hold their notions close.

Present clustered thorns
to the air, saying:
Here's my view of the
world. My simple chi.

*—24 January 2020*

Acupuncture involves needles placed along a body's energy meridians. A saguaros cactus, of which there are many in this area, has many needles in the form of thorns arranged in energy meridians. Those facts got me to wondering what a saguaro might be thinking, with all that energy flowing through it, and what all those thorns, like clusters of acupuncture needles, might signify.

# Morning Blessed With Cooking Utensils

there's the ladle
catching the sun's light
with a glint in its eye

cast iron pan
seasoned by years
has seen it all

wooden spoons
worn and smooth
ready to mix it up

modern blender
monolithic and aloof
above it all

the grater leaning
against the chopping
block quietly efficient

measuring cups
nested into an orderly
and accurate hierarchy

spatula trying
constantly to turn
over a new leaf

oh the knives
sharp-witted with
cutting remarks

garlic press
crushing it
as always

and the big yellow bowl
holding the streaming
sunlight just for me

*—25 January 2020*

Much of the charm of poetry, for me, is finding the extraordinary in the ordinary. For this poem I took a gathering of perfectly ordinary objects, cooking utensils and tried to see them in a different light. I even added the light of the early morning sun, when it streams in through my kitchen window and lights everything up in a way that doesn't happen during the rest of the day.

# Single-Minded Master of Measuring

The inchworm moves
in consecutive arcs
on trees and bushes
in forests and parks.

The inchworm measures
without leaving marks
or footprints or tracks
or giving off sparks.

The inchworm is quiet
so it never barks;
it's like those stealthy
fish known as sharks.

The inchworm's devoted
to task without larks,
constantly counting
in light and the darks.

*—26 January 2020*

---

I don't question the muses. When they say to write about a subject, I listen. The last few days, inchworms have been in my thoughts. It felt like the universe wanted me to write about them. Some light verse seemed in order. The inchworms I have seen always display an arc. So I began with the word arc. Light verse usually benefits from rhymes, so I wrote down all the rhymes for arc that I could think of. I ended up with a list of about a dozen or so. Some of them seemed tough: how was I going to get in sharks or sparks in a poem about inchworms? By determination, that's how. Make it work!

For those who want to do as I do, think of a word, then write down all the rhymes for that word. If you can't find at least ten or so, then move on to another word. Now use your rhymes to guide you through the poem. It's a fun exercise and can result in some pleasing verse.

# Missing the Mark

ground loop
shakin' coop

wheezy dupe
lucky goop

holy hoop
brunt stoop

plea soup
swindle scoop

*—27 January 2020*

Sometimes rhymes take hold of my imagination, and I can't let them go. Yesterday it was rhymes for "arc" which I deployed throughout the poem. Today it was rhymes for "soup."

I started by writing down all the rhymes for soup that I knew. Then I turned them all into two word phrases: Pea soup, single scoop, round loop, chicken coop, and so on. I arranged the phrases into two line stanzas and was pleased by the musicality of the poem, especially when I read it out loud.

It felt like a pretty good poem in itself, but then I decided to take it one step further and play around with the phrases. So I revised the first word of each line to make it a close variant of that word. Thus, "pea" became "plea," "single" became "swindle," and so on. The poem still retained its musicality, but now it was also something of a puzzle and a bit surreal. Just my kind of thing!

Rhymes are mysterious and powerful. A lot of modern poetry, including most of mine, dispenses with rhymes, but it is often worthwhile to explore the dynamics of rhyming, how it shapes a poem and gives it character.

# The Surest Sign of Fall

arrived when
I walked to
work at the
library and

passed the
oak tree
there and
heard the
acorns falling
on the roof

each one
making a
dry rapping
sound like
drum beats

calling for
the cold
of winter
to come
marching in
on icy feet
and snowy
strides

*—28 January 2020*

This poem describes what actually happened in October when I lived in Stevenson, Washington. I would hear the acorns falling on the library roof. It was a sound I grew to associate with fall. And the coming winter.

# Cherry Crisp

Best to cut the cherries in
half to liberate the juices.

Spread them out in the pie pan.
Add a sprinkle of cinnamon.

Stir in a bit of maple syrup.
Set that aside for the moment.

You might want to admire
all those red half spheres

crowded in on one another
like some field of red tulips.

Now take a few generous
spoonfuls of coconut oil.

Melt them in the microwave
or the stove top until

the oil is clear and liquid.
Add the oil to a big scoop

full of quick cooking oats.
Stir that around until the

oats are coated with the oil
then spread the mixture

as though it were an overcast
sky onto that field of red

tulips you planted earlier.
Slide the whole creation

into a three hundred and
fifty degree oven to sun

bake the oats and the
cherries for about an hour.

Eat it warm or cool and
consider serving it with

a scoop or two of ice cream
because, well, ice cream!

*—29 January 2020*

Recipes are a kind of poetry. They employ stripped down language, are replete with imagery, and evoke strong reactions. For one thing, they can spur people into cooking things.

Consider taking your favorite recipe or just one you know well, and turning it into a poem. Try to find images you can associate with the recipe and try to stay away from over-accurate amounts or portions. Make it free and loose. Make it a creative experience.

# Hives

We lived in a village then, with
all the men, like in the old times.

We wore coverings made of
prints dotted with flowers.

So much to struggle against.
There were shoes, but not

enough of them. The roads
meant everything in those days.

They were the way out for some,
but not enough of us. Rocks

everywhere. Nothing to eat.
Fathers found ways to be fathers,

but only if it suited them.
There were so few good times

and the brothers were attracted
to firearms for many reasons.

Bees found holes in the ground
and grew colonies of immense

proportions. They filled the air
with too much noise. Too loud

the buzzing. Then the volleys
of hail pummeling everything

we knew. We cried sometimes
as the welts rose up on our skin.

Bruises flowering on our limbs.
The bees searching for the

real flowers, becoming confused,
and zeroing in on the blooms

on our necks as we fled with arms
windmilling and legs churning.

*—30 January 2020*

There are many techniques for writing poems. Here's just one. Take a poem you like and write or type it out with generous space between each line. Now look at each line and write a riff on that line in the space beneath it. Don't try to make your riffs harmonize with one another, just concentrate on that one line and write a line or two of your own. Then go on to the next line and do the same thing. Continue in this way until you get to the end. Now erase the original lines, the ones that aren't yours. What you have left is a brand new poem inspired by the other poem, but completely yours.

    Today's poem was composed in that fashion. I took Natalie Diaz's poem "Why I Don't Mention Flowers When Conversations with My Brother Reach Uncomfortable Silences" from her collection *When My Brother Was an Aztec* and used it in the way I described above.

# Visions of Random Variations

they were a macabre
blob

bits of free
debris

an isometric
kick

in other words:
herds

*—31 January 2020*

Another trick to writing a poem: open a book at random and place your finger on a page. Write down the word under your fingertip. Do this twice more. You now have three random words. Use all three in a poem. I did that this morning. The book was Mary Kinzie's *A Poet's Guide to Poetry*. The three words I extracted from her text were "macabre," "isometric," and "debris."

> # February

# Horse Sense

The speed of light
they say is a constant

thing. The speed of
a horse more the thing

that varies from hoof
to hoof. Some will look

for ways to translate
the pounding rhythms

that mares and stallions
beat out of the ground.

What are they saying?
What meaning do they

convey in the blinding
glare of the sun at

dawn? Shadows rippling
over rocks and grass,

their flight a constancy
light cannot touch.

—1 February 2020

Another poem from three random words. The words are "horse," "light," and "look." I chose them from a copy of Angela Carter's *Burning Your Boats*.

# The Face of Kindness

I didn't have an envelope so I
constructed one from a sheet of paper
I found tumbling on the freezing wind.
I asked the clerk at the post office for
a jar of glue to paste it closed. He eyed
my shabby coat with sympathy and put
a roll of tape on the table between

us. "No glue," he said. "But this will work fine."
I hesitated. He pulled off a length
of tape and applied it to my makeshift
envelope and he was so kind about
it I had to tell him the letter on
the inside was to my daughter asking
her for money to help me through the cold.

And then I pulled out the stamp I had saved
and he took it and stuck it onto the
letter and looked up at me and told me
"Good luck. I hope it all works out for you."
And he did not turn away or scrunch his
nose or furrow his brows or fix his gaze
blankly on the spot three feet behind me.

*—2 February 2020*

I asked my loyal Facebook readers to give me three words that I would use in one of my daily poems. This is the result of the first suggestion, from Marshall Shapiro. His words were: "Envelope," "Table," and "Coat."

# Interruptus

To produce a snarling litter
of baby dinosaur critters,
a male T. Rex and a female T. Rex
must engage in snarling dino sex.

No doubt such activity was progressing
as the atmosphere the comet was ingressing.
And so the T. Rexes were interrupted
in producing that which nature intended.

Now no dinos exist on the planet
except petrified in rocks like granite.
Blame the comet not the dinosaurs:
cut down in the midst of their love roars.

*—3 February 2020*

Today's poem was composed based on Kim Antieau's three words: "Comet," "Litter," and "Sex."

The very first thing that came to me was rhyming sex with T. Rex. So I figured I would go with something humorous. Next was the comet. I knew that scientists speculate that a comet impacted the Earth and killed all the dinosaurs. So I had my plot. The rest was finding interesting rhymes and making them work in metrical lines.

This was a fun one.

# Escaping Finding Spring

I spring out of bed.
The squabbling geese
outside my cell will
give me no respite.

I hear them fighting,
the sound springing
from their throats.
Odd gurgling sound,

like water from a spring.
But I know what it means.
My friends have arrived.
This is the season of life.

The door springs open.
My comrades spring me
from my confinement.
I hold a mattress spring

in my hand. A weapon,
of sorts, defending the
indefensible. We get to the
getaway car. The engine

springs to life. I tell my
liberators I would spring
to their defense at any time
I am so grateful. They tell me

it's not necessary, but it would
be nice if I would spring for
dinner. I tell them I have no
money and they slap me on

the back, like it's a big joke.
We know, they say, we know
you're penniless. This causes
tears to spring from my eyes

and I spring forward to hide
the shame I feel, reaching
for them with the fierce
fight I remembered in the

geese: letting nothing keep
me from seeing the cool
sweet life of flowering plants
in the early days of spring.

*—4 February 2020*

Another triplet of words from one of my Facebook readers: Judy Bane. Her words were: "Geese," "Squabbling," and "Spring." My first impulse was to play on the meaning of the word spring. It has quite a few. I tried to incorporate as many as I could into the poem.

# Gentle Sky Accepts the Hurt

Stomp the ground and weave the dirt.
Grief is that which we move through.
Gentle sky accepts the hurt.

We're always on such high alert
for loss and pain and troubles new.
Stomp the ground and weave the dirt.

But worries cannot ever avert
the random acts that we will rue.
Gentle sky accepts the hurt.

Yet fate does often seem to assert
that hope is always close and true.
Stomp the ground and weave the dirt.

For if belief is short and curt
then life is but a dark bleak view.
Gentle sky accepts the hurt.

Existence will eternally exert
its constant churning vibrant zoo.
Stomp the ground and weave the dirt.
Gentle sky accepts the hurt.

—*5 February 2020*

---

This one came from my sister Nancy's three words: "Gentle," "Stomp," and "Weave." Two lines came to me immediately: "Stomp the ground and weave the dirt," and "Gentle sky accepts the hurt."

I had been reading Kiki Petrosino's collection *Witch Wife*. She often writes villanelles, which requires two lines that rhyme and that can be repeated in a poem.

Since my two lines rhymed, they could serve as the basis for a villanelle. A villanelle is a relatively constrained form. It is a poem of six stanzas. The first five are three lines long, the last one is four lines long. It has a rhyme scheme: aba aba aba aba aba abaa. It also calls for the first line of the first stanza to be the last line of the second stanza and the last line of the fourth stanza and the penultimate line of the sixth stanza. The last line of the first stanza is also the last line of the third, fifth and sixth stanza. Also, each line in the poem should have the same metrical length.

It has a lot of rules! Probably the most famous villanelle is Dylan Thomas's "Do Not Go Gentle Into That Good Night." His repeated phrases are the title and "Rage rage against the dying of the light."

To make my villanelle, I wrote out my two repeating lines and then wrote rhymes for "dirt" and "hurt." I wrote the second line of the first stanza, then listed all the rhymes I could think of for "through." Using both lists, I looked for appropriate words that would serve the developing theme of the poem, which seemed to be that hope is necessary to navigate life's troubles and that the universe has its own rules and ways that have little to do with our hopes and desires.

I managed to get the repeated phrases and the rhyme scheme right, although I did not adhere strictly to metrical length. I went with my ear on that aspect of the villanelle.

# On the Menu at the Zombie Café

Braaaaaaaaaaaaaaaaaains
of course, is the mains.

But there's also lightly sautéed pancreas
served on a bed of shredded lettuce.

Some nice pickled entrails
will fill you up without fails.

A burger of fancy grilled lung
garnished with slices of fresh tongue.

An assortment of lovely uvulas
for discerning zombie dinnuhs.

Crunchy deep fried sphincter
a bargain at fifty cents per.

Don't forget the braised liver
it will disappoint, like, never.

And for dessert some baked gall bladder
will satisfy and make you fatter.

*—6 February 2020*

Another suggestion from one of my Facebook readers, Mary Katherine Ray. Her three words were: "Pancreas," "Sphincter," and "Uvula." Ugh. Well, I asked for it, so I guess I can't complain. Mary Katherine did end her suggestions with "lol" which I took to mean she expected something humorous. So I tried to think of something funny to do with body parts. The idea of zombies came to mind. Though horrific, they are also somewhat comical, at least to me. They walk in a funny way and they like to say braaaaaaaains. At least some of the ones in popular culture do. Also, they eat brains. But surely they would like some variety in their diet. From there it was a quick leap to menu items from a restaurant catering to zombies.

It might not be much of a poem, but I hope it gives you a smile.

# The Dark

A bird will never
light on your finger—

A storm will never
snuggle up to you—

A fear will never
find a way out—

A hope will never
take root—

A task will never
hook into you—

A child will never
be your friend—

A joy will never
capture your heart—

A sky will never
drop your jaw—

A talent will never
astonish and dazzle—

As long as you keep
your shadow enwrapped.

*—7 February 2020*

---

Rachel Slick's three words "light," "fear," and "shadow" were the impetus for this poem. Not much to say about this one. I do believe most of us benefit from understanding the dark impulses we might harbor—not to act on them, but to know they are there. It helps us become whole beings who can then see the wonder all around us.

I obviously employed a repetitive construction, and I wanted readers to feel like they could come up with their own phrases, their own path to enlightenment through understanding the darkness inside and around them.

# The Point of Cactus Thorns

My cousin the cactus
thought I was too bare,
so it gave me some thorns:
they're stuck here and there.

My cousin the cactus
had sharp points to share:
Be careful around me,
you must take good care.

My cousin the cactus
said if you dare
to draw close or hug me
you'll feel pain most rare.

My cousin the cactus
was forthright and fair.
By ignoring its warning
it's thorns I now wear.

—8 February 2020

We were cutting trails through some cactus fields here on our property and I neglected to take care of myself as I should. I was having such a good time that I didn't notice how many thorns I was picking up from all the cactus I was cutting down. In other words, I was ignoring the warnings of nature. Which is generally not a good thing to do. Thorns are there for a reason. They protect the plant.

I will be more careful in the future. In the meantime, I had fun writing this poem, working it to get all the rhymes on care and dare.

# The Army's Limitations and Failures

the king
tends to cling

the knight
won't smite

the pawn
runs a con

the bishop
will slip up

the queen
is mean

and the rook
can't cook

—*9 February 2020*

---

I learned to play chess many years ago from my father. For a while I was besotted with the game. I read books of strategy and played over famous games. I regularly attended meetings of the local chess club, entered tournaments, and kept up my rating and my membership in FIDE (Fédération Internationale des Échecs). Though I never achieved a very high rating, I enjoyed playing and grew to love the beauty of the game.

    I stopped playing some time ago and did not pick up the game until relatively recently. Now I play blitz games on my phone through the Lichess app. At any time of day or night, I can fire up the app and in less than ten seconds I can be playing some player from somewhere in the world. It's marvelous.

    This poem came from considering chess pieces and their various characteristics. It's also an example of my current interest in rhyme. As I tried rhyming certain of the chess pieces, I discovered that I was beginning to delineate their weaknesses rather than their strengths. As I said before, I don't argue with the muses or with my creative urges and directions. I went with the deficiency theme and pared the stanzas down to their barest minimum.

# Be Who You Are

The rain
will explain

itself never.
It, forever,

just is
wet biz.

*—10 February 2020*

It's supposed to rain here later today. In the desert, that counts as news. I was thinking about what rain signifies. The moisture, the darkness, the life-giving qualities. All these are part of it. But what is rain to itself? Nothing but rain. No further significance needs to come from it. I came up with 12 words that I hope evokes that sentiment. Also, note the rhymes. I am on a rhyming roll.

# The Force Seize Suns

Whine tar walks on
icicle legs, stilted
cold and frozen dawn.

Spraining lifts up fresh life,
sprouting green with
relief from strife.

Some mar burns the air
we breathe, blowing heat
over sweating hair.

Awe tum drips leaves
from trees, reds and
yellows, deep rich weaves.

*—11 February 2020*


Having some fun in a punny way with the four seasons.

# Storyteller

My beautiful pen,
stuffed full of blue ink,
with my writing hand
it's always in synch.

Sometimes my pen
will give me a wink
and tell me that
it's made out of zinc.

It will insist
it skates on a rink
and is friendly with
a woods-dwelling mink.

It says it can fix
any cracked sink,
or remove the source
of a nasty bad stink.

I don't give these claims
much heed or a blink.
Their boastful nature
keeps my pen in the pink.

So on my pen's lies
I won't be a fink,
I'll just be glad
it's stuffed full of blue ink.

—12 February 2020

I'm dealing with a little head cold today. Not doing much of anything. No grant writing, no working around the house, no editing, no brush clearing, no furniture assembling, no cooking. Nothing. I read Shel Silverstein's book *Falling Up* all the way through. He is something of a genius. His poems are sprightly and macabre and funny. He comes up with amazing unexpected rhymes, which I love. And he has whimsical and odd stories to tell in his poems. In Silverstein's world, thing are always going wrong in horrible ways, but the way he tells it, you laugh rather than cry. At least I do. I imagine some readers would cringe at his poems.

Today's poem is inspired by Silverstein. I tried to emulate his light touch, and made sure there was a fanciful situation in it. I started with a list of rhymes for ink, and used the ones I could make work for the situation of a talking pen.

# Mirror

Floating in the glass:
the same life as mine.
Fluidly real
but only
intermittently.
When I blink
it disappears.
Otherwise it slides
about like a puppet,
with me
holding the strings.
Lift my arm,
wobble my hand,
it's all a dance,
two partners in
perfect harmony.
A kind of flattery,
some high praise,
an image that
wants to be
exactly like me.

—13 February 2020

---

I started with a word: "unfamiliar." I immediately considered how sometimes when people look in mirrors, they say what they see is unfamiliar to them. They expect to see a different version of themselves.

Mirrors are potent tropes for stories and myths. When the queen looks into the mirror and asks it who is the fairest in the land, the mirror answers! It's crazy!

In the poem I wanted to take power away from the mirror and put it back into the hands of the viewer. Whoever looks into a mirror, after all, is the one in charge. Without the viewer, the mirror has nothing.

# Valentine's Day

"What color my eye?"
she asks her guy.

"Why, your eyes are brown,"
he says—with a frown.

Her eyes are blue.
The color's not new.

They've been that hue
since they first grew.

She looks at her guy
with a heavy sigh.

He has no defense,
but from this day hence

he knows it is wise
to remember her blue eyes.

*—14 February 2020*

Kim and I were driving down Speedway late tonight, and we heard an old Elton John song where the person in the song does not know the color of his girlfriend's eyes. Kim said she couldn't believe he wouldn't know the color of her eyes. Then she said that I knew what was coming next. I knew. She wanted to know if I knew the color of her eyes. I guessed brown. I was wrong. They're blue. I have no defense and offered none, but got this poem out of the exchange.

# The Many Annoyances that Accompany the Life of a Mythic Icon

The thing is,
someone climbs
up your hair,
no matter how
long it is
or how strong
you are,
it's gonna hurt.
Plus it takes
all day
to clean and dry.
I'm going
bankrupt just
on shampoo
and conditioner
even though
I buy in bulk
at Costco.
You ever try
to comb
or brush
hair this long?
I bet not.
I can't find a
hairdresser.
They put up
a CLOSED sign
whenever I
darken their
door. Just as
well. I wouldn't
be able to
afford their
prices. I find
nests in my hair.
Truly. Birds live

in it. They
love the feel,
the way it flows,
how it keeps
them warm
and protected.
Maybe that's why
I keep it so long.
It's a way to stay
in good graces
with the wild.

—15 February 2020

Pretty basic idea here. Take a well known icon and subvert the myth surrounding them. I chose Rapunzel. I could have picked any number of other mythic or pop figures. If you do this, really try to upend the received and common view of the icon. Make Bart Simpson a cultured guy, Smokey the Bear an arsonist, Bugs Bunny a carnivore, or Mickey Mouse a burglar. You get the idea. It's fun to look at icons in new ways.

# Working Hands

As I was falling
with nothing to hold me,
a passer by
handed me a set of wings.
I gave it back, with thanks,
and began building my own
from my cache of will power,
hope, and intention.

*—16 February 2020*

Today I gave my two-week notice for my job at Natural Grocers. I started working there in August. We needed the money then, and I was glad to get the job. But I'm starting to write grants for non-profits now, and I expect and hope that that will sustain Kim and me better than the minimum wage job at Natural Grocers did. Also, with Covid-19 beginning to spread around the country, it seems wise to not have a job which puts me in constant contact with the public.

    It's a risk to quit a job. Losing guaranteed income every two weeks can be scary. But we have some savings, and we have other sources of income, so this seems like the right time to take the leap. Today's poem is a reaction to my quitting. I'll be taking a leap into the unknown and, as the saying goes, I'll be building my wings on the way down.

# The Kinship of Life

Heard screams. Howls.
Went to the front door.
Coyotes? Wolves?
Neither. Branches
brushing against the
metal roof, encrusted
sunlight clearing
its throat, feeling
its voice. I stood
rooted for a thousand
seasons, ear turned
to the sky, listening.

*—17 February 2020*

Five minutes ago I heard coyote howls at the front door. "Do you hear that?" I asked Kim, who was in another room. "I do," she said as she came down the hall, camera in hand, ready to take a picture. The coyotes sounded like they were not more than 30 feet away, serenading us with their songs. Alas, it was dark, no way to see them. Kim's camera was no use. But we listened, together, for a few seconds, then the coyotes stopped, and, presumably, moved on.

I sat down to write my daily poem. I imagined a similar scene, only it wasn't coyotes howling but rather tree branches on the roof. My idea was to take a real life event and turn it around into something other than what it was. So instead of animals making the sound, I imagined a plant making the sound. Plants are just sunlight transformed, and they tend to grow slowly and invite extended rumination. I tried to indicate that effect in the poem by having me listen for a length of time reminiscent of a tree's lifespan. The piece is an attempt to distill a moment into something larger.

The title came last. I wanted to tie everything together. All living things are part of the same network of existence.

# At the Bird Bath

Flurry of feathers.
Some squabbling over territory.
Beaks raised to the sky.
Guys posing for the ladies.
Everyone wary of predators.
Water slopping over the edges.
Beaks dipped into the tiny pool.
Kim a respectful distance away.
Camera in hand.
Too many moments.
Can't capture them all.
Snap, snap, snap.
Wings carrying subjects away.
Bird bath still as a pond.

*—18 February 2020*

We have a couple of bird baths in the back. They are mostly idle, but every so often a small flock of birds will descend on them and antics often ensue. Kim watches for those moments and when they occur, she is there taking pictures. I wanted each line of this poem to be like a snap-shop, a single moment in time.

# Shoes

So many ways
to cover the soles,
impossible to
list them all.

There's horse, snow,
and baby,
orthopedic, tap,
and dress.

Also tennis, running,
and golf,
plus bowling,
saddle, and slip-on.

You've got your tango
and ballet, and you can
pair them up with
platform and skate.

And don't forget
climbing and boat,
and dance, derby
and high-heeled.

There are surely more, and
more to be invented,
but in the end, do we really
need our soles so augmented?

*—19 February 2020*

I wrote the title first. Shoes. Simple. Then started thinking of all the different kinds of shoes. So many. The ones in the poem are just those that can take the word "shoe" after them. There are many other kinds of shoes, but I restricted myself to this linguistic type. Then I played around with them to get a good rhythm.

I used this title earlier in this book, on December 25.

# Between Appointments

A skin tag
frozen off
without any fuss.
The patient grateful
for the service.

I bid her farewell and
leave the examining room
and pause in the hall.
The picture
hanging on the wall
next to me
depicts a mountain.
It should be scaled
by a clown, maybe,
the rainbow trickster
with nothing up his sleeve,
looking for his lost balloons.

But it isn't.
It's just a mountain,
clad in white snow
and green conifers,
reflecting sunlight in
a golden aura,
the valley below
rich with life,
as though the mountain
is its benevolent provider,
a force for good,
something that could
fix anything.

Five seconds
to take this in,
then my hand on the
next doorknob.
Deep breath.
Forced smile.

> Eternal search
> for comforting words.

—20 February 2020

When I'm at a doctor's office, waiting for the doctor, I always wonder what it is like for them going from one appointment to the next. Dealing with a minor ailment one moment and maybe a life-threatening condition the next. I imagine it must be emotionally difficult.

I also often wonder about the art that hangs on walls in medical offices. They often seem so bland, perhaps purposely so. What might it convey to a doctor between appointments, though? Maybe nothing. Maybe something profound. I chose the latter for this poem.

# Premonition

someone
maybe your ancestor
maybe mine
once looked up
at a milky sky
or a bright blue sky
or a blank sky
and felt a lurch
in their stomach
thinking how
in something like
ten thousand years
or so
everything was
going to be
precariously
balanced
between life
extension and
life extinction

*—21 February 2020*

Are we living in an apocalyptic age? We might be. Climate change could kill us all, or, at the very least, make life miserable.

I have heard of people having premonitions of deaths. They get a feeling that something is wrong, and then, later in the day, for example, they hear of a relative who died at the same time they had the premonition.

I wanted to extend that notion to the planet. If life is dying on Earth, then maybe someone had a premonition about it? Maybe someone a long long time ago.

# Disgust

I see it on some faces
when I ask for a small donation
to a worthwhile charity.

It's disguised shame, I think,
and a silent accusation: I have made
them uncomfortable

thinking about what they have
and what others don't. Privilege
is a heavy burden to bear.

Not enough attention
is given to this fact. This
hard truth of life.

—22 February 2020

---

Natural Grocers, my employer, often partners with other agencies to try to raise money for worthy causes. This includes organizations like The Organic Farmers of America and the Jack and Jill Foundation, which offers financial support to students in traditionally black colleges. Natural Grocers asks their employees to ask customers to support these causes. I do this while working the cash register. Most people are very gracious. They will give a buck or two, sometimes more. Others say simply no, they are not interested. But some folks will be visibly upset with you for daring to ask the question. I can see the contempt in their manner and expression. I feel the disgust rolling off them. I noticed this today while I was asking for support for Jack and Jill. It was very revealing. The moments of disgust seemed to me to be begging for immortalization in a poem, which is what I did here.

# Why We Welcomed the Invasion

Thousands of
mosquitoes arrived
and chose

to take their blood
from the
flood of ghosts

who all sat in
the saguaros, waiting.
They took the sting

out of the
stars and helped us
forget our scars.

*—23 February 2020*

Last night I had a dream about mosquitoes trying to sting ghosts but having no luck. The ghosts just sat there, not even noticing the mosquitoes. I liked the image and played around with it to get today's poem.

# Caricature

Elongated breaths
and drawn out
presence, smoothing

to picture in
your wide mind.
Exaggeration

rarely hurts
anyone, even
pretend hurt

like in a cartoon.
It's good to
stretch ourselves.

Be free like
rubber bands.
Frame the

world in surreal
meanderings
never quite

completing the
circuit, never coming
all the way home.

*—24 February 2020*

Towards the end of the day I began to think about my daily poem. A word came to me: caricature. Didn't know what to do with it, but I turned it over in my mind. Caricature is a drawing with features of the subject exaggerated. But what if you could just exaggerate your features or qualities in real life, without benefit of an artist? What would that look and feel like? That's the sensation I was trying to evoke in this poem.

# Empty Nest

"My friend died," my
mother told me

on the phone. A
week earlier

someone broke
into her

friend's house
and her friend,

her terminally ill,
85-year old

friend, screamed
at them to

get out of
her house get

out now. And
they did, leaving

behind a wrecked
door frame and

broken glass.
The police told my

mother's friend
she couldn't stay

in her house that
night. But she did.

Nothing was going
to make her leave.

A week later
my mother's friend

died in her house,
the one she

defended with
the power of

her own voice,
raised to warrior

volume. My
mother told me

all this with pain
and pride in her voice

and I listened
carefully to the

epic tale, every
turn and twist,

a tragedy and
a eulogy both.

—25 February 2020

On my morning hike I passed a nest in a saguaro. It was empty. I wondered what bird had made it and if that bird would return this season.

When I came to write my daily poem, I tried to do something with nests. I wrote a few verses in which I imagined one of my shoelaces woven into a nest. That didn't get me anywhere interesting. Nothing was catching fire. I wanted to leave the nest motif behind, but my mind kept coming back to it.

Then I remembered a conversation with my mother a couple of weeks ago. She told me about her very good friend and what happened to her in the last week of her life. I tied that in with the notion of an empty nest and came up with the above, almost a found poem, but not quite.

If you listen to people talking, you will often find that what they say has a poetic quality to it. All you have to do is write it down.

# Feathers and Lyrics Don't Mix

The trouble with
song birds is
not a single
one of them
ever knows any
of the words.

—*26 February 2020*

This morning the song birds were everywhere outside. So many of them. So many different melodies. It was delightful, of course, but as I listened, I wondered if any of them knew the words to their songs.

    Note that each line is exactly three words long. And there is an internal rhyme: birds and words.

# Days of Empire

We were bold explorers
in those days, raising
our flags, symbols of
our power, where the
people could see them.
Later, when the flags
grew tattered from
the wind, we pulled
them down and replaced
them with more durable
versions. The people
were not impressed.
Instead, they climbed
the flag poles and pulled
down the flags and
used them as blankets.
Then they broke up
the flag poles and
burned them in their
fireplaces. It was a cold
winter and times were
bad. We walked the streets,
shivering, and endured
the taunts of the people
we once tried to help.

*—27 February 2020*

How is power used? How is it misused? One of the things power does is try to expand its reach. It is rare for an entity with power to give it up. The issue for me in this poem was to imagine how people who are subjected to power might react. They would, if possible, take the symbols of power and use them for their own purposes. Which, I suppose, is kind of a long-winded way of retelling the poem.

# The Kitchen I Grew Up With

No dishwasher, which was
an odd thing for a house
built in the seventies.

The workspace was cramped,
with little room for dirty
dishes and a cutting area

much too small for anything
big, like a Thanksgiving meal.
The fridge stood like a silo

in the middle of everything,
with a narrow closet of shelves
behind it, odd afterthought.

The stove and microwave
took up what seemed like
an entire wall. The whole

design was disjointed, with
three islands separated, like
a small archipelago of

appliances, each seeking some
connection to the other.
When I walked through it

or stood in it or pulled out
the cutting board and chopped
an onion or peeled a carrot

or looked out the window as
I washed dishes, there was the
feeling that its true unity came

from whoever was in the space.
Whoever sensed the separate
outposts and, by task and

presence, stitched them together
into a semblance of order.
We made a meal of them.

*—28 February 2020*

All writing is about memory. And memory is a notoriously unreliable source of information. Does that mean you shouldn't use it? Of course not. Memory is all we have. It helps to try to make it accurate, if you can. But it isn't necessary. My method in this poem was to take a familiar location from my past—the kitchen of the house I grew up in—and try to remember what it was like, what it evoked. I let the memories come freely, not trying to evaluate them or edit them. What I quickly discovered is that the kitchen I remember was weirdly inadequate to making meals. It was not designed particularly well, and it was kind of small for a family dwelling. And yet, we made many meals in that kitchen. My mother still lives in the house and uses the kitchen every day.

# Entropy

THE MATERIAL WORLD
ThE MATERIAL WORLD
ThE MATeRIAL WORLD
ThE MATeRIAL WORlD
ThE MATeRIAL wORlD
ThE MaTeRIAL wORlD
ThE MaTeRIAL wORld
ThE MaTeRIaL wORld
ThE MaTerIaL wORld
The MaTerIaL wORld
The MaTerIaL woRld
the MaTerIaL woRld
the MaterIaL woRld
the MaterIal woRld
the materIal woRld
the materIal world
the material world
the materialworld
thematerialworld
thematerilworld
theaterilworld
theateriworld
theaterworld
theaterword
theateword
heateword
heatword
eatword
atword
aword
word
ord
od
o

*—29 February 2020*

Entropy is a descent into disorder. Science tells us that everything in the universe is always on a path to entropy. That is, we are always on our way to decay. I wanted to convey this in a poem and decided a line of text gradually decaying into nothing would do the trick. So I began with all caps, then reduced each letter to lower case, one at a time. Then I removed the spaces between words and began erasing letters, one at a time.

An example of concrete poetry, a form I am not usually fond of, but that's no reason not to try one out and see how it goes.

# March

# Biology Class

My lab partner wasn't much interested in
looking through a microscope. I, on the other
hand, was so fascinated by the wriggling
critters I saw through the eyepiece that I
moved closer for a better look and accidentally
knocked the instrument off the table. It fell to
the floor and shattered. The slide with the
critters went skittering into a corner. The
teacher raised his eyes from another student's
scope and looked directly at my lab partner,
who shrugged his shoulders and glanced
over at me, now red-faced and full of regret.
The teacher came scurrying over to our table.
He moved like the single-celled creatures I had
just seen: his pillowy limbs swinging, jostling
with the air, striving for an unseen horizon.

*—1 March 2020*

---

I started this poem as a series of short three-line stanzas, but the form seemed wrong. Too drawn out and light. I wanted some density to it. Objects through microscopes often feel dense to me. They evoke a feeling that there is so much to the world that we don't even know about, much less understand.

The scene I describe didn't actually happen, but it was something I was always afraid of in any lab class. What if I broke the equipment? The very thought was scary to me.

I liked the idea of turning the teacher into something resembling a microscopic creature. I wanted to end on that image. It seemed very strong.

# Gravity

the weight of the

words falling into


place is just a



massive move




toward the





bottom

*—2 March 2020*

Like "Entropy" from a couple of days ago, I wanted to try to evoke the sense of gravity. Things falling accelerate as they go. So I added blank lines between lines to illustrate the notion of the poem falling toward a gravity source.

# The Chairs

have thoughts of their own.
Like, what if we all decided
to break, just as the mayor's
delegation prepared to sit
down? Or what if we all
gathered in a circle and made
ourselves look like stone
henge? Or or or what if,
just talking here, just spit
balling, what if we made
ourselves into kindling and
burned our selves all up in
the fireplace and turned into
smoke and rose up through
the chimney up into the air
and we just floated, like
clouds, from place to place,
now wouldn't that be some
thing? Flying chairs. A flock
of us, roaming the atmosphere.
Freedom on the rise. Try to
sit on us then. We dare you.

—3 March 2020

Formula for a poem: take an inanimate object, then write down what that object might be thinking.

I chose a chair because Kim and I were just trying to attach a seat to a chair frame, and we were having difficulty making it work.

# #RhymesWithRhymes

Green limes
Twin primes
Annoying mimes
Good times
Filthy grimes
Warm climes
Icky slimes
White rimes
Thin dimes
Perfect crimes

*—4 March 2020*

I keep coming back to rhymes. I wanted to find words that rhyme with rhyme and then use them in short lines that have some musicality to them. The idea was to encourage a reader to see these words in a different light: clichéd, to an extent, but fresh when deployed in a rhythmic poem.

# Flutterby

The moth is like
the phoenix, always
rising. Smoky wings
carry it up in
swirling eddies
to orbit light
bulbs, those
surrogate moons.
Sometimes they
wander through
doorways, with
their uncertain
gait, jittery
intruders,
happenstance
visitors, not
searching, exactly,
but finding
shelter from
the chaos
in your soft
warm sweaters.

*—5 March 2020*

We get lots of moths in the spring here in the desert. They fly around the outdoor lights and get into the house, no matter how careful you are about opening and closing the door, or how fast. Their random flights ensure that some of them will get into the house, even though I don't think they particularly want to be indoors. It just happens.

## Uneven Ground

The gate with
the broken latch

hangs open on
its ragged hinge

and keeps to
itself like a

twisted tree that's
barely rooted to

shifting soil as
though yearning for

some sense of
a sure footing.

*—6 March 2020*


I'm always looking for connections between things. Is a gnarly old tree like a broken gate? Maybe. Maybe not. But I wrote this poem to make you think it might be.

# Friction

Melting mountain snow ripples flowing over fish gills.

*—7 March 2020*

I'm reading Robert Hass's *A Little Book on Form*. In the first chapter he discusses one-line poems and makes the assertion that the haiku, which is relatively well-known in the west as a short three-line poem, would be more accurately rendered in one line. In Japan it is generally presented in one line.

He also says that the one-line poem, though common in other cultures, is mostly untried in the west. He gives some few examples, but they function as exceptions, not representatives of a tradition.

It seems to me that a one-line poem is barely a poem at all. Billy Collins says that a poem, because it has ragged lines, always brings you back to the poem by making you turn again and again after each line. This is something prose lacks. So a poem is self-conscious in a way that prose is not.

Then what of a one-line poem? It cannot bring you back again and again. It starts and ends with no turning. Unless you include the title, I suppose.

Thinking about Hass and Collins inspired me to try my hand at a one line poem. I wanted something mysterious, perhaps a bit illogical, and I wanted it to have something to do with nature. I could have broken it up into three lines:

Melting mountain snow
rippling flowing
over fish gills.

But it would be a different beast if I did that. I like the one-line version. It makes one think of a straight shot down a mountainside to the creek or river in the valley, where the water that was once snow nourishes a fish, which is a creature that could never exist on a mountain. At least, that's what I hope it does.

# Avian Encounters

Birds always delight me, but why should that be so?
Tough to explain, but easy to say: birds always delight me.

*—8 March 2020*

I'm continuing to read Hass's *A Little Book on Form*. In the second chapter he takes up two-line poems. He says once you get to two lines, you've created a relationship and if you're conscious of form, you want that relationship to be harmonious. So, for example, in the Western tradition, the unifying relationship in a couplet is most often meter and rhyme. For example: "I think that I shall never see / a poem as lovely as a tree."

But there are many other unifying relationships for a couplet. For example, he mentions the Bantu tradition of southern Africa in which the couplet does not require harmonious meter or rhyme, but instead relies on similar images. One of his examples: "An elephant was killed by a small arrow. / The lake dries up at the edges." I did not see the connection here until Hass explained it. The soil of a dried lake bed resembles the skin of an elephant. Wow! That's cool.

Another couplet form he discusses goes something like this: "Statement of feeling. A question. / An answer to the question. Another statement of feeling." That's the form I employed above. This particular technique often ends up with more or less identical first and last phrases, as I did here.

I'm enjoying Hass's book. It's like reading about how to build things. He takes the simplest piece of poetry, the line, and uses it like a brick to build up poems little by little. It's an interesting way to look at the process, and it's inspiring me to try my hand at some of the possibilities he discusses.

# Otherwise Mark it With an X

Jagged line joining sky to mountain:
this is where the signature of nature
weaves up and down and in and out.

*—9 March 2020*

Continuing on to chapter 3 of Hass's book on form. Here he takes up the issue of three-line poems and poems composed of three-line stanzas. Just as the two-line poem introduced the idea of relationship, the three-line poem introduces the idea of complexity. It is a weaving and opens up the possibilities of complex relationships.

The three-line poem can also be a syllogism, that basic unit of logic. "x is y. All y are z. Therefore x is z." Some short poems are actually syllogisms in disguise.

Hass calls three-line poems a weaving together of ideas and/or images. I liked that and took the idea of weaving for this three-line poem.

No rhymes in today's poem. Hass talks about rhyme in his book. I think he sees it as a hindrance because a couple of times he has talked about the modernists and how they freed forms from rhyme. He also calls English a rhyme-poor language, unlike other languages where rhyme is very common. I have heard others make the claim that English is not rich in rhymes, which seems paradoxical to me. English borrows from just about every other language in the world and has the most abundant vocabulary of any language. I believe Italian is one of the rhyme-rich languages. Probably Spanish as well. I'm sure it's no coincidence that a lot of the rhymed forms like sonnets and villanelles come from romance languages.

I like coming up with with rhymes for poems, but I also see where it can be a hindrance. A kind of straight jacket which one might want to escape from. I suppose that's what the modernists did in their day: escape the confines of constraining rhymes.

# Dinner at the Assisted Living Center

The old ones waiting for their evening meals.
Their hands resting on laps or table tops.
Concentrating their will to lift a fork.
In chairs sturdier than their occupants.

*—10 March 2020*

Chapter 4 of Hass's book takes up four-line poems and four-line stanzas, known as quatrains. They allow for a rhyme scheme of some complexity, if that's what you want to do in your poem. They also give some elbow room to develop a theme and, in his view, they are the final building blocks of larger poems. He contends that the vast majority of poems are made up of one-, two-, three-, and four-line units. The sonnet, for example, can be seen as three four-line units with a concluding two-line unit.

    I like the idea of building a poem, in the same way I like the idea of building a wall, or a house. It feels like I'm making something sturdy, something that has a chance of lasting.

    My four-line poem came from observing some of the folks I got to know at the assisted living center where I used to do outreach for the library. For many, ordinary daily activities were difficult. But they were fierce in their determination to keep trying, no matter what.

    This is a metered poem with each line 10 syllables long. Notice also that the poem could have been written in a different order. In many different orders, actually. Here's an experiment to try: Write each of the lines on a slip of paper. Then drop the slips into a hat and draw them out one at a time at random. The first one you draw is the first line of the poem, the second slip is the second line, and so on. Try it. There are 24 possible arrangements of these four lines. Any order you come up with will make a coherent poem with a slightly different sense to it.

# Three Haiku

prickly pear thorns cast
sundial shadows across
spring green cactus lobes

moon over low clouds
desert still as winter trees
cool breeze trembling quail

pause on dusty trail
low sun gilds saguaro arms
sparrow turns golden

*—10 March 2020*

The city of Tucson held a haiku contest. The deadline was today. I didn't know about it until today. Kim saw a note about it on Facebook.

Entrants were to write up to three haiku on the theme "living in the moment." The above were my three entries.

Haiku is one of the best known forms. It is a poem of three lines. The first line has 5 syllables, the second has 7, and the third has 5. In Japan, where it originated, it is traditionally a nature poem in which a season should be evoked in some way. I was pretty explicit with the winter and the spring references in the first two, less so with the third one.

Postscript: the contest appears to have been cancelled due to the Covid-19 crisis.

# The Plague Year

Each step tentative.
Personal space now
stretched to feet instead
of inches. All our
interactions so
altered now, as though
tiny bits of matter
have infiltrated
everything, like
grains of sand in gears.
Grinding life to a
slow pace resembling
stately funeral
processions, all of
us wondering what
will be coming next.

*—11 March 2020*

The coronovirus has hit the world hard. China has hundreds of thousands of cases with many deaths. Deaths also here in the United States. All of Italy in quarantine. Universities closed. Public gatherings canceled. All of us told to restrict contact with other people and avoid crowds. It is sobering to realize how quickly the world turned upside down. It was only about two and a half months ago that the virus was first announced by China.

Kim and I have withdrawn from much of the world. We are holed up here in our house, going out only to buy groceries or hike the park.

This poem is my reaction to the pandemic so far. No one knows how long the world will be disrupted. It feels like we are all waiting.

# Late Afternoon Emphasis at the Chapel

Sunlight streams in
through high windows,
slanting against the
opposite wall like a
line of italicized text.

*—12 March 2020*

One thing I notice here in the Sonoran desert is the shadows that appear late in the afternoon when the sun is low. They seem like otherworldly apparitions. Sometimes a line of shadows will suggest some message, as though the sun was trying to write something.

# At the Recital

The notes rise
up from the
piano like cinders
from a fire.
The pianist aflame
with passion, the
keys singed and
crackling. Our ears
burning, the hall
about to burst,
and no end
to the inferno,
no way for
the sparks to
be snuffed out
on this night.

*—13 March 2020*

This poem was inspired by my friend Michael Manning's piano recital here in Tucson. Michael is an accomplished pianist and works hard at his craft. It shows. His concert was glorious.

Live music is about sound, obviously, but it can also be about other sensations. That's what I tried to convey here.

# Body Language

Spine mingling.
A head for fig years.
Bend me your ears.
Elbow your ray in.
Toe the brine.
Anoint a finger at.
Nosing aground.
Stoked to the bone.
Hand it aloft.
Heart welt.
Grow with my gut.
Bake your neck.
Head of the brass.
West foot forward.
Rest foot forward.
Chin sup.
Eye brow grazing.
Chest lumping.
Back baking.
Face the few sick.
Nose to the blind stone.
A tongue crashing.
Stomach learning.
Duel of thumb.
Knuckle blunder.
Bone of Confession.
Kin by a hair.
Dwell-heeled.
Bake it on the chin.
Skin in the blame.
Hand me town.
Boss my palm with silver.
Foot ruse.
Dust by the skin of my teeth.
Song in the tooth.
Ear to the downed.
A nose forgiveness.
A leg hup.

—*14 March 2020*

The idea was to write a poem about the body. I started writing a list of body parts and noticed many of them were parts of idioms or common sayings. It seems we often measure the world through our own bodies. And why wouldn't we? The body is our way of being in the world.

So I switched gears and began writing down sayings that feature body parts. That might make a good poem, but it didn't seem imaginative enough. So I began tweaking the sayings a bit, and I liked the result. I spent the day thinking up body idioms and tweaking them. This poem took me most of the day, off and on, to write.

# The Constellations

After the sun sets each night
it likes to throw off sparks
that gather into images on a sky
blackened by light deprivation.

It's the perfect dark stage
for all those mythic dreams,
a comfort to our fiery guardian's
long night of slumber.

*—15 March 2020*

The idea here was that maybe the constellations in the sky are actually the dreams of the sun. A wild idea, but it felt like the start of a poem, so I went with it.

Mind you, this was after I started a good half dozen or so poems that just didn't gel into anything interesting or usable. But I had my self-imposed deadline: write a poem by the end of the day. I kept pressing on, hoping something was going to spark on my notebook pages. Eventually it did, and this is the result.

# We Are Our Ancestors

Used to be I could seize
a fish right out of a
lake and take it up to
a tree to eat but now
all I have is these blunt
fingernails. Evolu
tion's failure. I miss the
feel of my sharp talons
in concert with my beak,
tearing the fish open.
Now I stick a worm to
a hook and drop it in
the water. And wait as
the fish swims around and
laughs at me while I watch
a hawk high on thermals
turning wide circles with
the ease of cutting blades.

—*16 March 2020*

I started writing this in my notebook, but it did not catch fire. I had the idea of talons evolving into fingernails and how disappointing that would be to a hunting creature. But I couldn't find the point of view it should be in. A naturalist? No. The fish? Definitely no. I made a few half-hearted tries, then decided to move to my computer.

Once I had a few lines on the screen, I saw the way to go. I would be the hunting creature, who got transformed into this non-hunting human. Once I had that entry into the poem, I powered through the rest in a few minutes.

The lesson here, I guess, is that the medium matters. If it's not coming alive to you on paper, try a screen and see what happens. Or if the screen isn't working, move to paper and see what happens. You could get something good that way.

# An A to Z of Free Advice

Accepting life and decay can take some concerted effort.
Before opening the package, shake it for clues.
Creativity will almost always assert itself willingly.
Decide early on what is the best shirt to wear.
Every decision will lay down a forking path.
Feel your way through the bad times and you'll prosper.
Grade your efforts with a generous spirit.
Heave out the tired and the out-moded when you can.
Icicles have their metaphoric significance.
Justice is an ideal goal you can't rely on.
Keep the spirits in a cool dark place.
Lean on strength when you can, weakness when you must.
Move everything aside to find the truth.
Never do anything just to make the sky happy.
Over and over is not such a bad way to learn a skill.
Put the toys away when you stop playing with them.
Quit telling yourself you need more than you already have.
Restate your purpose every few weeks in a different mode.
See with your ears sometimes, just for the perspective.
Take the garbage out to the bin with a sense of joy in your
    step.
Unlearn the lessons that never taught you anything.
Very often it is the bad times that we remember with fond-
    ness.
Weaponizing love hurts everyone involved, including you.
Xylophones have their place, just as your uncommon soul
    does.
Yip yip yip is not a bad song to sing sometimes.
Zest doesn't come just from lemons.

*—17 March 2020*

My try at a classic form: the abecedarian. I'm sure I don't have to point out to you that the first letter of each line forms the alphabet.

    This was a fun one to do. I didn't start out with the thought that each line would be a bit of advice, but that's how the first two lines went, and I just continued the mode to the end.

# How Do You Talk to Someone Who Has Been to Hell?

You rose on the deceitful seductive winds of war, but I
was privileged to choose a different path. You saw
foreign life and lives, and many deaths. How does the
experience sit with you and your heart? Were you your best
at all times? Did you connect with the varied minds
all around you? I have heard some of the stories of
those times, those harrowing excursions into danger. My
own heart trembles to think so many of your generation
were called to such trauma. It must have destroyed
something real in you. Or am I being cruel by
bringing up these memories, these old tales of madness?

*—18 March 2020*

---

The idea here (taken from a prompt in Diane Lockward's *The Practicing Poet*) was to take a line from a famous poem and use each word in that line as the end word for a new poem. I chose the opening of *Howl* by Allen Ginsberg: "I saw the best minds of my generation destroyed by madness."

Then it was a matter of filling in each line to end on Ginsberg's successive words. I had not planned to write about a veteran returning from war, but that is the point of such exercises. It gets your mind going in fresh directions.

# An Optimistic Outlook on Life

I startled the lady bug. It
spread its wings and flew away,
but its spots fell off. I collected

the spots and put them
in a small jar and now I'm
waiting for the lady bug to

return for them. I'm sure the
lady bug will come back for
its spots. I know I would.

*—19 March 2020*

I was doodling in my notebook. Writing down lines, ideas, titles, attempts at stanzas. Really, just fooling around, not trying for anything, when I wrote down lady bug and immediately thought of the spots on a lady bug and I wondered what would happen if those spots slid away.

# The Merry Maker

creates all the uncountable molecules of the air we breathe
and the water we drink.
The merry maker makes birds who sing
and trees that shade.
Snakes that hiss
and cats that purr.
Ground that holds us up
sky that waters us
the moon that follows us
and the light that delights us.
The merry maker giveth food and love and hope.
Plus a heart to give thanks
and a brain to understand.
The merry maker does not discriminate
but will rather pollinate
innovate
stimulate
elevate and
cultivate.
The merry maker is the Johnny Appleseed of abundance
spreading seeds of gratitude
like clouds of chocolate dust.
Nom nom nom!
Music? Yeah. That's the merry maker at work. Sing it!
The merry maker gives us pain to warn us of danger.
Well, heck, merry maker, thanks for that chunk of misery!
Don't expect to *see* the merry maker
cuz they work in the dark, or high in the air, or deep in the ground.
Next time you doubt the merry maker
look up at the stars
or down at the dirt.
It's all the same to the merry maker:
it's all about abundance
and a soul dance
romance, strong stance, horse prance, and lucky chance.
The merry maker is happiest
when you take the gift, all the gifts, wrapped or unwrapped,
doesn't matter.
Give thanks if you feel the urge

but know the merry maker is happy either way.
The merry maker spills the light of the sun onto us
every morning of every day.
The merry maker makes time for everyone
24/7/365.
All right, merry maker, you go. Fill the world up, merry maker.
You be you, OK?
And we'll be we.

*—20 March 2020*

Another prompt from Diane Lockward's book *The Practicing Poet*. This one was to write a gratitude poem. The model was Thomas Lux's poem "The Joy-Bringer." The idea here was to be exuberant and vary the syntax, line length, style, and mood, to give a feeling of abundance just by looking at the shape and extent of the poem. I went all out with it. I hope.

# Wading Into a Lake in Early Spring

The freezing
ooze between
the toes. The
water circling
your numb
calves. A coil
of green snake
winding by,
seeing you
with bright
open eyes.
Your hands
clutching opposite
upper arms to
quell the
shivers but
you know
it won't work.
Winter still
lives in the
lapping
waves, still
sends you
back to
the shore,
back to
a beached
existence,
wet destiny
postponed
for a few
more weeks,
snake envy
seizing you.
It looked
so much
at home,
so much
a part of
the realm.

*—21 March 2020*

I remember wading into Lake Ramsey where I grew up in Sudbury, Ontario in early spring. Maybe not March but April or May. The water was cold, and seemed it would remain cold for a long long time. I remember the snake. Bright green spiral at home in this realm in a way I could not be.

# Road Hockey

No one kept score.
The passing cars
stopped the game

while we moved the
nets to one side.
The drivers smiling

at us, like we
were doing the most
normal thing in the

world: passing a
frozen puck from
stick to stick,

mimicking the players
we saw on television.
How they glided

across the ice like
winged heroes.
The way they raised

their arms after a
goal, holding up our
impossible dreams.

*—22 March 2020*

---

I remember playing hockey in the road, at night, with snow falling. It was clearly an incredibly dangerous thing to be doing, but we did it, the kids in our neighborhood. When cars went by, we moved the game to one side. It was not an inconvenience, just part of the activity. So many of us played hockey. It was practically a national religion. Road hockey had the advantage of not requiring a lot of equipment, like skates, or a rink, for that matter. The street was our rink, and it served us well.

# Solar Powered

lizard skin
exposed to sunlight:
blistering speed

*—23 March 2020*

Here in the desert, the lizards are appearing again after a long winter absence. I see them while walking our property and hiking trails. They move incredibly fast over all kinds of terrain: sand, grass, rocks, and up tree trunks, and even up stucco walls and especially wooden posts and fences. They do not seem to have an in between speed. They are either still as stones, or moving so fast it's hard to follow their motion. I like seeing them in the spring when they first come out. It feels like they are true denizens of the Sonoran Desert.

# The Old Mermaids Take You On a Tour of The Sanctuary

**Sister Sheila Na Giggles says:**

For a twisty path
there's just one place to start.
Meander on over
to the labyrinthian heart.

**Sister Dee Dee Lightful Mermaid says:**

Gather your wits
and don't lose your marbles.
The next stop comes
at a rocky ensemble.

**Sister Bea Wilder Mermaid says:**

A place to hang out
and a place to get dry.
You'll find it easy
if you stay spry.

**Sister Lyra Musica says:**

Lend me your ear
to knock on the door.
That should be enough,
I won't say anymore.

**Sister Laughs a Lot Mermaid says:**

The trip is tabled
behind the casita.
Don't worry, to visit,
you won't need a visa.

### Sister Bridget Mermaid says:

Swing on over
to the next station
for a cushy relaxing
mini vacation.

### Sister Ursula Divine Mermaid says:

Don't sweat it,
you're well on the way to completion.
The former lodge
is what you are seekin.'

### Sister Ruby Rosarita Mermaid says:

Next is a house
for quail and creativity,
where time is spent
completely blissfully.

### Sister Sophia Mermaid says:

At the end of a path,
a table and chair.
Some peaceful relaxing
is what you'll find there.

### Sister Magdelene Mermaid says:

Don't worry about getting
benched 'neath a tree.
You'll love the shade
most certainly.

### Grand Mother Yemaya Mermaid says:

The rabbits love it
here in the dirt.
What more can you say
this is the desert.

**Mother Star Stupendous Mermaid says:**

Follow the 8-fold path
on the driveway island.
There you'll find
you'll be enlightened.

**Sister Faye Mermaid says:**

Next is a sign
of things to come.
We offer you love
and a hearty welcome.

*—24 March 2020*

---

This one takes some explaining. Tomorrow is Kim's birthday. With the prudent social distancing which we are practicing now that the Covid-19 virus is on the rise, we won't be doing what we usually do on our birthdays, which is going out to some recreational venue and then eating at a restaurant.

So what I did instead was make a little scavenger hunt here on our property, which we call The Sanctuary. When we first came here 16 years ago, before we bought it, we fell in love with it, and it inspired Kim to write *Church of the Old Mermaids,* a novel set in and around Tucson and this property. In it she created 13 Old Mermaids, characters who were washed up on the new desert when the old sea dried up. Kim gave them all whimsical names which I have used here.

I put each of the rhyming quatrains on a small card and tomorrow I will deploy them around the property and have Kim do the scavenger hunt, going from one to the other, as directed by each quatrain. At the end, there will be a card for her, wishing her happy birthday. The last few years I have written a poem for Kim especially for her birthday. This time, I will have the poem distributed all over our property. Hope she likes it.

If you're interested:

The twisty path is the labyrinth we built in one of the corrals.

The rocky ensemble is a collection of marble blocks we arranged into a kind of mini Stonehenge.

The place to hang out is our clothesline.

The knock on the door is a brass knocker in the shape of an acorn on one of our doors.

The table is a metal table and chairs we recently bought and put behind one of the apartments on the property.

The swing is beside the pool and it has several cushions on it.

There used to be a sweat lodge on the property and now it is the site of two tables and a chair.

The Quail House is a small studio where we used to write our novels when we came to the property before we bought it.

We cut a path through some of the cactus and at the end of this path is a small table and chair under a tree, which is a pleasant place to sit and be with the natural surroundings.

Another spot under a tree, this one with a bench instead of a table and chair.

Another corral on the property (it used to have horses) we call the rabbit corral because there are almost always rabbits running through it.

At the house end of our driveway stands a mesquite tree, and under it an ocotillo plant, each stalk of which has 8 sides.

As you come up our driveway, you see a sign that says: "The Old Mermaids Sanctuary."

# At the Car Wash

Hands off the steering wheel.
Foot off the brake.
Transmission in neutral:
I am the passive passenger
here for a cleansing, nothing more.

Sudsy bristle wheels
come down from above
rolling and scrubbing
away all the dirt.

Soapy tears stream down the
windshield. Remember crying
the first time I went to the barber shop.
Thundering rumbling machinery
all around, working the grime loose.

A shower of rinsing water,
mini rain storm, pelting the roof.
Then the blower,
peeling away the film of water
like melting plastic.

And now, at the end,
a clear view, like when I clean
my glasses and the world presents
itself to me anew

and different and I want to remember
this freshness
for as long as I can
but you know I will forget it
soon enough
as it becomes
the new normal.

*—24 March 2020*

I kind of like going to the car wash. You're in this small storm thundering all around you, and then you come out the other end and your car is clean. Marvelous! It also gives you a small meditative space for a few minutes. I tried to indicate that in the poem.

# We'll Never Be Fast Friends

The roadrunner runs down roads and driveways
and paths and trails and black-topped highways.

The roadrunner has no time for lolly gagging
it's always on the move and will never be lagging.

Roadrunner, sometimes I wish you'd slow down,
so I could say hi and around we could clown.

But roadrunner you've got your expeditious ways
so keep going fast and enjoy your swift days.

—25 March 2020

We see roadrunners here on The Sanctuary. They always move fast. They are very charming and I like seeing them. I'm told they are considered mystical creatures by the native peoples here. Their feet leave Xs for footprints, which means when you come across roadrunner tracks, you can't tell which direction it was running in.

Once I saw a roadrunner on the property with a baby rabbit in its beak, which it then methodically struck repeatedly against a rock, presumably to make sure it was dead before it ate it. It was a little shocking to see this. Nature red in tooth and claw is the old quote, I believe. To which I would add: and beak. I was not quite so charmed by roadrunners after witnessing that particular brutality.

But my revulsion passed and now I like seeing them on the property again. Time heals all, I suppose, or erases enough that we forget or are numb to small atrocities.

They are comical-looking. Probably what inspired the roadrunner cartoons, with the coyote chasing after it. But roadrunners are also fierce warriors. If they encounter a rattle snake and they get into a fight, the roadrunner almost always wins. That's pretty impressive.

# Falls Creek Falls

Hesitation
at
the
top
then
a
tum
ble
as
the
wa
ter
turns
wed
ding
cake
white
and
leaps
from
the
rocks
fly
ing
su
per
fast
twist
ing
in
to
ropes
and
strands
and
balls
of
water
crash

                              ing
                              into
                              the
                              pool
                              at
                              the
                              bot
                              tom
                              then
                              rip
                              ples
                              crawl
                              ing
                              to
                              the
                              edge
                    dazed with arrested motion
                   looking back to the top asking:
                       Did I come from up there?

                                         *—26 March 2020*

Falls Creek is an actual creek we used to hike to when we lived in Washington state. A trail snaked along the creek and at the end of it a 500-foot waterfall tumbled down over rocks and ended up in a pool at the bottom. It was a destination falls, so impressive that the creek was named for it.

    What I did here is pretty obvious, I guess, turning the poem into a kind of waterfall of words that collect at the bottom in a pool of stillness.

# My Eyeware

arm wrestles
the sun

bending light
toward my

eyes just
enough to

elbow away
the blur

*—27 March 2020*

Where do I find poetry? Well, it can be anywhere, really. Like eyeglasses, for example. Seemingly ordinary objects, they perform magic, taking the light that the sun puts out and bending it so that people can see clearly. They are little miracles that you see everyday on all kinds of people.

Today's poem tried to look at eyeglasses in a slightly skewed perspective to illuminate the miracle they are.

# Hypnagogic

That slightly unreal
state of mind
that comes between
wakefulness and sleep
for just an instant:

isn't that
kind of like
the moment
when the Earth,
all misty and at loose ends

from tending
to the water
and helping all the
creatures survive
one more day,

slips over into
a state of mind
where it can
let everything go
for one eternal instant?

—28 March 2020

The hypnagogic state of mind is always an odd thing. Are you awake or asleep? How can you tell the instant when you slip from one to the other?
    I then applied this state of mind to the Earth. It has to sleep sometimes, too. Doesn't it?

# All The Chandeliers Above All the Pews

They had to weigh hundreds of pounds,
    all thick metal bands and heavy wooden beams.
During monotonous hymn singing
    when I was all of eleven years old
I would sometimes wonder
    what would happen if they all detached
from the ceiling and fell
    on the congregation below, all those
worshippers who felt secure and reverential.
    Would God save them all from
death? Truly, this is the question that plagued
    all of my thoughts in those moments.
Then the collection plate's journey around
    the chapel, and when it had visited all the
pew kneelers, the minister held the full plate
    high before a stained glass of Christ, all
shimmering with red and gold light, offering
    all the contents, all the money to
the divine, as though saying: "Here is
    all of our blood, please don't kill us yet."

*—29 March 2020*

I have a very strong memory of the events in this poem. I recall very clearly the imposing chandeliers that hung over us when we went to church on those Sundays more than 50 years ago. If a memory sticks with me that long, it's a good bet that it would be a good subject for a poem. And here it is.

## Passing the Torch

Firelight travels from the flaming
center of the aloe plant

to the tip of the ocotillo
where it flares wide and bright,

glowing against the sky, then
to the fish hook barrel cactus

lighting the bright burning
blossoms and red thorns

to pierce the dusky air and,
still not finished, journeys

next to the Christmas cholla
dotting it with red light berries

scattered in with the slender
green tubes and finally, at odyssey's

end, settles on the clustered
cactus fruit turning it dazzling

yellow, the light a siren call
for passing birds to lance

their beaks into the flesh and
pull up the heat of burning life.

*—30 March 2020*

Kim and I were taking a walk around The Sanctuary near dusk and we noticed how the blossoms growing out of the aloe plants looked like torches in the setting sun. But they weren't the only ones. The ocotillo plant in the front of the yard also displayed a bright red blossom. It felt like the plants were passing light from one to the other. When I sat down to write my poem I started with this image: the passing of a torch from one desert plant to the other.

I wasn't sure when I started where the journey would end, but as I envisioned the light going from plant to plant I saw it ending at the bright yellow fruit that clusters at the top of a barrel cactus. They always look like they are trying to light up the sky, calling birds to come eat them. It felt like the right stopping point.

With this poem I moved my daily poems from my Facebook page to the Patreon page that Kim and I maintain. The decision was based in part on having to generate some income since I quit my Natural Grocers job and my grant-writing gigs were drying up due to the economic slowdown due to the Covid-19 pandemic. Folks could spend as little as $3 a month and get my daily poems in their email. If they wanted my commentary as well, that would cost them $10 a month. Our Patreon supporters also got Kim's photographs and other writings from both of us.

# Dirt Road Hill

The one with the rapid rise
where the car careened
up and over, our stomachs straining
and lurching, floating free
it seemed, until we dropped down
again, all four wheels whirling
over dust and rocks, our guts gaining
a hold on the wicked world
once more because then there
came the lingering longing
ache to go over that dangerously dicey
blind hill again, at which any animal
or person on the south side
might be crossing where we
could not see. The uncaring urge
holding onto us, more malevolent
and so much bigger than we wanted.

—*31 March 2020*

---

There was a dirt road near our house when I was growing up. It was mostly unused, but there was this hill on it. People used to drive on the road way over the speed limit, just to get the thrill of going up and over that hill. It was like a roller coaster. I remember driving with my dad, begging him to drive fast over the hill, just so I could feel the floaty sensation in my stomach.

Even as I asked, I knew it was dangerous. The hill blocked any driver's ability to see down the road. If someone was crossing the road on the other side of the hill, or if an animal was there, or if a car was stalled, we would have hit it soon after we crested the hill.

But that fact, obvious to any driver, did not stop them from taking the hill at high speed.

What I remember most about the experience was that, even knowing the danger, I wanted to take the ride up and over. It was a lesson: your instincts do not always lead you in the safest direction.

No rhyming in this one, but I did alliterate the last two words of every line, rather in the manner of the opening lines of "Kubla Khan" by Samuel Taylor Coleridge:

In Xanadu did Kubla Khan
A stately pleasure-dome decree:
Where Alph, the sacred river, ran
Through caverns measureless to man
Down to a sunless sea.

# April

# Consolation

I see the birds up in the trees
and also lots of buzzing bees.

So very many bugs with wings
that fly around like regal kings.

I do not have the gift of flight,
that knack is missing from my birthright.

So instead I admire the critters soaring
and remain down here where life's more boring.

But sometimes I dream of catching air
and gliding over the landscape fair.

I take in all the glorious views
and thereby banish all my blues.

I swoop and dive then catch a thermal
rising slowly 'til the hour's nocturnal.

That's often when I wake up beaming
from all the fun I've just had dreaming.

And then I rise from bed still grinning
'cause I hear birds and they are singing.

*—1 April 2020*

---

I've had flying dreams all my life. They are usually lots of fun. The freedom is incredible and makes living in two dimensions on the flat Earth somewhat pedestrian.

I chose rhyming couplets this time around for its comic effect and the quick rhythm it gives the lines. My intention here was to have a little bit of fun.

Birds, especially, are among the most charming of nature's creatures, not only for the fact that they fly, but also that so many of them are consummate performers, singing their songs anywhere at any time, serenading us all with clear pure notes and the most pleasing of melodies.

# Submerged

The tree in
my backyard catches
sunlight pouring from
the sky and
replaces it with
an irregular cloud
of shadow you
can't pop no
matter how hard
you try.          Instead,
you might want
to take the
time to swim
in that twilight,
as you would
in an underwater
world where you'll
find coral and
swimming fish.          We
call them rough
bark and shimmering
leaves in the
shadow of the
tree but by
any name you
choose they are
wondrous strange if
you wipe away
the grayish water
and find the
right eyes to
see them with.

*—2 April 2020*

On really hot days, walking under a tree and into its shadow feels like entering another world. Shadows seem like two-dimensional objects plastered to the ground or some other surface. But in fact shadows are three-dimensional. They occupy space between the object and the ground. They could be seen as holding darkness in an irregular net.

    I noticed this the other day when I was walking around our property and ducking in and out of the shadows that the trees were creating. Then I heard from an old friend who told me about his SCUBA diving adventures, how marvelous it was to fly through the water and observe all manner of interesting things there. I put those two things together— the idea of 3D shadows and the spectacle of underwater treasures— and saw a correlation between coral and bark, and fish and leaves.

    Once I had that connection, the poem came pretty rapidly.

# Synesthesia

Red on the tongue is sweet like honey.
Green tastes more like a bite of crunchy bacon.
Yellow partakes of the bitterness of arugula.
Pink is always known to be extra salty.
Blue has the heft and crunch of a peeled carrot.
White will remind you of a hot bowl of chicken soup.
Gray evokes the comfort of a peanut butter sandwich.
Brown is the nose-dripping assault of a hot pepper.
Black arrives with the nuttiness of a mild cheese.
Orange brings the wake-up tang of vinegar.
And purple always adds a touch of peppery sharpness.

—3 April 2020

The idea here was to take one class of things (color) and treat them as another class of things (taste). I tried to scramble expectations by, for example, having pink be extra salty when it is commonly associated with sweetness.

I worked rapidly, as is my usual mode and came up with color/taste pairings I found intriguing and unexpected. This was a fun one to write.

# Skeleton View

I know you're in there
even though I've never seen you.
Not even a tiny glimpse.
Did you know that here
on the outside
you have a reputation?
You wear black robes
and carry a scythe
and are known to reap
lives,
to actually snatch them
away to some place called death?
But how could you know this,
bathed as you are in liquid red,
holding up the flesh suit I wear
like an obedient butler?
My guess:
you don't know much of anything.
You're the worker bee
always on task
sturdy and dependable.
Skull down,
you are focused on the job at hand:
giving shape where it is needed.
No time for death,
you have a life to support,
a duty to dispatch.

*—4 April 2020*

We are now in the thick of the Covid-19 outbreak. Thousands of deaths, and tens of thousands of cases, with no end in sight, and experts telling us it is going to get worse before it gets better. Kim and I have not left our property in a week. The last time either of us was in town was when I got groceries. That was Sunday. Today is Saturday. We have opted to have our groceries delivered this week so we don't risk exposing ourselves to anyone with the virus. It's likely this could go on for many more weeks.

Life has slowed down. Where before I felt like I could do a dozen or more things in a day, it feels like I can handle about four or five and then I feel lethargy overtake me and I nap on the chaise lounge or spend time playing chess on my phone.

Like many people, I have been thinking about what might happen if I get the virus and end up dying. And that got me to thinking about symbols of death in our culture, which led to thoughts about the grim reaper, commonly depicted as a skeleton in black robes.

Skeletons may be symbols of death since you generally don't see them unless the owner of them has died. But in everyday life they are far from avatars of death. We need our skeletons to hold us up and to produce white blood cells. When concealed within us, as is right and proper, they are robust symbols of life. That's what I was getting at in today's poem. Love your skeleton! It is as much a life-giver as is air, blood, nourishment, and shelter.

# The Meaning of Doves

The doves bring twigs
to the wooden beams
supporting the shelter over our porch.
They want to construct a nest
where no nest belongs.

I push the twigs off the beam.
They fall to the concrete,
but the doves return
with more twigs.
No no no I tell them.
Your eggs will roast in the sun there.
Your children will never hatch.
You need to build somewhere else.

We saw the dead eggs last season.
Sad little white globes.
The doves sat on them
for weeks and weeks
but nothing hatched from those
cooked spheres.

We don't want that futile
sadness again.
Wielding my broom
I push the twigs to the concrete once more.
The doves flutter to the ground
and watch me
with dark eyes waiting.
The urge to make a home
and create life
their only priority.

They are persistent,
these doves,
but then,
being symbols of peace,
I imagine they would have to be.

—5 April 2020

This morning Kim and I were out walking and noticed the doves had returned to the porch and were attempting to build a nest.

We try not to interfere with the wildlife here. We let critters dig their holes, walk their walks, and eat whatever they want. We don't try to remove the rattlesnakes, and when bees swarm, we let them do their thing until they move on.

But the doves are different.

One of them built a nest last year where she really shouldn't have. Right in the sun. The eggs she laid never hatched because they couldn't take the heat of the sun. They got cooked.

So now, when we see doves bringing their building materials to places that are going to be under the full bore heat of the blazing Tucson sun, I take a broom and push the twigs away. I do this several times a day until the doves get the message and move on to somewhere else.

When I do this, the doves give me the stink eye. That look, full of bewilderment, befuddlement, and contempt. At least, that's how it seems to me. They are not happy with my interference, and I can't explain it's for their own good and the good of their offspring.

# Wrecked

A misshapen mass
left on the trail:
an interrupted meal?
We approach warily,
the charcoal fur,
not keeping anything
warm or camouflaged
anymore, showing
red along the edge.

The limbs at a wrong
angle, the head flopped
to one side, eyes closed,
mouth set in a grim
expression, hoping the
ordeal will soon be over.
It's a hard life when
every moment brings the
possibility of being
someone else's dinner.

What to do now?
If we leave it
some other animal
will come take it.
We know this.
But the urge to
get a shovel and
bury it is strong.

No personal connection,
really. Not a relative,
no one we knew. And
yet. Some modicum
of respect seems due.
Honor the life now gone
by returning it
to the ground.

*—6 April 2020*

This one took a while. I tried writing out a few lines on various subjects. None of them sparked anything interesting. Then I googled "poetry prompts" and scrolled through a few results. I tapped on a link more or less at random, and the first prompt it gave was "write about something that happened to you last week."

That's simple enough.

A while ago we found a dead creature during one of our walks. Right there in the middle of the path. Was there poetry in that? Well, sure. The two great themes of literature (and life, I suppose) are love and death.

One of the first writing instructors I ever had said something like: "If it isn't about love and death, then why write it?" At the time that seemed too narrow a view of writing, but as time has gone on, it seemed more and more correct. Love and death are the most consequential things we experience in life. And in writing, the two most popular genres are romance and mystery. One deals with love, the other with death. These are the subjects that grab people and make them want to read on.

So this is a poem about death and the fact that death is what all living things eventually share.

# Keeping a Secret

The moon
sees all

but never
tells. It

just moves
on and

then it
is gone.

*—7 April 2020*

We're told that the full moon tonight will be a super pink full moon. It will be at its closest approach to the Earth in 2020, which means it will look about as big in the sky as it ever does. This full moon, according to *The Old Farmer's Almanac,* is named in honor of the pink wildflower known as ground phlox, which blossoms around this time of year.
    The moon has always struck me as a kind of beacon in the night, the way it traverses the sky, then slips over the horizon to its hiding place. Then it also waxes and wanes, hiding from us at times in what we call a new moon.
    So this exceptional full moon got me to thinking about the moon again. As it travels overhead, it's easy to see it as a gaurdian watching over us. Or, maybe, spying on us. At least, it was easy for me. That's where the poem came from.

# The Peculiar Psychology of Snow Storms

In winter the snowdrifts came in long waves,
blown in bleached white from a powdery sea.
Spindrift would roll off in clouds mistily,
and the flakes pile up in bluish round caves.
I'd watch winter's march come close to the house
while I stayed cozy behind double panes.
The whitecaps arrayed in stately long chains,
so solid and fierce, they could not be doused.
Those swells were not completely unyielding,
not one of them reached my dwelling's flat wall.
A wide gap remained between brick and squall,
green grass on the ground as though it was spring.
Why did the storm not complete its journey?
No way to tell, snow is all mystery.

—8 April 2020

My first attempt at a sonnet during this yearlong project of doing a poem a day. This daily poem took me much longer than usual.

I found the sonnet is a demanding form. It requires 14 lines, ten syllables per line, and a strict rhyme scheme. I chose abba cddc effe gg, although different types of sonnets can have somewhat different schemes. The sonnet originally comes from Italian, which I understand is a very rhyme-rich language. English is not, which means finding the rhymes is more challenging. Shakespeare, of course, wrote many sonnets, and it is probably due to him that sonnets became an English tradition at all. I spent a lot of time on my dictionary app looking up rhymes for my end words, which, I'm willing to bet, is not the way Shakespeare did it.

Besides the rhyme scheme, a sonnet also usually has a "turn" somewhere in the middle, where the poet looks at the subject in a different light, or from a different perspective, or even changes their mind about what they have just written in the lines above. The technical term for this turn is *volta*.

My turn occurs in the ninth line where I begin to show that the snow storm, which up to then has seemed too strong to resist, actually does have some weakness. Then I show how the snow doesn't quite smother the wall, because it doesn't quite get to the wall.

I remember seeing this phenomenon when I was a kid and wondering why the snow didn't get to the wall. I'm sure it has something to do with wind currents and eddies and how they interact with stationary objects during a storm, but even knowing this, the gap between snowdrift and wall has always been a source of fascination to me. It feels like the snow just kind of went so far and then chose to stop for reasons of its own. Maybe just to be different. Maybe to psych out the wall. Maybe something else.

In any case, that feeling I had that the snow had some motives for its action seemed like the right subject for a poem, and the sonnet form seemed to fit, so I threw myself into sonnet mode and came up with today's verse.

# Flashback

We walk down the wash,
sandy memory of a river.

Our feet leave labored tracks—
another memory laid over the

channel. The tree branches on
either side lean close. The

wind picks at them and
they hiss in response, recalling

the quiet rush of flowing
water that will always return,

like an image from childhood:
indelible, as faithful as sunlight.

*—9 April 2020*

We have rivers and creeks where we live in Southern Arizona, but they are dry most of the time. Seeing water in them is a very rare occurrence that comes only with substantially heavy rains.

We walk down these washes. They are sometimes ankle deep in sand and gravel and walking them can be laborious, like walking on beach sand. Progress is slow and it makes you notice the world around you a little more than you would walking down a trail or a path.

What I notice are the trees and the agave plants on either side. They often seem to be trying to tell me something, as plants often seem to do. When I listen, I don't really hear anything understandable, but sometimes they get my imagination going and I come up with odd observations that I then put into poems.

Which is what I did today.

# The Loneliness of the Jigsaw Puzzle Piece

Five lobes:
two blobby
arms: a
skewed bubble
head: and
two balloon
legs striding
out of
the disheveled
pile and
across the
table to
its one
true spot:
shoulder to
shoulder with
its comrades:
all interlocked
to create
the partially
assembled landscape:
all of
them unique
and exactly
the same:
hoping for
the grace
to blend
in with
this crowd.

*—10 April 2020*

With so many us now self-isolating in our houses and apartments, there must be a lot of lonely people at home.

As I considered that state of affairs, I imagined the opposite: what if people were jammed up close together? What would that be like? Loneliness might then be replaced by annoyance. Hard to say which would be worse.

That led to thinking about jigsaw puzzles. How the pieces join up in just one way, and how that might be a metaphor for people in close proximity. Especially when some puzzle pieces look a lot like human figures. The ones with five lobes, anyway.

# The Rincon Mountains

most evenings they
pull a blanket

of sunlight over
themselves all the

way up to
their chins just

to keep warm
through the night

*—11 April 2020*

---

The Rincon Mountains are a small range here in the Southwest. I see them through my office window. They present an interesting jagged line against the sky. In the late afternoon they take on a ruddy color as the sun sets directly across from them.

If I look slant at that color covering them, I can half convince myself that it isn't so much sunlight on them as it is an actual physical object, like a quilt or a blanket.

Once I have that in my head, I can't shake the perception away. At least, not for a while. Not that I want to. It's pleasing to imagine the mountains sleeping snugly under a blanket of light.

# Red Coat Concert

The cardinal sings
and from its beak rings
a single pure note
repeated by rote.

Oh cardinal why
will you never try
another heart song,
what could be so wrong?

You might try a lilt
or even notes spilt
in cascading streams
as though from weird dreams.

How 'bout a blues line
or folk song sublime.
A rousing gospel
to inspire people.

Rock and roll anthems
are known to grab thems.
Certain love ballads
make people feel glads.

But cardinal please
don't pay mind to these
crazy opinions
and odd suggestions.

There's no need to change
your acoustic range.
It is perfection,
a pure confection.

Keep singing your song
and you can't go wrong.
And I'll keep my ear
tuned to your good cheer.

*—12 April 2020*

Each song bird I hear on The Sanctuary has a particular melody or notes that it sings again and again. I actually like hearing these. They lend a certain charm to life here.

This morning I was listening to the cardinal. It belted out a song of three identical notes and did so again and again. I had this fleeting thought: what if the cardinal could learn a new song? But no, there's no need for that. It has the song that works for it.

Still, the thought led to today's poem.

# Please Stop Soon

Coming home from a crafts class
at the YMCA.
Me carrying some popsicle stick construction
in a brown paper bag.

I'm cutting through a parking lot
when two older guys, teens,
walk up behind me and ask what I'm
doing and I quicken my pace.

Start running.
I hear their footsteps
slapping against the pavement,
me slipping between parked cars

them keeping up.
My sleeve catches on an
antenna and the bag goes flying.
I pause, fatal error.

One of the guys grabs me
by the back of my jacket.
I'm not tall yet,
still small enough to be prey

to these two thugs.
We're all three breathing heavily.
I'm the only one scared.
He turns me around,

his grip on my jacket strong and sure.
*What you got in the bag?* he asks.
I start crying
the tears roll off my eyes and fly

up above the three of us,
beckoning me to follow.
*Come on*, they say, *it's safe up here.*
I'm shaking, ready to take off.

The other guy stomps on the bag hard.
The popsicle sticks snap.
The guy holding my jacket pushes me hard
so I fall on my ass

sprawled on the parking lot
and taste salt in my mouth
filling up with blood
from my bit tongue.

Disgust on the face
of the one who pushed me.
He spits on the pavement
near my feet.

And then they turn and run from me
like I'm a dangerous animal.
I get up slowly.
No lesson to be learned, no moral

to tuck away in my mind
for strength in hard times to come.
But tears remove irritants.
One of their major functions.

I take shallow breaths,
wipe my face
think how will I tell my parents
what just happened.

Feel my tender heart
still going like crazy, me hoping
for the shaking in my hands to stop,
please stop soon.

—13 April 2020

Another prompt from Diane Lockward's book *The Practicing Poet*. The task here was to take an event from childhood that had some victimization and/or revenge element to it and tell that story.

As best I can remember, all the details in this poem happened to me when I was about nine or ten years old. I am aware, of course, that memory can be faulty. Which means some of the details here might not be quite right. But the gist of it is true. A couple of older guys chased me and pushed me to the ground and I was very scared.

The part about tears flying up and calling me, that part didn't happen, but it felt right for the poem. I wanted an escape, but none was available. Easy to imagine the tears offering me one, since, in the end, I reasonably certain it was my crying that chased the bullies away.

# King Arthur

The crown,
let's face it,
is an annoyance.
It's heavy
and won't stay put
unless you hold
your head *just so*.
And then you look
a little stiff,
like being king
is this great *burden*.
You envy the knights,
going out on all these
great adventures.
Sure, they might get killed,
but in the meantime
they feel alive.
Flying on horseback,
swinging mighty swords.
Might for right.
Isn't that the phrase?
Someday you'll toss
the crown aside,
saddle up your favorite steed,
and travel the countryside.
The court will wonder:
Where's the king?
What happened to Arthur?
They'll pick up the crown.
It'll have a dent
where it hit the wall.
They'll hesitate.
Then try it on.
While your horse's hooves
are pounding the dirt
and you're taking in great gulps
of bracing air,
they'll feel the dead weight
of all that gold
pulling them down.

*—14 April 2020*

One of my favorite books of all time is *The Once and Future King* by T. H. White. In fact, I love this book so much that I've only read it once. I have such fond memories of it that I'm afraid to read it again, in case it is not as wonderful as I remember it. I have reread other books from my teen years, and I found almost all of them wanting. So this particular book will remain safely encased in my memory.

I thought about this book today as I was taking my morning walk and listening to *History Unplugged*, a podcast by Scott Rank. Today's episode was about King Arthur, who is almost certainly fictional, but who has been featured in countless books, poems, movies, and comics. This gave me the idea to write today's poem about King Arthur.

I sought to humanize the myth just a little bit. I wondered what aspect of being a king would be annoying. I immediately settled on the crown. That heavy appendage of monarchical power that had to be a real pain to deal with. Or so I chose to imagine it for the purposes of this poem.

Having power is an intoxicant, so I have gathered from memoirs of world leaders. But it is also, paradoxically, a diminishment. A world leader's life is no longer private, and world leaders generally can't just go where they want to go.

So the poem is about a leader who throws aside the accouterments of leadership to taste a little bit of freedom, at least for a little while.

# Heart Attack

They tell us here
to be wary
of pack rats getting up
under the hood of your
car and chewing through
the wires.
There are horror stories,
lots of them.
We put a light under the car
to scare away the critters:
they favor darkness
and don't show themselves
if there is any light.
We are also advised
to periodically lift the hood
and check for evidence of
pack rat activity.
When I do,
I am cutting open the car's chest.
I see the hoses
like veins and arteries
leading into and out
of the engine block.
This loop
must be the aorta.
That tube
possibly the superior vena cava.
The sinewy wires
bundled into neat stacks
and nestled snugly
into the chest cavity
appear intact.
No pack rat attacks here.
The car's heartbeat
still strong and true.
I close the hood,
like sewing up a wound,
and am fleetingly aware,
as I shuck my surgeon's gloves,

of my own heartbeat,
keeping the jaws and teeth
of death at bay.

*—15 April 2020*

The first week we moved here, a couple of people told us that if we want to keep pack rats from crawling up under the hood of our parked car and chewing through the wires, we needed to put a light under our car every night. Others suggested placing bars of soap under the hood. Online sources suggested copious spreads of rat killer on the ground around the car, but we weren't about to do that. We saw ads for devices that emit a sound which, supposedly, pack rats can't stand. Another possibility was to lift the hood of our car each evening and hang a light above the engine.

We opted to put a light under the car and plugged it into a timer so that it came on at night and turned off during daylight hours. This has worked for us so far—fingers crossed.

I wanted to describe the situation with pack rats and cars. As I wrote, I felt like I needed a metaphor for the car's engine. I settled on the heart—the maze of hoses under a hood has always reminded me of the veins and arteries associated with hearts.

# The Cabinet

*They call me the carpenter,*
*I craft goods from a tree.*
*People tell me I'm an artist,*
*I just build what I see.*

I get a hammer and some wood,
a saw and lots of nails.
I plan to build a birdhouse
to protect those wings and tails.

Once the birdhouse is completed,
I'll install it on a pole.
A little bird will find it,
and fly inside the hole.

But before I quite get started,
here comes a bride-to-be.
She wants me to make for her
a cabinet for a fee.

So I say to this young lady:
"I can make the furniture.
But first I make my birdhouse,
then I'll do your job for sure."

I could tell by her demeanor
that my offer would not fly.
She wanted her cabinet pronto,
a delay would make her cry.

She said "I came to see you,
because you are the best.
I've travelled such a distance,
I don't mean to be a pest."

I sighed and said I'd help her.
The birds will have to wait.
I built her what she wanted
and made sure it was not too late.

She counted out some dollars
as she took the cabinet.
I asked her how much money
was in the bundle I'd get.

She asked me, "Are you saying,
that you can't do your sums?"
"No Miss," I said, "I don't know,
'cause I'm blinder than ghost hums."

She said she was so sorry.
She just had no idea.
I told her not to worry,
as she drove off in her Kia.

Then I heard a bird above me,
chirping their house should be next.
I worked hard to make it happen,
so they could build their nest.

*They call me the carpenter,*
*I craft goods from a tree.*
*People tell me I'm an artist,*
*I just build what I see.*

*—16 April 2020*

---

I'm reading a collection of interviews with songwriters conducted by Paul Zollo. *Songwriters on Songwriting* features such well known names as Paul Simon, Bob Dylan, Joan Baez, Carol King, Madonna, and many others.

I've heard many people say you can't make a living as a poet, but that is not true. All of these songwriters are poets. They use rhyme, meter, assonance, imagery, and all the same tools that poets use. They just set it to music.

There's all kinds of craft advice and tips in these interviews. For example, Paul Simon says he never starts a song with an idea of where it is going, or even what it is. When he writes a song he is trying to find out what the song itself is trying to say. He has no control. He just follows along wherever it wants to take him.

I highly recommend this book (and its sequel, *More Songwriters on Songwriting*) to anyone who wants to write poetry. Heck, to anyone who wants to write anything.

I wanted to try my hand at something that might approach the form of songwriting. Today's poem is what I came up with. Not sure it's a song at all, but, following Simon's suggestion, I let it go where it wanted to go.

# The Nature of Chaos

It was me who unleashed the plague,
me who started the wars.
No need to look any further
for the perpetrator:
it was me, it was me, it was me.

That volcanic eruption
that filled the sky with ash?
Yup, that was some of my best work.
Oh, such fun I had with lava.
It was me, it was me, it was me.

Remember the hurricanes
that swept the houses away?
And surely you recall,
the tornadoes that tore up all.
It was me, it was me, it was me.

The floods and the avalanches,
the mudslides and the earthquakes.
So many ways to destroy
all that you have built.
It was me, it was me, it was me.

Now don't think I regret
a single awful star
that I have sent down to
the Earth from my throne afar.
It was me, it was me, it was me.

And please don't think to try
to understand my mind
or psychoanalyze
the demons in my head.
It was me, it was me, it was me.

You are the sort of folk
who likes to find some reasons
for every bad occurrence

and all the dismal seasons.
It was me, it was me, it was me.

But for me I think there's beauty
in the grand ballet of destruction.
You won't persuade me otherwise,
so best to find your shelter.
It was me, it was me, it was me.

Now someday maybe I'll tire
of wrecking all I see.
Then it might be your turn
to bring the structures down.
It was me, it was me, it was me.

You might say it will never happen,
that you would not be so.
Perhaps that may be true,
but only time will tell.
It was me, it was me, it was me.

And if the fates determine,
that your role in the future,
will be the agent of ruin,
then you might repeat with pride:
It was me, it was me, it was me.

*—17 April 2020*

---

Another lesson from songwriting: Repeat phrases for good effect. The last line of each stanza here is exactly the same. I hope it adds a sense of coherence to the poem. I also played around with rhymes in this one but did not maintain a regular rhyme scheme, preferring instead to let the rhymes occur with some irregularity and a certain amount of chaos.

I will say that one of the things that I do not like in popular songs is when the singer sings the same line over and over again. Some songs are exactly that: one line repeated for much or most of the length of the song. That just gets irritating. On the other hand, a strong chorus repeated a few times through the song can bring it all together both harmonically and thematically. I hope that's what I did here.

# Shadow World

In the late evening,
when the stars have drawn up
the light of the day
for their own purposes,

we vertebrates,
so proud of our spines,
feel a shiver,
partly from cold

but more
to mourn
the loss
of the luminous sea.

Animal sounds are everywhere:
owls gathering breath for the hunt,
crickets chirping anomalous joy,
pawed things scratching at the ground;

all seep out
from dark corners,
filling the void, finding a way
to keep on swimming.

—*18 April 2020*

---

We swim in sunlight all through the day. Then when night falls, the sea of light disappears. I remember when I was a kid, I wondered where the light went. Once, when I looked up at the night sky and saw the stars, I figured that's where the light went. It was obvious. The light was gone from down here, but up there the stars had light. Seemed perfectly clear.

Day and night does definitely have a different feel. Day is open, free. Night feels closed in, constricted. This is lessened, a little, by the presence of artificial light: streetlights, car headlights, and so on. But night still feels like a wild place.

Today's poem takes a lot of these feelings and observations and tries to craft something coherent from it all. I wanted to evoke the sense of life finding different strategies for survival after sunset, and what that feels like to someone like me, used to daylight as the default mode of life.

# Light World

In the early dawn
when the sun has drawn down
the light of the stars
for its own purposes

we vertebrates
so proud of our lit spines
all atingle with thoughts
shuttling up and down

raise ourselves
to greet
the lighted
dreamscape still clinging to our beings.

Animal sounds are everywhere:
finches singing up the sky,
lizards skittering across the sand,
insects buzzing the air awake;

all leap out
from illuminated recesses
filling the space, finding a way
to keep on flying.

*—19 April 2020*

A companion to yesterday's poem. Darkness and light, two faces of the same coin. Much of this poem is the same as yesterday's: the structure, much of the wording, perhaps even the meaning.

If any poem should have a companion poem written for it, this would be it.

# My Word

starts in my lungs
as air moving up
my windpipe

gathering meaning
all the way to the top
where it whirls

and twirls on
the dance floor
of my tongue

then spins out
from the dance hall
of my mouth

still moving
still grooving
humming and buzzing

carrying a piece
of my thoughts so
you know what I mean

—*20 April 2020*

Casting about for a subject today, I tried to think of a very ordinary thing, with the intention of presenting it in a unique manner. Nothing more ordinary than uttering a word. But the sequence of events that have to happen for that to occur is actually quite intricate. So I tried to show some of that. Then I tossed in a metaphor—a word as a dancer—and liked the image of the mouth as a dance hall and the tongue as a dance floor.

# Tick Talk

The tick is a bug
no one wants to hug.
It sucks up your blood
like pigs in the mud.

Ticks are pleased to take
from your crimson lake
and won't ever feel
it's a forbidden meal.

They're stealthy and sly
and will always try
to quietly land
on your outstretched hand.

Or in your hairdo
or on your back too,
and have no regrets
'bout pouncing on pets.

These bloodsucking goons
become red balloons,
as they with great joy
drink up and annoy.

No point in praying
for them to take wing.
They'll dive right back in
and chomp on your chin.

So here's my advice:
they are worse than lice.
If you observe one,
then crush it for fun.

*—21 April 2020*

Some years ago I wrote a series of poems about different bugs. I wrote light verse about crickets, spiders, houseflies, and a few others I don't now recall. During this current project I've written about a tarantula and an inchworm.

These poems always have a rhyme scheme and are meant to be humorous. Or at least entertaining. Today I recalled some of those bug poems and remembered I had always wanted to write one about a lady bug. Because, well, lady bugs are cute and most people kind of like them. But no rhymes were coming to me for lady bug poems, so I changed direction and considered a bug that pretty much no one likes: the tick. Ticks are blood suckers and they carry disease. What's to like?

Well, maybe crushing one of these parasites would feel good. So that's where I went with this bit of verse.

# Languages Everywhere

I wade into the creek,
my bare feet wrapped in
mountain glaciers.

So cold, I feel nothing.
Not even the cries
of melting ice.

Everything numb
and comfortable
against the night.

Later the pin pricks
as I warm myself, stars
I picked up like pollen,

many of them with
things to say. I sit by
the fire and listen.

*—22 April 2020*

This one came from remembering a particularly cold creek I once waded into when I was a kid in Northern Ontario. It was so cold that it numbed my feet in seconds and made me gasp. It felt like I was wading into some other realm, one with a different language that I didn't fully understand.

# Moon Beats

Deerskin drum bearing a mottle
of dark and light seas like the moon.

Beater strikes the Sea of Tranquility
crushing the eagle into the crust.

Hits the man right on the nose
eliciting a startled look with wide eyes.

Coaxes the frog to get moving and take
that leap back into the pond.

Raps the knuckles of the hands
pressed on the moonscape to make prints.

Thumps on the rabbit's ears turned up,
as always, listening for predation.

Knocks over the pile of firewood
painstakingly collected that day.

Moves to separate a woman from
the anvil she used to beat cloth into shape.

Shakes the leaves off the tree
planted there in the time before time.

All the myths and fables, the tales and stories,
they fall out and tell their truths, beat by beat.

*—23 April 2020*

---

We have a deerskin drum that hangs next to the fireplace. As I was doing the weekly vacuuming this morning, I noticed it hanging there and saw that it had patches of darkness and light on it, rather like the surface of the moon. That was interesting. I had never noticed that before. I continued to do my cleaning but told myself to remember the moon image on the drum, so I could write a poem about it.

# The Shelter of Trees

I sit under the tree
while it oozes leaves
slowly from its pores.
I listen to the green
medallions slurping up
sunlight. Straight, no

ice. In the evening
the bark resounds
across the fields
like a call to arms:
The rain is coming!
Prepare yourselves

to gather up the
moisture while
we can. In the
morning the trunk
is swollen wide
with water. I return,

sit on the damp ground,
wait for fall. Then my
friend will shower
me with melancholy
confetti, heralding
the coming hibernation.

*—25 April 2020*

I often wonder what trees think about. I am convinced that they do think. After all, besides the biological processes of growth and reproduction, what else do they have to do? They can't go anywhere. They never get a different view of the world. They've got to think about something while standing there being buffeted by the wind and getting rained on and then getting cooked by the sun. Or maybe not. Maybe it's just me thinking about them.

# It Clung to the Branch for a Long Time

I do wonder
while trying
to remember
if I saw
the same finch
in this tree
last week
if the finch
in the tree
this week
still remembers
how to fly.

*—26 April 2020*

This morning I saw a bird some distance away perched on a branch. It stayed there for a long time while Kim and I ate breakfast in the backyard. After breakfast we remained where we were, observing the bird for some time. After a while I did remark that I don't often see birds sitting in one place for such a long time. Did it forget how to fly? It was an offhand remark, meant to amuse, but I wondered how memory might work in a bird. People forget things all the time. Wouldn't a creature equipped with a bird brain forget things as well?

Maybe not. Maybe a simpler brain keeps everything neat and tidy, unlike some people who have a whole lot of stuff roaming around our brains, getting in the way of one another, and straining our capacity to keep everything straight.

These are the musings I indulge in while watching birds in trees.

It wasn't a finch in real life, but rather some yellow bird I could not identify. I like the sound of the word "finch," however, so I used finch in the poem.

# Falling

Petals of palo verde blossoms
snatched up by ants and laid
out in a wide yellow path

like Dorothy's route to the
Emerald City. Pine tree
pollen gathered into clumps

of light brown capsules like
someone spilled a bottle of
pills onto the ground. Snow

in the higher elevations or
in the height of winter all
gathered up into thick layers

of white. Owl feathers
mottled brown and white
laying on the ground

after descending a long way,
signs for a naturalist tracking
raptors across the sky.

Eyes turned up to see what
can't be seen, not anymore.
The passage of everything

descending through the air
landing at our feet. Arousing
curiosity's eternal pull.

*—24 April 2020*

---

So much falls from the sky, or the air. I wanted to highlight some of those things and maybe make us wonder about them just a little. I chose items I have seen or experienced, and I tried to tie them to color as an organizing principle.

# The Ground

Erosion and gravity
working together put
all that dirt here.

Then I come along
with my shovel
and displace piles

of it just so I can
stick a post into
the ground. Tiny

ornament, like a
metal stud stuck
through the lip

of the Earth.
The planet's version
of styling, maybe,

or my impertinence,
making it wear
such a hindrance.

*—27 April 2020*

---

Last night as I was falling to sleep, I had an idea about—well, I'm not sure anymore. What I remember is that I told myself I had a really good subject for a poem and that I should remember what it was so I could write it when I woke up.

Alas, in the morning the subject has gone. I only remember something about burying. I don't remember what was being buried or where or how or when. Just burying.

Well, OK.

Maybe that was enough. I treated it as a prompt: "Write a poem in which something is buried."

So that's what I did.

# A Memory From Age Seven

The headlight beams
climbing up the walls.

Strange light beasts
I never invited in.

They arrived on their own
every time a car turned

the corner on the road
just outside our house.

Lost illumination, unable
to negotiate the curve,

tumbled across the yard
into my bedroom window,

and then forced to look
for a home in my house.

My urge to trap them in jars
and keep them on my dresser.

Would they howl in the night?
Sprout shoots of glowing

embers? Try to escape the
glass cage? Scowl at me?

I never found out. They
got to the ceiling and just

withered to shadowy nothing
like evaporating dreams.

*—28 April 2020*

Today marks six months of writing a poem a day. Half way through my project. Have you been following along and doing a poem a day as well? It is not required, of course. If you just want to read along with what I'm doing each day, that's perfectly fine.

If you have been doing your own poem-a-day-project, take an inventory of what you have learned up to now.

Here's a few things I have learned.

First, I don't have to have inspiration to write a poem. If I treat it like a job or a task, I can come up with a subject and lines. If I wait for inspiration, I might never do my daily poem.

Second, I can write under most any circumstance. I have written my daily poem on my computer, in a notebook, on my phone, and on a scrap of paper I found on the floor. I have written in my office, in the living room while the TV was on, outside by the pool, and in the car while it went through the automatic carwash, and another time while I was waiting for the folks at Jiffy Lube to finish an oil change.

Third, writing a poem a day is lots of fun. Trying out new subjects and new approaches is a blast.

Fourth, writing a poem a day heightens my awareness. I am always on the lookout for an arresting image, or a good line, or a good metaphor, or a unique perspective on the ordinary. This project has helped me see the world in new ways.

# Prism, Mirror, Lens, Dust

My story begins in the dirt, such distant origins
    buried in deep time.
The Earth is a grimy lens refracting the truth of so
    many past events
to my inquiring eyes here in the peculiar aspect of
    time I call the present.

My story's middle is a brief gift given by a seemingly
    benevolent universe,

but I am wary of treating the gift as eternity. It is
    merely the prelude
to my story's end, completed circle, all three hundred and sixty degrees,
back to the dusty lens, refracted through the present
    into the future.

*—29 April 2020*

---

I sometimes think of poetry as a lens. Each poem takes a certain aspect of the world and refracts it through the lens of language to create a different view of that aspect. It's artificial, in its own way, but then, language itself is artificial. Something made up by people. We have no direct perception of the world. It all comes through our senses, our brains, our thoughts, our words.

# After Basho

inside the courtyard
the lizards cannot know
cactus is blooming

*—30 April 2020*

Marie Mutsuki Mockett had a piece on *The Paris Review* website yesterday about reading Basho to her 10-year-old son. Basho lived from 1644 to 1694 and was the most famous poet of the Edo period in Japan. He is considered the preeminent master of the haiku form to this day. Mockett quotes one of his poems in the article: "Inside the temple, visitors cannot know, cherries are blooming."

As I was reading the article, skimming it, actually, I came to this poem and it stopped me immediately. Nine simple words, but they evoke so much mystery and reinforce the notion that there are many worlds in the one world we know.

After I read it a few times, it reminded me of our own house here, with the walls in the back, meant to keep out snakes and other critters, but also, of course, forming a courtyard. I presumed to borrow Basho's wording and structure and use them for my own purposes, bringing a little bit of his sensibility to our desert setting.

# May

# Banquet

Air seasoned by bird calls.
Salad of leaves filling the blue bowl of the sky.
Breath of wind cooling the hot platters of rocks.
Forking branches spearing ripe fruit.
Shadow of cloud guests falling on the table of ground.
This is making a meal of what you have.

*—1 May 2020*

After reading some Basho and enjoying his pared down approach to poetry, I reflected on what I considered important in poetry. I came up with two things: clarity and mystery.

I prefer poems that make their imagery plain. But I also prefer poems that have something hidden behind the imagery.

In today's effort, I sought to make food and eating imagery from common and familiar natural objects and occurrences. But I also wanted an element of mystery. Who is putting on this banquet? The poem doesn't tell you, but I hope to make you think about it and maybe try to discover for yourself who or what that might be.

# Walking in Memories

the sandy wash
recalls the rush
of flowing water

*—2 May 2020*

I was getting ready to write today's poem when a cactus wren came to my windowsill and spent a half minute or so exploring. Its beak was open and it looked up and down and left and right repeatedly and hopped across the window. It looked like it was trying to find a way in, but the glass, of course, prevented that.

When it was gone, I figured I would write a poem about a cactus wren. But it flew across the yard and into the wash. I took that as a sign to write something about the wash. After all, the cactus wren led me to it.

Washes here are what other parts of the country would call a creek, stream, or river. They are dry most of the time. In fact, almost all of the time they are dry. They only fill up when there is a heavy rain, like during monsoon season. Lots of folks, including Kim and me, walk washes when they are dry. They form a natural hiking path and they can meander for quite a long way. They are very sandy, as a rule, which makes walking rather slow, which means it is often a meditative or contemplative activity.

I wondered what they would think of water. They don't see it much, but maybe they miss it? I went with that and tried to make it simple but evocative.

# To You, Reading This Poem

I am the same age
as you, no matter
what age you are.

I know the same world
as you do, no matter
where you have lived.

I cross the same river,
bleed the same red,
endure the same pain.

Walk the same ground,
dance the same steps,
shelter under the same sky.

Love what you love,
inhale the same air,
reach for identical dreams.

Look up at the same stars,
blink at the same sun,
sit down to congruent meals.

I wrap myself in the same
blankets you use, sleep and
snore just like you.

Hear the same music,
smell the same flowers,
taste the same tears.

I age as you do,
approach the same wall,
give thanks to kindred spirits.

Sigh with uncanny similarity,
speak the same languages,
yearn for the same wings.

—*3 May 2020*

Of course, the sentiments in this poem are not true. Everyone has a different experience of life. And yet. We also have experiences that are congruent with those of others. This poem, in a way, is a series of questions. Are we all the same, or are we different? Like so many other questions, the answer begins: It depends.

It depends on so many things: your age, your class, your health history, your family, your loves, your battles, and so on. Everyone has a unique set of those. All that is true. It is also true that many of us share emotions and thoughts and yearnings. Or, as an old saying has it: "I'm unique, just like everyone else."

This poem began with the opening stanza. I had the idea that the writer of a poem might identify so thoroughly with their readers that they would feel as though they were the same age as the reader. So I begin with a fantasy, and go on from there, laying down more and more consequences of that initial idea.

I was somewhat troubled by the many repetitions of the word "same." I tried other constructions and terms, just to vary it, but it seems to me it is the best word for most of these lines, so I didn't try to strain the lines with thesaurus terms for "same."

I do like how it flows and I'm happy with how it ends.

# Ocotillo Thunder Strike

Bouquet of lightning bolts:
tipped with sizzling flames,
sparked with electric leaves,
ragged with rows of thorns
to shock you into awareness.

*—4 May 2020*

Kim and I were walking a long trail in the park this morning and we passed a clutch of ocotillo, long stalks reaching to the sky that bend and curve in such a way that they reminded me of lightning bolts.

Any time something like that happens, I seize it as a poem in the making.

So later in the day, after I had let the image sit with me for a while, I composed this short five-line poem evoking the idea of ocotillo stalks as thunderbolts, all striking the same spot, creating a kind of bouquet.

# Air as Light

One night we
pulled the push
pins out of

the sky and
left bright holes
we called stars.

So when the
stars turned to
dust we took

deep breaths to
fill our lungs
with the tales

they had to
tell us. Then
we took turns

and dreamed the
same dream each
night we slept.

*—5 May 2020*

The moon, a couple of days from full, is hanging in the sky outside my window as I write this. The rabbit is clearly visible in profile, looking to the left, its ears big and stretching to the top right edge of the moon's disk.
    Observing this rabbit in the moon led me to consider the night sky and how it could easily represent some other thing than what it is. For example: the stars. What are they? Well, giant balls of burning gas, of course. But that's not what they look like from here. From here on planet Earth, they look like tiny holes in a black material. Pinpricks. Once I had that image, the rest of the poem fell into place, as it often does.

This is a metered poem. Each line is exactly 3 syllables long, and since each word is one syllable, each line is exactly 3 words long.

# Rooted

Plants in the ground
don't think much
about travel, except
maybe in the way
we think of flying.

It's a dream, a flight
of fancy that might
entertain on a lazy
evening when the
breeze is pleasant
and the air sweet

with the scent of
flowers. We think
of making wings
in our workshops
and donning them
to sail the air and
they—
  —well, maybe
they gaze at the dirt
in movable flower pots
with a heady sense of
longing, wondering:
*What if I could sink
my roots into one
of those? Would I?*

*—6 May 2020*

When I see plants, I often think about their inner lives. What is it like to live all your days with only one view? Do they ever yearn for a different way of being?
 I don't know the answer, but I don't need to. Sometimes poems exist to ask a question, not necessarily to provide an answer.

# After Upsetting the Apple Cart

All the apples
rolling down
the hill, each
following its
own separate
path.

One of them
became a meal
for rodents.

A larger one
rolled to a field
and took root
and became a
tree the kids
liked to climb.

Another ended
up in a jar
of applesauce
on a grocery
store shelf.

A particularly
red one spent
a sunny
afternoon on
a teacher's desk.

Some
were baked
into pies, some
were bitten
into by Adam
and Eve, and
one of the

green ones
never learned

a thing and
remained
as fresh and
innocent as
the day it
was picked.

*—7 May 2020*

I like to eat apples with the skin on, though I know many choose to peel an apple before eating it. I use a small paring knife to cut off pieces of the apple. My favorite variety is Macintosh. They are only available for a month or so in the fall, and I look forward to that every year.

The phrase quoted in the title is one I've heard all my life, though I have never actually seen an apple cart, except in movies. I assume they were (and maybe still are in some places) a common way of selling apples. The saying has always felt like a warning to me: Don't mess with things as they are. Even if they are bad, things could get worse. Much worse. I suppose that's true, but things could get better, too. The status quo is not something that should be slavishly adhered to.

# Bring Me the Head of the Band

They can always tune up on the ocean.
Sea birds sometimes eat plastic garbage
and then it fills up their stomachs and they die.

I saw a display of all the stuff they found
in one pelican's stomach there on the Oregon coast
near Newport. Toothbrushes. But it wasn't my fault.

In the past people didn't live so long.
Nothing bad happened to them, besides death.
Maybe that bothered them, I don't know.

The dead look at life differently.
They see what was and don't look to the future.
Only to the past. Or maybe the eternal present.

The moon is a cold hard rock. Sometimes a hot hard rock.
There's no atmosphere, so what are you going to do
when you get there? Just gasp in the cold and the heat?

The stars are very bright, but no one would want to stick
their hand into the flaming future they hold.
It isn't the sort of thing I would recommend to anyone.

*—8 May 2020*

Today's poem came from an exercise in Steve Kowit's book *In the Palm of Your Hand.* He suggested doing some automatic writing for a stretch of time. I set my timer for 10 minutes and then just began typing. In automatic writing the idea is to not think. Just write. The first words that come to your mind. Just put them down one after the other. Don't worry about meter, or logic, or any kind of sense at all. It's all about getting words out with no pauses or reflection.

When my 10 minutes were done, I had about 600 words. I went back over what I had written and tossed out what seemed uninteresting. I kept what caught my eye or my mind, did a minimal amount of rearranging, and formed three line stanzas out of what I had left. I took one of the lines I produced and employed it as the title of the piece.

I view what I produced as a kind of picture of what was in my head, slightly photoshopped to remove the blurs and the pesky bits of dust and debris that sometimes mar a picture. Not sure if the result is interesting to anyone else, but there it is. A poem mined from my unguarded consciousness.

# Scavenger Hunts

1.
a rock
a thorn
something dry and brittle
a yellow flower petal
a piece of plastic trash

2.
a thought
an emotion
a shiver
the beating of your heart
the itch in your sole

3.
the cold hard truth
the future
justice
hope
a reason to cry

*—9 May 2020*

Kim sent me an essay from the *Paris Review* website by Sabrina Orah Mark titled "Fuck the Bread. The Bread is Over." Like many of us right now she is staying at home with her family. She has two sons and is homeschooling them. The essay is about how the priorities in her life have changed with the advent of Covid-19. Things that seemed important just a few weeks ago now seem irrelevant. The title comes from her mother. It was her response when Mark told her on the phone that she can't get what she needs to make bread anymore.

   It's worth looking up and reading. One of the things she had her sons do, when she had more or less run out of homeschooling ideas, was a scavenger hunt.

   I took that notion and reworked it for today's poem. I started out with a concrete scavenger hunt: things that one could touch, physical objects. Then with the second hunt I moved to the personal with inner phenomenon: thoughts and internal processes, things that can't really be held but are intensely personal. Finally a third hunt for ephemeral concepts, things that are important, but somewhat elusive.

The idea is that the most important things are not things at all: they are concepts, abstractions, beliefs, and convictions.

When I was composing this, I tried to pare down the items to their bare bones. I felt brevity was an advantage here. I also kept to three hunts. Any less and my point would be missed. Any more and my point would be diminished.

# Escape Never Ends

Upon waking I find
brushes and paint
along with the ability

to draw. Without questioning
this turn of events
I produce a mural

on the wall of a sun lit
beach seen from the
ocean. I step into the

mural and swim to
the island. As I walk on
the hot sand the warm

air dries my clothes.
The tide laps at my feet
erasing my footprints

behind me. Day fades
into evening. I find a
banquet laid out

next to a pleasant fire.
A table a short distance away
bears paint and brushes

beckoning me to a canvas
on an easel next to the fire:
blank, white, textured, and new.

*—10 May 2020*

This one is pretty straightforward. The person in the poem takes the magical opportunity to create their own reality, but in the end finds the means to create a newer reality. The implication is that no reality will ever satisfy.

The impetus here was some of the work of René Magritte. He painted enigmatic and sometimes paradoxical canvases that invited viewers into his worlds. These worlds were often fantastic constructions. I wanted to evoke some of that sensibility in this poem.

# Parabolic Memory

A leather pouch
an elastic strap
a heavy stone:
when I was
a kid I shot
a slingshot.

No Goliath
in our neighborhood,
and I was
no David.

Loading the stone
into the pouch
nothing more than
and exercise in—

—what?
Phony nostalgia?
Fake reenactment?
Counterfeit power?

A long reach
to remember
now the lengthy
beautiful arc
of the stone
across the sky
carving an
eternal and
classic path.

*—11 May 2020*

When I was growing up a few of the kids in my neighborhood had slingshots. Some of them tried using their weapons to shoot rocks at birds. They never succeeded in hitting one, thank goodness.

I remember handling one of those slingshots, even tried my hand at shooting a rock. I deliberately aimed away from any living thing, including a tree, letting the rock fall in an empty field. I seem to remember my friend, who was with me, grabbing the slingshot from my hand and asking me why I wasted a shot. It didn't feel like a waste to me. I enjoyed seeing that rock sail over the field. It was glorious.

This poem came to me as I was listening to a lecture given by Professor Anne Curzan on the subject of linguistics in which she said that many words with "sl" are negative words. Consider slug, slag, slur, slam, and so on. Thinking about "sl" words made me think of slingshot, and that led to a memory of shooting a slingshot when I was, if I remember correctly, about 11 or 12 years old.

# Hai Tech Ku

umbrella unfurls
convex surface reflects light
to jet plane's pilot

automobile's brakes
screeching sounds to shiver spines
brake pad replacement

electricity
flows to refrigerator
so many ice cubes

microwave oven
turntable frozen dinner
bell rings robot song

red laser pointer
dances on white board surface
more power point slides

laptop keys faded
latest update loads slowly
need new computer

youtube videos
streaming the antics of cats
wifi still working

*—12 May 2020*

Traditional haiku are about the sights, sounds, and feelings of nature. Most deal with animals, plants, landscapes, and so on and also evoke some season of the year, either explicitly or more subtly.

My idea here was to do the exact opposite. Write haiku about the unnatural world, the tech heavy world we live in, with computers, microwaves, airplanes, and so on.

So I did a few of them.

I wasn't sure what to call this. I considered "Hai Tech," "High Tech Ku," and "Hai-tech Ku," but eventually settled on "Hai Tech Ku."

# Before the Ax

When the blade
is broken
from its handle
the power of
the chop
is only potential
and the tree
trembling in
the wind does
not shake
from fear.

*—13 May 2020*

Sometimes I get phrases stuck in my head. Today it was "Before the flood." Not sure where it came from or what it means. It could be from a song. Or something I read. I didn't look it up, just decided to let it be there, doing what it needed to do.

Later in the day I played around with the phrase. "Before the dance." "Before the flight." "Before the birth." And so on. One of the variations I came up with was the title of today's poem. Something about it caught my attention and all the other variations slipped away. I stuck with the title and late in the day quickly wrote out the poem to go with it.

No rhymes in this one but a lot of alliteration: blade/broken, power/potential, potential/chop, tree/trembling, and from/fear. I used these on purpose to give the poem a sense of cohesion.

# No Going Back

Mourning dove, what are
you grieving with
your wooooo-wooooo?
We once mistook you
for the passenger pigeon.
Is that what your cry
is for? Are you calling
for your fellow creature
made extinct? Next time
I hear you, maybe I'll
pause a moment and
remember your lost kin.

*—14 May 2020*

I asked Kim to suggest a subject for my day's poem. We were outside and had heard mourning doves with their plaintive call. Her suggestion was "Mourning dove."

Prompts are like improv. You never say no to an improv and you never question it. Same with prompts. You just go with them.

I didn't know a whole lot about mourning doves. We have a lot of them here on our property. Their wings make a distinctive whistling sound, and they occasionally take baths in our birdbaths.

I googled them and discovered that at one time they were thought to be passenger pigeons. Unlike passenger pigeons, however, they are not in any danger of extinction. There are estimated to be close to 500 million of them in the United States alone. Still, the fact that they were once mistaken for a species that is now extinct gave me a road into the poem. They are mourning for that lost species. At least, that's the conceit of the poem.

# Abstract Concrete

Misery sculpts misshapen bronze.
Happiness looks for well-worn lawns.

Beauty flies on raven wings.
Pity prefers loud cell phone pings.

Honor guards the king's gold stash.
Hope expects mere smoke and ash.

Courage moves in zigzag paths.
Anger marinates in tepid baths.

Deceit hordes coins from public fountains.
Compassion looks for routes up mountains.

Pride wears tired worn-out hats.
Honesty spends time with homeless cats.

Regret arrives in ill-timed waves.
Love fills all the cozy caves.

*—15 May 2020*

---

I'm reading John Carey's *A Little History of Poetry*. In his chapter on Elizabethan love poets, he says one of the distinguishing features of Shakespeare's art "is that abstract nouns are made agents, performing real acts."

When I read that I immediately saw it as a writing prompt. I then made a list of abstract nouns and paired them up to counterpoint or emphasize their meanings. Then I wrote rhyming couplets for each pair, giving the abstract noun in each line some concrete thing to do.

I'm not sure if the result is silly or not, but I had fun doing them.

# On The Eternal Power of Kings and Queens

Past monarchs claimed rights on the innocent,
as knowledge was never for peasants meant.
But now we vote to elect our leaders
and so we must be thinkers and readers.
That we now make law is mere illusion,
secret meetings spawn most legislation.
And those in power still claim rights to kill.
Despite our franchise we are fodder still.

*—16 May 2020*

---

As a rule people in power don't want to give up power. This is true even in democracies and republics, where the people are supposedly in charge of who has power. I certainly don't claim this as an original thought. I bring it up here merely to illustrate how this poem began.

I wrote down a few short lines in my notebook to solidify the concepts in my mind. Here they are:
*The populace under monarchies can remain innocent.*
*But in a democracy we are expected to know what's going on.*
*Yet many secrets remain—the populace is still ignorant.*

I mulled over these words for a time and wondered how to turn them into a poem. In poetry, all the art is in how you say a thing, not necessarily in what the thing is.

I settled on metered and rhymed verse, partly because I've been reading about the old English poets in Carey's *A Little History of Poetry*, but also because a poem with an argument seemed to call out for a somewhat old-fashioned way of writing poetry.

It took me about half an hour to compose the lines. Early on I wanted the last four words to be: "we are children still," and worked toward that goal. But after the poem was done, I decided the word "fodder" worked better than "children," though I debated the two for a while before settling on the word that felt more chilling to me.

My rhyme scheme for this one is: aabbccdd, a group of four rhyming couplets pressed into one stanza. I considered separating out the couplets by adding a blank line between each one, but felt it would detract from the flow of the whole. Each line is exactly 10 syllables.

# That's Entertainment

Cottontail rabbits hop there and here,
then freeze their fast motion
for three quick heartbeats,
before swiftly renewing their speedy commotion.

The feathered folk at the bird bath
sit on the rim,
dip their beaks thrice,
then fly on a whim.

The lizard so still it mimics a rock
then builds up its power
with three quick pushups
before zipping away, its expression a glower.

*—17 May 2020*

We see all these critters here at our place, and they behave more or less as I have described in the poem. The idea for this one came when I noticed that many of the birds that drink from our birdbaths do so 2 or 3 times. Sometimes 4, but most often, if my limited observations mean anything, exactly 3 times. I decided to take the theme of three things and extend it from the birds to other creatures. I kept a primitive rhyming scheme for each stanza (xaxa) but let the meter fall where it may. I didn't try to regularize that at all. The title says it all: It is great fun observing wildlife and noticing what they get up to.

# Mix Tape

The beaks
of the cactus wrens
tapping at my window
play a melody
I've never heard.

*—18 May 2020*

Cactus wrens come up to my window often and spend a few seconds walking back and forth across the pane. I watch them from inside. They will often tap the window with their beaks, creating something that at times resembles a tune. Today's offering is a simple observation poem. I saw something in nature and reported it here in five succinct lines.

# Remember, It's a Poem, Not a Glass

Memory drives a sedan.
Amnesia walks on crippled feet.

Sleep opens brightly wrapped packages.
Insomnia heaves trash out the window.

Health drinks in the colors of the world.
Sickness tries to paint with charcoal.

Love sees the future rising.
Indifference understands nothing.

Wealth lifts your chin.
Poverty scans the ground for coins.

Strangers are your friends.
Neighbors keep to themselves.

Optimists see this poem as half-full.
Pessimists see this poem as half-empty.

*—19 May 2020*

---

Like "Abstract Concrete" from a couple of days ago, here are further instances of some abstract concepts doing concrete things. This poem began with a random phrase, namely: "Memory drives a Mercedes." As often happens, I don't know where this came from. I've never been in a Mercedes and would probably not recognize one if I saw it. All I know is that they are considered luxury cars. I was probably attracted to the alliteration of Memory/Mercedes. Those kinds of things tend to catch my attention.

After I had typed that line out, I deleted "Mercedes." Didn't want a brand name in the poem. Nothing wrong with that particular option, but it just didn't seem right as the first line for whatever I was going to turn this into. I typed in sedan instead, losing the alliteration, but giving the line a more universal appeal, I hope. My next idea was to contrast Memory with Amnesia. If memory drove a car, what would amnesia do? Well, drag along, I guess. Try to keep up, but not succeeding. Hence, "Amnesia walks on crippled feet."

I was aware that I was being maybe a little too obvious or logical by contrasting the first words in those lines. Logic is often the assassin of poetry. Poems generally need some degree of illogic or wildness to them. You need that leap of craziness to make something really memorable and to draw readers into being co-creators with you. So I continued composing non-rhyming couplets in a vein similar to the first one, I tried to make my abstract/concrete comparisons a little bit out there. It's the best way to make a memorable poem.

That's what I think today. Tomorrow I might change my mind.

# Weighing My Options

As I stepped through the doorway
the threshold grabbed my hat
handed it to gravity's hands
which then pulled it down
to the space between outside and inside
and as I stood on that narrow band
and looked down at my hat
my scalp exposed to the air
I imagined the gods
high up on their gilded perches
looking down on me and laughing
and that felt good
felt right
so then I bent down
retrieved my hat
wished the gods well
told them I was glad
that I could give them a laugh
when the threshold
not done with me
pulled my glasses off my face
and dropped them
onto the indefinable place
where acceptance meets rejection
and I stood for some time
observing the blurry world
wondering which I would choose.

*—20 May 2020*

---

I don't normally take a nap, but today I felt like one. When I woke up I was a little bit groggy, as often happens after I nap and which is the main reason I generally avoid them. So I had some lunch and then it felt like time to write my poem, so I asked Kim for a prompt. She suggested "doorway."

OK. Doorway. I first considered breaking the word into two: door way. The way of the door. The way doors do things. Well, doors are open or closed. So I put down this line: "The door way is an open and shut case." I let that sit for a while. It didn't have much to it, so I deleted it and tossed out the idea of a door way of doing things.

Then I remembered my hat tilting on my head as I went through the front door a few days ago. The hat did not quite fall off my head, but it almost did. So I imagined the scenario that didn't happen: namely that my hat fell off and I had to pick it up. I incorporated the idea of a threshold, since that's what all doorways are, and the rest of the poem came in a few minutes.

It's not exactly a report from my life, since I did not drop my hat or my glasses, but it feels like something that could happen and that feels more than good enough for the poem.

# Celestial Navigation

on the trail
to falls creek

the familiar
end of a

fallen tree
cut by chain

saw blades
is a harvest

moon showing
the way forward

*—21 May 2020*

When we lived in Washington state one of our favorite hikes was on a two-mile trail that led to a 500-foot waterfall. In the summer we would often take that hike weekly and sometimes twice a week. The trail followed the creek up to the falls and wound through tall trees and past rocks, over smaller creeks, and through talus fields. It was always a fun and invigorating walk.

    We got to know the landmarks of the trail quite well. I remember at one point, maybe a third of the way in, there was a large log that the trail builders had left behind. It showed its cut end to hikers on the trail, and it was brighter than the surrounding woods. Not white, but definitely less dark than the bark or the ground. It often reminded me of the moon, leading the way forward. A kind of landmark (or skymark?) in itself.

# Life is an Illusion, Right?

One morning
you look up
and see a wall
you had not seen before.
There's a mural
on the wall
displaying a scene
from a dream
you just had
in which you built
a house made of clouds.
You put out your hand
to touch the wall
but it recedes from you
moving along the ground
like a brick snake.
That's when you stop
and assess the situation.
Your hand hanging
in the air
the wall taunting you.
*Tear me down*
*turn me to dust*
*if you dare.*

*—22 May 2020*

I was leafing through the June 2020 issue of *The Atlantic* where I found a poem, "Tree Beyond Your Window," by Michael Collier. Here's the first line: "One day you look up". The rest of the poem involves his observations of a tree and the life around it. I read the whole poem, but what really stuck with me was the first line. It's the perfect introduction to a poem, a story, a myth, a fable, or, well, just about anything. I imagined someone absorbed in their own world. Then, prompted by some mysterious process or event, they look up and see — what? It could be anything. They could see the world for the first time, an event they had never noticed before, a visitor, a calamity, a miracle, anything.

So I started today's poem with a variation of that line.

Then I let the poem go where my imagination wanted it to.

# All Natural Disasters are Personal

With a crackling sound
the shivering ground
wrecks the ancient mound.

Our watches unwound
and we find a hound
at the broken pound.

Then the rain comes round
as though mercy found
paths to healing bound.

—23 May 2020

I was watching an episode of the PBS show *Nova* about volcanoes. At the beginning of the program I heard the word "ground." My mind latched onto that word and I wondered how many rhymes it had. Quite a few, I realized.

    Once I had them written down, I saw I could make a poem out of them. So I wrote down a few ideas, settled on a five syllable line, and got as many "ground" rhymes in as I could.

# Creatures of the Night

They flow out of my—
Collect on the—
Howl at the moon's—
Make pacts with—
Cavort and dance until—
Get into fights over—
Frighten the inhabitants of—
Destroy the shops of—
Scout around for—
Eat the remains of—
Fly to the top of—
Take in the view at—
Growl at—
Scrape claws over—
Bleed onto—
Lick the wounds of—
Hold court in—
See the sun rising over—
Meander back to—
Settle in until—
Remember the freedom they—
Vow to repeat the—

*—24 May 2020*

No poem (or any writing, for that matter) is complete until it is read and understood by someone other than the writer. Today's poem takes that concept and stretches it a little by making it more or less meaningless unless the reader provides the final word or phrase of each line.

    My initial impulse with this piece was to take the phrase "creatures of the night" and play around with it a little. I imagined night creatures as dreams that escaped me and got outside of my head and—what? I wasn't sure. What would dream creatures do if they could escape the mind of the dreamer? Hard to say. I tried a few options. I won't quote them here because it might influence you in your choice of the endings of the lines.

# Sing What
# You Know

I remember seeing
swallows on a
5-staff stretch of
power lines, each
of them resembling
quarter, half,
or full notes and
inadvertently
composing
a melody that
no doubt sings
the praises of feathers
and beaks and
the harmonious life
of the flock

*—25 May 2020*

---

Birds perched on power lines often resemble notes in musical notation. How to turn that into a poem? I didn't think it was enough to just state the fact. So I contemplated what birds might accidentally compose. A song about themselves might be a good guess. Maybe something extolling the virtues of their characteristics, such as feathers or beaks. And hey, what about the fact that they fly in flocks, together, in perfect harmony, moving, sometimes, similar to a cloud of particles in which each member knows the movements of every other member.

    I liked the way harmony slipped into my musings and decided it would be there in the last one or two lines to bring the whole notion of music and composers full circle.

# The Fates of Orange

Destined to wrap some citrus
with a thick snug skin.

Painted on plump pumpkins
in satiny picture perfection.

Embedded with quiet care
in the flesh of crunchy carrots.

Riding autumn's lazy leaves
down to a lush lawn.

Snug in every round rainbow
hugging fellow colors in iridescent rapport.

*—26 May 2020*

---

Kim noticed that we were short of fruit in the house. A line came to me: "The Fate of an Apple." I liked it, but I had covered the subject of apples more than once in the past six months.

So no apples this time. Well what about oranges? The Fate of an Orange. But that didn't catch fire, so I considered the *color* orange instead of the *fruit* orange. That's when things started cooking.

The title became "The Fate of Orange," and I played around with alliteration in this one, having the final two words of each line in each couplet begin with the same sound. It's not exactly rhyming, but it has some of the same feel as rhyming and gives each couplet a pleasant coherence.

# Long Time Friends in the Neighborhood

The front of the
old house: droopy
windows for eyes,
scratched up door

for a nose, mouth
almost closed tight.
Only a few streaked
stair teeth showing.

Shingles weathered
to pale gray, and
paint more a peeling
memory than a

color. But a steady gaze
across the street.
Two old-timers
having a face-to-face.

*—27 May 2020*

---

Started out trying to write a ghazal, which is (according to Lewis Putnam Turco's *The Book of Forms*) an Arabic form comprised of a series of couplets—at least five, but no maximum. All the second lines of all the couplets have the same word at the end. The syllable immediately preceding this word should rhyme with every other second last word of every second line in the poem. In addition, there should be one couplet (usually at the beginning or the end) in which the first line has the same constraints as all second lines in all the couplets. The lines usually have ten syllables or more.

    Well. It actually sounds a lot more complicated than it really is. Or so I thought.

    I figured I knew the form well enough to try my hand at one.

    Wrong.

I was able to come up with one couplet, but the next one proved to be quite difficult. I was not able to do anything that felt the least bit competent. So I dropped the idea for now and moved on.

Casting about for a subject, I remembered something I read a long time ago about our perception. We are hardwired to see faces in things at the slightest provocation. So, for example, many people see two surprised faces in a standard wall outlet. Take a look at one and see if that is true for you.

Houses, too, can look like faces.

Which is where today's poem came from.

# Freezing Point

Icicle prison on those cold winter nights when
the day's ice-melt froze in long brittle ropes.

They draped over the lip of the roof and
crawled down the front of the windows

in prismatic bars. When we went outside
we'd gaze in wonder at these stalactites of

hardened water. Our breaths puffing out
white clouds as we gripped one of the

unicorn horns and broke it off with a
sharp snap punctuating the harsh air.

They'd stick to our warm mittens as though
the woolly fiber would cradle them in safety.

*—28 May 2020*

---

It's a hundred degrees here today. No chance of seeing ice, obviously, but something about the heat made me think of the opposite: winter days in Sudbury, Ontario, where I grew up. One of the wonders of winter was the giant icicles that sometimes formed when a relatively warm day, marked by melting snow and ice, was followed by a cold night. That's when these amazing eight-foot icicles would form, hanging from the lip of the roof. I was always intrigued by these. They had a rare beauty and they were ephemeral, seldom lasting more than a day.

# I Sing Nature Electric

The trees in their rooted life ask only for a solid
    place to make their stand in a rain of sunshine.
Around us the songs of all the birds coalesce into
    the harmonious and peculiar voice of the air.
We pull the blue sky down to the ground where it
    drapes itself over the hills and rivers and lakes.
A long way on the other side of the horizon the edge
    of the sea kisses the edge of the continent.
Our gaze follows the white blade of the mountain
    rising from the valley to a sharp chiseled peak.
The ants carry yellow petals along the ground creat-
    ing a golden path to the hill that is their home.
We watch rabbits climb up a bush and pluck clouds
    from the sky and stick them on their rear ends.
The continents move at breakneck speed across the
    globe floating on molten rock like it's nothing.
Some of us leave footprints as we walk while others
    possess ankle wings keeping them always aloft.
When snow arrives we expect quiet as it accumu-
    lates and we are surprised when it asks for direc-
    tions.
After the rain deposits a coppery smell on every-
    thing we remember what it was to make mud
    pies.
No one warned us that nature would one day stop by
    and expect some cookies and a cup of tea.

*—29 May 2020*

---

I generally write a short line, as I'm sure you've noticed. Today I decided it would be a good challenge to try some long lines. I took as my inspiration some of the long rambling lines of Walt Whitman. The title is a variation on his "I Sing the Body Electric."

# Travel Writing

Curiosity took me
out of the sea
and onto the shore
wet with brine.

After drying myself
in the sun I began
walking across the
continent, no particular

destination in mind.
The forest canopy
sheltered me for a
time until I came to

a vast clearing
cut with rivers and
pocked with lakes.
I drank the wild

water, no fear or
hesitation on my
lips. A long day
of hiking followed

over flat lands
planted with wheat
until I arrived at
a wall of mountains

rising toward the
stars. Here I stopped
to wonder at the
improbable majesty

before me and then
it was one foot in
front of the other,
springing up the slopes

gathering the lapels
of my shirt against
the wind and snow
and cold. Then down

the other side to
a sun settling into
the sea, maybe the
same sea I came

from and maybe
not. I stood on
the sand, the tide
bringing brine

to lap at my
ankles. Here was
my ancient home
calling me back.

*—30 May 2020*

The continent I live on is obviously too big to cross by foot in one day. Nevertheless, it's a fruitful conceit to consider how I could. I tried here to highlight some of what I might encounter if I took such a walk. The shore on the east coast, the forests of the eastern states and provinces, the lakes and rivers of Ontario and Michigan, the wheat fields of the west, the rocky mountains, and then the shore on the west coast.

For those of you who are writing along with me, here is a prompt: Consider something that takes a long time, like an extended walk, or the building of a house, or the raising of a family. Then consider speeding up the process, like a fast motion movie. What sensations or experiences would be highlighted if you did that? Write about those things.

# Full Circle

In the end
I accept what

the middle brought

to the
beginning.

*—31 May 2020*

I have here on my desk a quote from Walt Whitman: "The secret of it all is, to write in the gush, the throb, the flood, of the moment. . . . You want to catch its first spirit—to tally its birth. By writing at the instant the very heart-beat of life is caught."

I largely agree with this sentiment. I know in my writing life that the pieces I write quickly with little thought are the ones that usually achieve the most success with editors and readers. This project is an illustration of that. Most of the poems I have produced here were written quickly, in the moment, with very little revision.

You might say the poems in this book were largely me writing down what I found in my head that day. For example, this one. I didn't know what I was going to write when I sat down. I just asked myself what was going on in my consciousness. I discovered something about circles. That led me to the term "full circle." And that made me think about causality, and, more specifically, backward causality: how current events might affect earlier events.

Impossible? Maybe. But if you can't have impossibilities in poetry, where else can you have them?

# June

# Epitaph for a Mechanic

Here lies, stained with oil,
Mac McKeven, wrapped in soil.
Fixed many an auto,
never won the lotto.
Now parked in heaven,
is poor Mac McKeven.

*—1 June 2020*

In Turco's *The Book of Forms* I found an entry for a minor form known as the literary epitaph, or mortuary verse. Otherwise known as terse verse for the long gone. Turco gives a few examples, including an amusing one from X. J. Kennedy called "Epitaph for a Postal Clerk." I found it clever and amusing. It is the inspiration for today's poem, which I hope you find clever and amusing as well.

# Epitaph for a CPA

Buried here under overhead dirt,
Alice Forts, accounting expert.
Her profit/loss now but a sum
in the cosmic debit column.

*—2 June 2020*

I couldn't resist another terse verse for the long gone.

# Epitaph for a Geologist

A cozy hollow six feet down
holds Harold Stone who cracks no frown.
Studied rocks all his years,
now among them, drinking beers.

*—3 June 2020*

I did another one, obviously. I like writing these terse verses for the long gone. Finding the rhymes, making the occupation mesh with the imagery of death, and doing it all in a few lines. What could be more fun?

# Do the Twist

Tree leaves
like perked
up ears

listen to
the wind
singing songs

from distant
cousins rooted
in the

same dirt
tendrils reaching
deep making

dance moves
in slow
motion spirals.

*—4 June 2020*

Walking along the wash the other day, I saw trees on the bank with their roots exposed where the water had washed away the soil. The trees looked OK, but seeing the roots in the open air looked somehow very wrong. I stopped and studied them for a moment, and saw that the roots took on a different persona in the open air. It was like they were happy to be free of the confining dirt. Maybe they were actually dancing? If so, what music were they dancing to? Why, the wind, of course. The wind has its own sense of melody and harmony. A little monotonous, perhaps, but still musical in its way. From there it was an easy step to imagining the leaves as ears, and then the imagery just fell into place and the poem was born.

# Clock Hill

Alarming how the soil
sails away under the steady

beat of rain. Half past
spring and the hands of

time have worn the swell
to a minute proportion of

what it once was. No chance
now to recapture chronology.

The entropic enterprise admits
only a slow seep into the future.

*—5 June 2020*


Time seems to go in only one direction. Things get older, not younger. That means most objects are clocks of a sort. They mark time by their degradation. Even a hill can be a clock.

# Advice

Life is a journey
so we've been told.
We're advised to grab it
and always be bold.

Don't bother with luggage
on this long trip.
Your only necessity
is water to sip.

Well that may be fine
for some Spartan types.
But we prefer more
for our days and nights.

We're traveling companions
on life's winding road.
We see wonders together
and share any load.

The end of the trail
is still out of sight.
We'll get there whenever
then sleep through the night.

Until that day comes
we'll keep stepping forward
and marvel at nature
as we journey onward.

—*6 June 2020*

I read this to Kim when I was done. She said "So that's a death poem?" I had to admit that it is, though that's not how it started out. I began with a common phrase: "Life is a journey." Like many such sayings, it can have different meanings for different people. I played around with the concept of journey. Trips involve things like luggage, sightseeing, and so on. I tried to incorporate some of those aspects into the poem. By the time I got to the end, I had to consider what the end of a journey is. In life, I suppose, it is death. But often for trips, it's a long sleep because travel can be tiring. I used sleep in the poem, conscious of other sayings, like the one that calls death the big sleep, and the one that calls sleep the little death.

I used rhymes in this one. My rhyming scheme for each stanza was xaxa. I've used that scheme before in these poems. It does seem to move the poem along at a brisk pace, which is what I wanted for this one, since it is about travels and journeys.

# The Persistence of Sunlight

The sun puts copies
of itself on my

field of vision
if I dare to steal

a glance at it.
Petty polka dot

reminders of its
immense power to

drown out the night.
Come on, sun, lighten up!

You must be part
of some constellation

viewed from a
faraway alien planet.

Just another tiny point
in the sky. Hardly enough

to illuminate a thought
never mind a world.

*—7 June 2020*

This one started out as "The Persistence of Vision," which was the original title. It's the biological phenomenon that keeps an image of what we see on our retinas for a brief time. It's not long, but it is long enough to, for example, allow us to see a film as a moving image, rather than a series of still photographs, which is what it actually is, projected on a screen at the rate of (usually) 24 per second.

Once I got into making some lines for the poem, it was pretty clear that the sun was going to be the protagonist, so I changed the title to what it is now.

The sun is immensely powerful. It is the engine of our planet, makes everything grow, and keeps us from freezing in deep space. But it can also be annoying. Case in point, is when you look at the sun and then get sunspots in your eyes that stay there for a long time.

In the poem I took that common event and tried to turn the sun into something not quite so powerful. Just another point in the sky.

# Hearing the Rainbow

Think of it as an orchestra of disparate instruments.
The loud bellow coming from red.
The startling Boo! of orange.
Applause of thunder rolling off yellow
Sound of sighing wind embedded in green.
Surprised by the sharp crackling of blue.
Charmed by child-like murmurs rippling off indigo.
Listening to the cardinal's song rising from violet.
Put them all together, without benefit of
a formal score, and you'll hear the music
of a symphony arcing against the sky.

*—8 June 2020*

We see colors, of course, but what if we heard them instead? I took an iconic image—a rainbow—and wondered what each of its colors might sound like.

# Another Point of View

A line of glue
laid down
on a sheet of paper.

Another sheet
placed over it,
glue trail
now a wet rippling path.

Watching it dry
is like waiting
for a drought
to come and drain
a river to cracked mud,

the water seeping back
to some place deep
in the ground
where tree roots
begin to build giants.

*—9 June 2020*

Glue? Really? Yes, glue. As I believe I have written earlier in this book, I don't question what the muses send to me. But getting a first line or a subject is just the first step. What next?

I have always noticed that when you put glue on a page, it dampens the paper and puts waves in it. So I took that image and turned the line of glue into a river.

The other thing that glue does is dry. So I made the river run dry. Where did the water go? Down into the earth, where it nourished tree roots. And paper, of course, comes from trees. So this poem is a full circle of sorts, beginning with paper and ending with the origin of paper.

# Ventriloquism

Just before her death
she told him
that any time he saw
a hummingbird
he should know
it was her
coming back
for a visit.

After the funeral
he put out
hummingbird feeders
and the hummingbirds
came and he
said hi to them
and waved at them
with tears in his eyes.

This went on for years
until one of the hummingbirds
darted close to him and
quite unexpectedly
he felt the air pushed by the
hummingbird's wings
on his skin and

remembered how she
used to wave a fan
under her chin
on hot days
and sometimes the air
from that fan
would touch his
face with
unexpected coolness.

*—10 June 2020*

I started with the title. I liked the sound of the word, and I have enjoyed some ventriloquism acts in the past. I don't think it's a popular performing art these days, but I could be wrong.

I wanted a different take on the word and spent some time searching for a situation that would allude to ventriloquism without actually invoking its classic rendition as a person holding a dummy and making it seem like the dummy is talking.

# Draft Dodger

Right now
this instant

all over
the world

new babies
are drawing

first breaths.
No choice

in the
matter. Resistance

only a
fanciful scenario

like escaping
to Canada.

*—11 June 2020*

---

I am reading some of the poems in Catherine Reilly's, *Scars Upon My Heart: Women's Poetry and Verse of the First World War*. I have no personal experience with war. My father fought in World War II when he was quite young. That was not an uncommon thing in Yugoslavia at the time. He did not tell me a lot of stories about his experiences, but I know he saw combat and he had been wounded.

    Reilly's book prompted me to consider writing a war poem, but I hesitated. Combat may be one of those things that one has to experience to really write authentically about. Though I don't necessarily adhere to that standard in other subjects. I write about all kinds of things for which I don't have firsthand experience. Nothing wrong with that, in my estimation. Many classic works have been written by authors with no personal experience of the subject matter they write about. Just to take one example: Hart Crane did not fight in the Civil War, having been born after it ended, but he wrote *The Red Badge of Courage*, widely considered one of the best novels of that war.

My copy of Reilly's book is used. It has lots of underlinings and notations in it. I usually don't like that sort of thing, preferring my books' pages to be unmarked, but here the previous owner marked most of the poems with one of three phrases: anti-war, pro-war, or neither. The book, according to this anonymous judge, has a very balanced mixture of the three.

It would be very difficult for me to write a pro-war poem. But as I considered some of the poems in the book, I did come up with some war-related subjects. One of them is resistance to conscription. Or, what we used to call it back when I was a teen, draft dodging. Living in Canada, we knew that many Americans of draft age came to Canada to avoid the war.

The title for today's poem was obvious, then, but as I started writing it, the whole notion of war dropped away from it, and I began to write about birth. This was completely unexpected, but that's a good thing. Don't want to be obvious, after all.

# Tree Bark

at night
I think

it happens
when we

don't see
or expect

it because
it's an

instinctive sound
deployed for

protection of
the tree's

flesh and
there are

also the
most eerie

of growls
I'm sure

that's what
I must

be hearing
in so

many of
my dreams

*—12 June 2020*

The first word that came to mind today was "Expedition," so I dutifully typed it out on the screen in bold letters. I tried to compose a line or two to go with it, but nothing came. I also remembered a poem I once wrote about putting together an expedition to go rescue someone who had checked out of life. Or something like that. It was a long time ago. In any case, I didn't want to repeat myself, so I deleted "Expedition" and typed out "Expectations" instead. This felt like it had more potential. I considered words that have more than one meaning, and how our expectations of the word color how we receive that word.

Which brought me to "bark." It's the covering on trees, but also the sound dogs make.

Once I had that connection, the poem more or less wrote itself.

# Bioluminescence

Some of
us say

we are
made of

star stuff
but the

true builders
of light

are the
fireflies, those

stellar mimickers
throwing out

constant glowing
constellations of

light into
the dark.

*—13 June 2020*

"Star stuff" is not my phrase. I remember Carl Sagan using it on his TV series *Cosmos*. Not sure if he made it up or not, but he seemed particularly fond of it and I remember it from his use some 40 years later. We are star stuff since all the heavy elements that make us up were created by fusion in the cores of stars billions of years ago, then spread across the universe when those stars exploded into novas. Before that there was just helium and hydrogen. At least, I think that's how the theory goes.

In any case, I liked the phrase and wanted to use it in a poem, so here it is.

# Envy the Cat

How she carries another world,
behind her eyes subtly blurred
when she chooses to visit.

It must be exquisite
to have this ready bit
of unreal reality

always there, no fee
required for entry,
just the will to check out

on occasion. No doubt
she protects her paradise,
with her air of being wise.

*—14 June 2020*

---

When we had a cat, I noticed that she would often "check out." Her eyes would be open, but there was nothing behind them. I always felt like that meant she was in her other world, the one she carried around with her, the one we could not see.

I was reminded of this while reading Kay Ryan's poem "A Cat/A Future" in her collection *Elephant Rocks*. Ryan took the same observation, more or less, and used it to comment on the unreadability of the future. I used it to say something about cats.

Lot of rhymes in this one, though the rhyme scheme is not regular at all.

# Isolation

The world keeps swinging around.
If I close my eyes
I can imagine the whole works
arrayed around me like a carousel.
That's the sort of illusion
we nurture in such times.
While the world dances
to the drumbeats of the heavens
I only produce virtual steps.
Store them up for later
like broth you make
and freeze for a future meal.
It's OK to wait
for the right opportunity.
The drumming will resume
any time I wish it to.

*—15 June 2020*

Many of us have been in isolation for a while now. Two days ago I woke up in a sweat. Kim said I felt very warm. I checked my temperature and it was 101. I immediately went to the urgent care to get tested for Covid.

The doc said I most likely don't have it. She says she does tests all day and very rarely gets a positive result. Still, she agreed it was best to get the test. So I did. Won't have the results for another couple of days at the earliest.

So I am in another level of isolation. I moved into the Casita, one of the airbnb apartments on our property. Been sleeping mostly. My temperature goes up and down, but has not returned to normal yet.

Anyway, it seemed a poem about isolation would be appropriate, so here it is.

# Tree Shadow

Fountain of gray rivulets
laid flat on the ground.
No water sound present,
just the image of arms
spreading wide and reaching far.
Filtered light through branching
trails, endlessly recycled paths.

*—16 June 2020*

I was sitting in the courtyard of the Casita this morning, notebook in hand, preparing to write my daily poem. It was a very pleasant morning. The air was clear, the temperature was relatively cool, and birds were coming to the mesquite tree in the courtyard, from where many of them then drop down to the bird bath for quick sips of water before they fly away.

I thought maybe a poem about birds might be right for today, but it didn't seize me, so I cast about for other inspiration and noticed that the shadow of the mesquite filled the courtyard, the branch shadows looking like the spouts of a fountain. Hmm. Maybe I could do something with that. I put the first line down: "Fountain of gray rivulets" and then was stymied for a few minutes. I wasn't sure how to go on. Should I make more explicit the connection in my mind between the ephemeral shadow and the more substantial fountain? Even though the fountain was not actually there, it had more weight to it, at least in my estimation, than the shadow. Yet the shadow was the subject of the piece.

I went for plain description in the next line, just to complete the opening image. Then it seemed useful to state that the fountain was a silent one. So I did that. In the penultimate line I used the word branching to make explicit I was talking about a tree, and also to indicate the branching spouts in a fountain. Then in the final line I again alluded to how fountains often recycle water for their effects, and this fountain of shadow appears to recycle light.

I had one internal rhyme: ground/sound, and a kind of slant rhyme with arm and far. The last three lines have no rhymes or slant rhymes. I wanted them to stand on their own without the effects of rhyming words.

# Urgent Care

Drink plenty
of fluids.

Be sure to get
plenty of rest.

Take Tylenol every
4-6 hours as needed

for pain or fever.
We come to work

to keep you safe.
Please stay home

to keep our
community safe.

*—17 June 2020*

If this sounds like medical advice, it is. It's part of the text they gave me at the Urgent Care when I went there a few days ago to be tested for Covid. So this is found poetry, an odd genre in which the poet takes existing text and forms it into lines and stanzas with the intention, I suppose, of demonstrating that even words not intended as poetry can be poetic if looked at in the proper way.

    This example begins with straightforward advice about drinking fluids and getting rest, then ends up with a poignant plea to please do one's part to keep the community safe, just as the staff at the urgent care center do. It's pretty good. I'm not even sure I could have done better if I tried.

# Puttulump Puttulump Puttulump

In horse country
I step off the

trail and wait quietly
for rider and steed

to pass. Rider
and horse both

nod as they go
by. I bask in

the power aura
of the beast. How

can such strength
come from eating

hay and oats? My
palm itches with

the urge to present
an apple slice or

a carrot to this
creature. But it

would nourish me
more than the animal.

Or so I have been
led to believe. I'll

bet no one ever asked
the horse's opinion.

—*18 June 2020*

Say the words of the title quickly and they sound like running horses. At least to me.

The rules of hiking trails in this part of the world is that walkers yield to horses. If you see a horse coming, you are to get a good distance off the trail and stand quietly, still as possible and not saying anything. All meant to keep from startling the horse. Kim and I are always more than happy to oblige the horses and riders.

I do sometimes wonder, as they go by, what they think of being beasts of burden? A human thought, I suppose, though not necessarily. Who of us knows what goes on in a horse's mind, or any animal's mind, for that matter?

# Manifesto

When the fires come
we will vanquish them.

When the winds blow hard
we will shelter from them.

When the rains bring floods
we will heal the earth.

When the earthquakes shake
we will stand up tall.

When the mountain erupts
we will welcome new land.

When the dust storm rages
we will reach for healing.

When the heart feels pain
we will know our strength.

*—19 June 2020*

Kim showed me a video on YouTube: "Wolf Totem" by The HU, a Mongolian heavy metal band. It's worth finding and viewing. It's modern and shamanic all at the same time. A unique achievement. The song is in Mongolian, with (I assume) native chants and beats, but it is subtitled in English on YouTube. The lyrics were my inspiration for today's poem.

# Volcano Breath

Imagine the doctor
asking the mountain
to take a deep breath
and hold it for
a few centuries.

The doc holds a stethoscope
to the mountain's slope
listening for congestion
and rumblings and such
as the mountain exhales.

The doctor takes cover:
the rocks and ash
fill the air, telling
the world the volcano is
healthy, strong, and fierce.

*—20 June 2020*

In one of yesterday's stanzas I made reference to an erupting mountain creating new land. That is, of course, exactly what a volcano does. We often view volcanos as natural disaster, with good reason.

But a volcano is also an expression of health. It's the planet asserting itself with strength and vitality. That's what I tried to express in today's poem. The doctor examination metaphor is probably because I've been under the weather the last week or so and have had a couple of consultations with doctors, one in person, and one virtual. As I have indicated throughout this project, it is rarely a bad idea to use the material you have at hand.

Today was also the day I got my test results: negative. I don't have Covid-19. Kim and I were both immensely relieved.

# Life Repair Kit: Items 1-5

*After Richard Brautigan*

1. Eat nourishing food.
2. Work at tasks that sustain you.
3. Love wholly and without reservation.
4. Eliminate all unnecessary baggage like excessive noise, over-stimulation, burdensome worries, and useless labor until you reach a state of outer and inner peace and equilibrium.
5.

—*21 June 2020*

Years ago, when I was in my teens, my aunt, who worked as a cleaner at a local cinema, found a book someone had left behind in the theater and brought it to me because she knew I was a reader. The book was *The Pill Versus the Springhill Mine Disaster,* by Richard Brautigan. At first I didn't know what to make of it. It appeared to be a collection of poetry, but odd poetry. No rhymes. Very short. Kind of koan-like much of the time. A lot of what appeared to be mini-memoirs thrown in. A lot of the poems were miniature philosophical statements or inquiries. It was an odd duck, at least to me, but here's the thing: it was compulsively readable. There was not a boring page in the entire book. I believe I read it through several times.

I learned later that the author was also a novelist and had a troubled life, eventually killing himself. What he left behind in his poetry was unique.

One of his poems that I remember was titled something like "Karma Repair Kit: Items 1-4." The first 3 items were sound advice. The fourth item was blank. I loved the idea of finding karmic peace to such an extent that the last part of the poem, which was to help you find that peace, became unnecessary. Self-referential in an intriguing way.

I obviously blatantly borrowed the title and the idea for today's poem (but not the words). To avoid charges of plagiarism and establish instead a sense of tribute, I put his name in the poem and have given this explanation for the poem.

# Shedding Souvenirs

In the woods
we're told to look for deer antlers

near fallen trees
because they sometimes break off

deer skulls
as the animals jump over the trees

and land
on their front hooves with a jolt.

Makes me wonder
what we lose when we step over

wonders
in our path, hoping for a more

direct route
to some destination we don't yet see.

*—22 June 2020*

---

I started out this morning looking up a word at random. That word was *granite*. My intention was to write a poem about that word. I've done this before, but today things didn't click. I wrote down some rhyming words for granite. I wrote a line: "A piece of it will snugly fit inside my mitt." Once I had that, I figured I was going to write a light verse on the subject of granite. Well, easier said than done. I really had nothing more to say about granite.

I tried to go on by writing something about how a bigger piece would be a hunk of rock that sunk. Nothing much there. I fooled around with a few other ideas about granite, but it became clear fairly quickly that there really wasn't anything there.

So I abandoned that route and thought about where I've seen antlers in the woods. Where did that come from? No idea. Maybe something in my brain got stirred up while I was trying to make granite stand up and do tricks for me.

In any case, the antlers were far more interesting to me. I did remember that a friend once told us that antlers tend to be found near fallen trees, for the reason I state in the poem's first half. What intrigued me was that a lot of folks are very interested in finding antlers in the woods, while the owners of those antlers, as far as anyone can tell, are pretty indifferent to losing them. The whole thing felt like a metaphor for not paying attention to what's around you, and I tried to make that explicit in the poem's second half.

# Rock Stars

Slate is great,
granite is lit,
and of wonder marble is full.

Pyrite has bite,
shale is hale,
and limestone will pick no bone.

Pumice gives bliss.
flint is mint,
and basalt has no fault.

Calcite is bright,
sandstone has tone,
and quartz is devoid of warts.

*—23 June 2020*

Yesterday I gave up on writing a poem about granite. Today the granite idea came back. I wasn't prepared to do a whole poem on granite, but maybe I could do a poem about rocks in general.

The title came to me immediately, then the first two lines. Which meant I had the start of a form. Short rhyming lines about different rocks. I googled common rock names and was surprised to find what looked like hundreds and hundreds of different kinds of rocks. Most of the names were completely unfamiliar to me, and, I figured, to most other folks as well. I scanned through the list looking for more familiar rocks. I ended up with about a dozen and set to work rhyming the rock names.

I played around with the form a little, ending up with three line stanzas in which the third line breaks the pattern of the first two lines by being longer but keeps the rhyme on the rock intact.

# Sleeping Mountains

Our rapid eye movements
are earthquakes
and volcanic eruptions.

Insomnia does not
normally plague us
but when it does,

you hear the rumbles
of thunder and lightning
raking our skins.

Sometimes we have night
sweats, fevered times
when our blankets catch fire.

But mostly we slumber
quietly, and dream of
becoming stately clouds.

*—24 June 2020*

The idea here is take two separate images (mountains and sleeping people) and see if there are connections between the two. This came to me last night as I was drifting to sleep. I've heard mountains be described as sleeping giants. When you look at a mountain range, you can sometimes see the outlines of figures and your imagination can make you see human forms, or something resembling a human form. So too with clouds. Most everyone has the experience of seeing faces or objects in clouds. Seems to me a mountain might see itself in a cloud as well.

# Summons

The buzz of the bees
unmistakable sound
a signal to those who know.

Pilgrims arrive
faces raised
to the boiling mass.

The swarm hangs like
a trembling egg
from the branch of a tree.

We hold
electric potential
between us.

Cross species
comfort a
curious mystery.

Let's close our eyes,
all of them, and feel
the power of life.

—25 June 2020

We've had a few swarms of bees on our property. They stayed for a couple of days, then moved on. Each time, the sound of them felt like something unworldly, and we felt compelled to go investigate.

Bee swarms bring out the mysticism in me. They are a remarkable sight and each time I gazed at a swarm, I wondered if they noticed us. And if they did, what they made of us. It's not possible to know, of course, but I speculated on a possibility in this poem.

# The Pleasures of the Seashore

I think nature
was feeling nostalgic
about windup toys
the day it created sanderlings
and set them down
on the beach to churn
up the surf
with wondrous constant speed
like sprightly feathered automatons.

*—26 June 2020*

I was looking for inspiration for today's poem by riffling the pages of David Allen Sibley's *What It's Like to be a Bird* and asking Kim to tell me when to stop. Well. She had me stop (completely by random) on the page that features sanderlings, which, by coincidence are just about my favorite birds in the world. We saw them often when we lived on the Oregon coast. They moved like windup toys across the beach at constant speed. Then they would stop, stick their beaks into the sand, and start up again. They were the most delightful birds, and I miss seeing them. I tried to give a flavor of their charm in today's poem.

# Sleeping Sparks

A dream of swallows
soaring with acrobatic grace

diving, twirling, gliding
through the night sky.

Scooping up stars
like they are insects

unaware of their fate
until the last second.

Then they deploy
a sharp and stinging

response against the
swallows, biting back

with piercing barbs, but,
alas, a moment too late.

*—27 June 2020*

---

Like yesterday, I riffled through the pages of Sibley's *What It's Like to Be a Bird* and asked Kim to tell me when to stop. She had me stop, at random, on the entry for swallow. We used to see lots of swallows when we lived in Washington. We knew the places around town where they built their mud nests, and we would visit them often to see how they were doing. Swallows have incredible acrobatic ability, and they are fast. They fly through the air scooping up insects, especially mosquitoes, so they are beneficial to have around. I imagined swallows scooping up stars instead of insects, and this poem is the result.

# Weddings

Soul mates
carving a slice
of eternity
as gifts for

each other.
Vows to love forever
gain strength
as years glide by.

Suddenly yesterday
is four decades ago
and the house
of mutual admiration

has so many rooms that
eternity feels like
the briefest of instants
in an immortal joy.

*—28 June 2020*

Today is the 40th anniversary of Kim and I meeting, and the 39th anniversary of our wedding. We remarked today that it sure doesn't feel like forty years. We have had and continue to have a love affair for the ages, and we are both deeply grateful for each other. I wouldn't want to ever be without Kim.

Today's poem is a tribute to our wedding but also a good word for all weddings. Weddings are statements of faith as well as love, where two people decide they will face the world together for all time. Thanks for the ride, Kim.

## Derailment

My scar resembles a train track,
the kind you see on maps

where little dashes across the
longer line indicate where the

ties go. The glass that made
that cut half a century ago

was like an engine slicing
across the landscape

of my skin, drawing up red
blood like it was squeezing

it out of the soil. My cry
at the pain, was it the train's

whistle warning all around
that there was danger and

you had to step back? Later,
at the emergency room,

the doctor bent over my hand,
laying down suture tracks,

his breathing a rhythmic click-clack
of steel wheels over gap-riddled rails.

—29 June 2020

---

A long time ago, when my family lived in Elliot Lake, Ontario, I was carrying a carton of glass pop bottles and tripped and fell on some concrete steps. The bottles broke into sharp shards, and one of those shards gave me a nasty cut across the base of the ring finger of my left hand. It took five stitches, and today I noticed that the scar is still there, a line about 2 inches long with little hatch marks along it where the suture threads must have been, but which, strangely, and for the first time, look like train tracks to my eye.

Once I had that image I wrote down a few similarities between scars and trains and did some editing and came up with today's poem.

# The Language of Light

It's all verb,
because light is all action.
Moving at an impossible speed,
filling the cosmic void
in all directions,
never standing still long enough
to be a noun.
We call it light,
but, really, no word can capture
what it is.
It'll never be an adjective or an adverb.
Those are much too passive,
with their supporting roles.
The action of light,
its movement and inexorable will,
is always the star.
Will always bring to everyone
an article of faith
as it illuminates the void.

*—30 June 2020*

---

I heard a phrase, I don't remember where: "The language of love." That was intriguing to me. What is the language of love? Surely it is intimate and private, something between two people. But love can express all kinds of things beyond romantic love.

I thought of other languages: the language of trees, the language of escape, the language of water, and so on.

Somewhere in that chain of thoughts came the language of light.

That one stopped me. It felt interesting and like it might lead to something.

So I wrote the first and second lines without even thinking about them.

From there I brought in other parts of speech and related them to light. I liked ending on an article.

# July

# Green Orchestra

The wind gathers its breath
and blows through instruments
made of leaves
and bark and branches.

This morning's program includes
a palo verde symphony
some pine tree overtures
and the mesquite fugue,
always a crowd-pleaser.

Later the saguaro thorns
will compose a serenade
from the wind
and the cactus wrens will
gather for the recital.

*—1 July 2020*

I was sitting outside this morning when a slight breeze came up, and I heard it swishing through the big pine tree we have in our backyard. When wind goes through trees, it can be an enchanting sound, like the tree is making its own music. I took that notion and tried to extend it and make it colorful and playful. I also liked the idea of birds listening to the music of the trees and cactus. They would be the perfect audience, very knowledgeable, since they are musical beings as well.

# Fairy Duster

Even if you
listen carefully
you can't always
hear the fairies.
They have such
soft voices. But
sometimes they
have a lot to
get off their
chests. Conflicts
and painful issues
to reconcile.
That's why they
use the fairy
duster. It does
a good job
of clearing
the air as
they air their
differences.

—2 July 2020

I asked Kim for a suggestion for today's poem. She looked at the latest painting we got from Rachel Slick, which features several different flowers. One of them is a fairy duster. So Kim suggested that as the subject of my poem. I immediately seized on the idea of "clearing the air," with its double meaning of getting rid of dust and resolving conflicts between people by airing their differences.

# Bell Rings

The church across the street,
five rings every Sunday morning,

calling the faithful. Before that,
the bell on my bicycle, made

active by my thumb, letting
everyone know I was there,

riding the wheels of freedom.
At school, the teacher, holding

a bell in her hand, ringing it
several times for the end of

recess: freedom over. And
sometimes, at quiet moments,

for no obvious reason, the
ringing in my ears, what is

it there for? What is it saying?
Another bell, at the resort

in the mountains, rung only
once at every meal, calling

the hungry to breakfast, lunch,
or dinner. The echo of it floating

up to the peaks, causing wildlife
to raise their heads for just an

instant before returning to
whatever freedom they know.

—3 July 2020

The idea was to write about something that happens throughout a lifetime, but in different contexts, and then try to find connections between them. I settled on ringing bells. The first image that came to mind was the bell on my bicycle when I was a kid. I remember ringing that bell as I rode my bike. It was a soft sound, but it seemed to fill the world, letting everyone know I was there, riding my bike. It was meant to be a warning device, but it was more than that. It was a proclamation. I rang it not only when I needed to let others know I was coming up behind them, but also just to hear it ring.

Other instances of bell rings are in the poem. As I put them down, the idea of freedom came to mind. Maybe from the phrase "let freedom ring." I'm not sure. In any case, once the concept of freedom emerged, I ran with it and it ended up settling, in the final line, on unexpected recipients.

# Feathered Friends

A lot of birds
spend time in the 'burbs.
They'll perch on curbs
like feathered nerds.

As far as words,
they mostly use verbs
as alarming blurbs
to warn their herds.

They always sing onwards,
and cause minor disturbs,
but their playful perturbs
are just melodic standards.

*—4 July 2020*

---

I have not done a rhymed poem in a while, so I wanted to do one today. I first noticed that *verbs* kind of but not quite rhymes with *birds*. I found that instantly intriguing. I wondered what I could do with this particular slant rhyme. I then wrote down all the rhymes I could think of for verbs. They were: blurbs, suburbs, curbs, herbs, and Serbs. In another column I wrote rhymes for birds: herds, nerds, words, and curds. I left out turds, because, well, that's just nasty to have in a poem.

    I started constructing the poem with four line stanzas, each stanza having the same rhyme scheme: abba. I changed suburbs to 'burbs because it sounded better to my ear. I liked that the non-rhyming words sounded almost like rhymes. That felt kind of cool. I got the first two stanzas fairly quickly, but I got stuck on the last one. I felt I needed a third one to bring everything together, but the rhymes I had left over didn't seem to do the trick.

    I then resorted to my phone where I found a rhyming dictionary and asked for rhymes for verbs and birds. I wrote down the promising ones: disturbs, proverbs, and perturbs for verbs, and thirds, backwards, cowards, onwards, and standards for birds.

    I then played around with those words on the ends of lines, maintaining my abba rhyme scheme.

I'm not sure the poem holds together as an evocation of birds and bird behavior, but I do like the sound of it, the way the rhymes ping off each other.

# Six Conditionelles

### Taking a Dip

If the pool could be cool
I would swim round the rim.

### Arboreal Likes

If the trees you would please,
take a wade in their shade.

### Wash Day

If a rug has a bug
a good clean makes it keen.

### Diminished Gravity

If the Earth had less girth
all our stuff would be fluff.

### Language Conjecture

If the birds could speak words
they would curse in free verse.

### Express Yourself

If the plants gave more rants
they would grow in the know.

*—5 July 2020*

I was flipping through Turco's *Book of Forms* and came across a fun little verse form called Conditionelle. Like many of these forms, explaining it is more complicated than just looking at an example and seeing how it works. But I'll explain it anyway.

A conditionelle is a couplet that begins with "if" and employs internal rhyme. It uses only one-syllable words, six-syllable lines, and often tries for humor. The metric form is given thus:

```
x x a x x a
x x b x x b
```

where the first x in line one is the word "If", all the other x's are one syllable words, and the a's rhyme with each other and the b's rhyme with each other. The form is attributed to David B. Axelrod, who invented it in the 1970s as a way to get school kids interested in poetry.

I intended to compose one conditionelle for today's poem, but they are so much fun that I went on to do five more.

# Make a Meal of the World

Fill my salt shaker with stars.
Fold the clouds into my soufflé.
Serve soup in a sky blue bowl.
Grind Mars to a cinnamon powder.
Grill burgers over the sun.
Cut the moon into onion slices.
Substitute comets for hot peppers.
Say grace to the bountiful heavens.

*—6 July 2020*

I woke up this morning with the title of today's poem in my head. I had no idea where this phrase came from. I don't recall reading it anywhere or hearing it at any time. I googled it to see if it is a famous quote. Google found one instance of its use. It is part of a sentence from *Firebird* by Marion Robinson. This was a book unknown to me until I googled the phrase.

In any case, I liked the phrase, and even if I didn't, it came to me in a dream (sort of) so I felt I should pursue it. I took the phrase literally and considered aspects of the world around us that could be likened to items we consume. The poem consists of my attempts to find those correlations.

# The Fans Above My Head

Spinning asterisks
trying for something
notable, as though
they are helicopter
blades inviting us
to raise ourselves
to a higher realm.

*—7 July 2020*

Now that we are in the heart of a hot Arizona summer, we have the ceiling fans on most of the time. They help cool things down. This morning I walked under one, felt its wind on my head and shoulders, as though it was trying to get my attention, and I knew it would be a perfect subject for a poem.

# Road Encounter

Two vultures
wings spread wide
giving sunlight
enough time to
paint a mural
on their feathers.

—*8 July 2020*

Kim and I took a drive to the Buenos Aires National Wildlife Refuge about 80 miles Southwest of Tucson. On the way back, we saw a half dozen vultures on the road, working on some roadkill. As we approached, two of them faced us and spread their wide wings out. It was like seeing some exotic peacocks. An arresting image. Now here it is in a poem.

# Echo

Palo verde pods
curled up like
snakes ready to
strike. I wade
through them,
step on them,
the crunches
sounding like
warning rattles.

*—9 July 2020*

We have lots of palo verde trees on our property. Palo verde means "green pole" in Spanish, and refers to the green bark characteristic of this tree. The bark, remarkably, performs photosynthesis, producing about two-thirds of the tree's food, the remainder coming from the leaves. The trees also produce pods of seeds that drop from the tree and dry up on the ground. They curl up and are very brittle. More than a few times I noticed that they resemble little snakes curled up in the dirt.

# On the Particular Frights Evoked by Certain Desert Arachnids

The spiders on the wall
ignite my sense of fear
mostly because they're all
large as a chandelier.

—10 July 2020

Last night I rescued an extremely large spider from the wall near the ceiling. It was so large that the wide jar I had barely fit around it. As I was engaged in capturing it, I realized that it looked kind of like a chandelier. Maybe that's why it liked to be near the ceiling. It was not the first such spider Kim and I have found in the house. We've captured a few others. They are very large and almost always are up high on a wall near the ceiling. I liked the chandelier image and decided to use it here. I chose rhymed and metered lines because I felt it added to the fun.

Each line is six syllables long, and the rhyme scheme is abab.

# Storyteller

You listen on still nights
when the wind has retired

for the evening. That's when
the trembling stops and the tree

is able to get some rest
from its constant motion.

But you don't push for a story
from the stately barked one.

Not yet. Instead you wait
until the tree is ready

to tell of its travels
and let slip a secret or two

it may have learned
when it spread its wings and flew.

*—11 July 2020*

---

My first attempt at a poem today was titled "The Filter." It involved a person listening to voices from the dead. That one went nowhere.

Next, I kept the title because I liked it for some odd reason, and wrote an abstract thing about voices getting clogged up in one's head so that it became necessary to clean out the filter. I made it seem more alien by creative misspellings of many of the simple words in the poem. That one, too, was very unsatisfying.

So I turned the page in my notebook and wrote out the word "Filter" in big letters. I asked myself why this word caught my interest. The other day I cleaned the filter in the air conditioning unit in one of our rooms. I also helped Kim clean out the dryer lint that accumulated in the dryer under the filter. Maybe I had filter on the brain.

I wasn't sure, not exactly, but as I considered it some more, I imagined wind as a kind of filter. It moves debris and dust around so it doesn't accumulate in any one place. From there, I imagined the filter gone. That is, no wind. What would the trees feel like when the wind stops moving their leaves and branches around? Maybe they would appreciate being left alone for a while.

Then it was a short step to imagining someone sitting near or even under such a tree, waiting for the tree to say something. I originally wrote it in first person, but on reflection, I changed it to second person. It seemed more universal. I also dropped "The Filter" as a title. It did not seem rich enough for the poem. I opted for "Storyteller" instead.

I also used this title earlier in this book, on February 12.

# An Itch

is just
a demand

for attention,
rather like

a child
pulling on

its mother's
skirt saying

pay attention
to me

or I
will make

your life
soooooooo miserable.

*—12 July 2020*

Itches have always puzzled me. What use are they? Why do we have them? Sometimes, when an itch is particularly bothersome and won't go away, it seems like an actual being asserting its will. And what kind of being? Well, the annoying kind. Like when a kid is whiny. That kind of being.

# The Breath of a Rock

You won't feel it
even if you
put your ear
to its surface.

All its inhalations
and exhalations
are mostly in
the spirit realm.

Subtle movements
of pure energy
you need your
heart to hear.

*—13 July 2020*

I thought about breathing this morning. No particular reason for it, and as I've said a few times in this book, I never question the thoughts and impulses that come to me unbidden when I'm preparing to compose a poem. Any thought can lead to a poem.

Once I had the notion of breathing, I flipped it and considered an object that doesn't breathe. Like a rock. But is it true that it doesn't breathe? Could it be that I just can't perceive a rock's breath? Maybe, maybe not. I accepted the possibility, however, and composed a reaction to that possibility.

# How to Be an Insect

*after Wendell Berry*

One.
Ignore what doesn't interest you.
Express yourself in your own individual way
using sound, color, motion, and deception.
Depend upon camouflage, annoyances,
wings, compound eyes, and buzzing.
Lots of buzzing.
Any creatures that don't like your ways of being,
doubt their sanity.

Two
Try living indoors and out
to decide what feeds you best.
Communicate quickly,
you have very little time.
What time you have
is not married to eternity.
Accept your three-dimensional life.
You have no other.
Know that sacredness
follows you everywhere.

Three
Question the wisdom of silence,
but accept silence when necessary.
Of the little revelations
that come from quiet moments,
make gestures that reflect
your understanding of those moments.
Always disturb serenity
for the sake of your right to life.

*—14 July 2020*

On my morning walk I was listening to my podcasts and Wendell Berry's poem "How to Be a Poet" came up. He calls it a reminder to himself. The poem is a series of observations about the creative life. What it takes to get inspiration, what to do with inspiration once it comes, and how to leave the source of your inspiration undisturbed. He favors silence. From what I can tell from the poem, he sees silence as something similar to a large room in which one can feel comfortable and be receptive to whatever might come by to fill the room and move you to something creative.

At least, that's what I got from the poem. I, of course, can only guess what Berry actually had in mind when he wrote and published it.

In any case, as I listened I wondered about other occupations or ways of being. I considered "How to Be a Mechanic," "How to Be a Cloud," "How to Be a Thought," "How to Be a Flower," and "How to Be a Contradiction." There are any number of variations on this theme. I could probably write a whole book of poems along these lines. In the end, I settled on insect. They are everywhere, they are nicknamed bugs because that's what many of them do to us, and they are endlessly fascinating. Their appearance, behavior, and sounds.

I used Berry's poem as a guide. I found it online and typed it out, then studied each of its three stanzas in turn, then wrote my stanzas as a response to his. I tried to agree with him where I could, and take exception to him where I thought I should. In particular, I tried to make clear that for an insect silence is often overrated.

I have no experience of being an insect, so this poem might be seen as me taking undue liberties with my imagination. I'm OK with that. Each poem is an attempt at something useful, entertaining, or enlightening. Until insects begin writing poems of their own, something like what I did here might have to suffice.

# History

Battles and dates
don't tell the whole story.
You need to know
the broken hearts
of the families.
The loss of limbs
and homes. How
sometimes in escaping
horror some committed
their own horrors,
throwing their babies
down a mountain
for the sake of
survival for
the rest of the family.
Such stories bring
only shocked silence
in response, as you
mentally turn back
the years
and wonder
what you would do
in the same
place and time.

*—15 July 2020*

The idea here was to take the concept of history, which is often a subject removed from everyday life, and make it as personal as possible. We are given a kind of sanitized version of the past, but as the past was unfolding in its own present, there were many awful decisions made by ordinary people in terrible situations.

# Jumpers

All grasshoppers have got
catapults in their knee.
When the weather gets hot
they snap their joint to flee.

Some grasshoppers have wings
colored orange or red.
They display these bright blings
when they fling out of bed.

Grasshoppers like to munch
any plant they may find.
They'll drool, chew, and crunch
and leave nothing behind.

Grasshoppers are well-named.
They hop in grass with joy.
But you could not be blamed
if you said they annoy.

'Cause when grasshoppers swarm
they are renamed locusts.
Dark clouds of them will form,
that's when they cause disgusts.

—16 July 2020

---

Once a week Kim and I each research a plant or animal that occurs on our property, and then give a presentation to each other on that plant or animal. My presentation this week was on the grasshopper. Since I had grasshopper lore and grasshopper facts in my brain already, I used some of what I learned for today's poem.

This one is metered and rhymed. Each line is six syllables, and the rhyme scheme is abab for each stanza.

# We Are Not Symbols

A thorn is not sharp-witted
with a cogent point to make.

A dove is not a pacifist and
militancy is not a hawk.

Bulls and bears are not
barometers of financial health.

An owl isn't wisdom
and an apple isn't temptation.

Dragonflies are not dream weavers
and bees don't personify labor.

See, we're all just here in the world,
being only our true wild selves.

*—17 July 2020*

---

Animals symbolize many things for many people. I was wondering what the animals might think about this. Would animals want to be symbols? I don't know, of course, but I can easily imagine that they would not. They were here long before they became symbols, and will likely be here long after their symbolism has passed.

# Perspectives on Power

Just as the lizard
pulls the tree trunk
through the air as it climbs,
so my feet push

the Earth away
when I bend
my knees and jump
high to meet the

cactus wren pulling
bright red saguaro
fruit to its
sharp darting beak.

*—18 July 2020*

Who has the power to move things? It's all about perspective. I can see the Earth pulling leaves to the ground by gravity, or I can see a bird pushing the Earth away as it takes flight.

Today's poem explores the ability to move or attract objects from a perspective slightly skewed from the norm. We all have immense power. It's just a matter of finding the place where we can wield it.

# Humming Cholla

Hundreds of
buzzing bees

wrapping the
cactus in

a sonic
cocoon. We

stand near
the sound,

let it
wrap around

us as
though the

buzzing exists
to warm

our curious
hearts and

electrify our
ancient spines.

*—19 July 2020*

While walking the land this morning, Kim pointed out that there were a lot of bees buzzing about. We heard the sound of bees everywhere. When we looked closer at some cholla cactus, we saw uncountably many bees swarming over them. We were puzzled by this behavior. None of the cholla was flowering, so as far as we could tell the bees weren't getting nectar. Why were they so interested in the cactus?

    We didn't have an answer. Instead we were mesmerized by the sound of them. Bees are fascinating creatures. Watching them hover over and around the cactus was a marvelous sight. And also a scary sight. Bees do have the potential to harm, though they don't normally do so. Like many creatures, if you mind your own business and leave them alone, they will mind their own business and leave you alone.

That's what we and the bees did this morning.

# Sunset Versus Words

In the evening when the sky catches fire
we watch the hot spark of the setting sun
ignite the fuel of the blanketing clouds.
We stand beneath the flames in silent awe.
Our words for colors fail us then. The hues
are more than orange and red and yellow.
But no point in groping for new language
at such a moment. It is enough to
breathe in the glorious sight around us.
Grateful for nature's unnamable blaze.

*—20 July 2020*

Today's poem comes from a prompt in Agodon and Silan's *The Daily Poet*. They suggested going outside and paying attention to the world one finds there. Notice the birds singing, or the smell of the earth, or the feel of the air. Then write, as a report on what you found there, a ten line poem of ten syllables each.

Yesterday Kim and I were outside around dusk and were greeted with a glorious sunset. The sky and clouds seemed to be ablaze with fantastic colors, some of which I had no name for.

I took that notion and developed it into today's poem.

# Comet

You are sky smudge,
unfocused sphere,
a bit of the milky way
torn off and thrown
against the sky.

Comet, you visit us
intermittently, like
a relative who shows
up every ten years
with nothing new to say.

You are mostly lost,
no tribe to call your own,
and when we pay you
no attention, you
leave in a puff and a huff.

No matter, don't worry,
we know you'll be back.
Trailing your thoughts
as though you are
a deep thinker and grand

entertainment. But comet,
you should know,
we see your pretension.
You're just a ball of snow
with some rocks you own

by retention. Fear not.
little comet, cold space
will preserve you. We'll
see you again when
the spirits move you.

*—21 July 2020*

There's a new comet in the sky that I understand is visible to the naked eye. In the Tucson area one can supposedly view it early in the morning. Unfortunately for us, that part of the sky is obscured by the Catalina Mountains to the north and north east. So I have to be content with seeing pictures of it.

In any case, It seemed a poem about comets might be in order. I tried to give the comet something of a personality and went for some bit of humor and incorporated some internal rhymes. I like the sound of this one. It's fun to read aloud.

# Surrounded by Life

Air
wet with humidity
wraps us.

Rabbit
deep in its form
cooling.

Tree
bright with sunlight
dazzles.

Sky
studded with clouds
inspires.

Ground
holding everything in place
assures.

Mountain
carving a jagged horizon
sees far.

Ocean
distant salty siren
at rest.

*—22 July 2020*

Some days no inspiration is forthcoming. That's what happened this morning. I sat down with my notebook and was not feeling the creative juices. When that happens, I usually start writing down random words. It's like dipping into my thoughts to see what's there. Kind of the way one might dip a ladle into a pot of soup and seeing what comes up.

Here's what I ladled out of my head, which I am transcribing directly from my notebook: "The wall The patio The pool The plate The shirt The shoe The expectations The treehouse Terrortory Territory."

None of that seemed particularly promising. Except for maybe Terrortory. A horror tale about property? Something to look at later, perhaps, but it did not seem promising for a poem.

I went on. Yesterday I saw a rabbit in a form under a shrub by the porch, lounging in the shade to get away from the heat. It was there all day. I wondered about the life of that rabbit and rabbits in general. How they rest, how they resemble pretzels when they run at full speed, their front legs way back and their back legs way forward.

I liked thinking about rabbits, so I tucked that away for a later time. Then, because we have been so humid lately, I wrote the following: "The air/wet with humidity/wraps us."

Hmmm. That looked promising. It suggested a form: a two syllable first line, a second line that expands on the subject of the first line, and a third line of two syllables that is a response to the second line, or a summing up of sorts.

So I continued in that vein, using my newly made-up form as a guide. I picked subjects from nature. I even used the rabbit which I had tucked away only a few minutes earlier. I kept going until the poem felt finished.

When I was done, each of the first lines started with "The." That did not seem particularly interesting, so I dropped it from every first line. Now some lines had one syllable, and others had two. I didn't try to fuss with that. The first lines, I decided, didn't have to have the same number of syllables. I did restrict each first line to one word.

The result is a series of observations about the life around me this morning.

# Full Circle

snake skin
shake skin
shake spin
take spin
take pin
fake pin
fake sin
cake sin
cake gin
lake gin
lake bin
rake bin
rake tin
bake tin
bake kin
snake kin
snake skin

*—23 July 2020*

So what the heck is this? Not sure, exactly. I started out with the two word line: "Snake Skin." I liked the sound of it. And it's something I've seen in nature: discarded snake skins. I wrote down a few half-hearted lines, but none of them caught fire.

Then, instead of considering the object named by the words, I examined the words themselves.

Snake Skin.

Snake rhymes with shake. So that's another line: shake skin.

I continued in this vein, alternating changing one of the words with each successive line. The result might not make a lot of sense (although some of the lines, like "cake sin" are evocative) but they sound cool when I read them out loud.

I also brought the series of lines right back to the first line, which explains the title. I also noticed that this is the second time in this book that I have used this title.

# The Dance

Darkness in the hall
before the big event.

Lights flick on
blinding the participants,

but not for long.
All are game to

try their moves on
the multifaceted dance

floor. See the couple
raising up the spirits

with their tango struts.
The lone ballerina

pirouetting a spiral
path from wall to

wall. Break dancers
spinning the dizzy world

around them. The line
dancers throwing down

rhythmic boot beats.
All the tap dancers

click-clacking their
universal language

of toe and heel
operating in harmony.

But the merriment and
joy and self expression

cannot last and soon
the movement slows

the breathing comes in
deep inhales and exhales.

Bent over, hands on knees.
And the lights snap off.

Darkness returns, only the
memory of motion remains.

*—24 July 2020*

Lots of things have beginnings and ends. In between, there can be much merriment and all kinds of partying. That was all I was trying to convey here, hoping that a group of varied dancers in a temporary dance hall could stand in for all those other events with beginnings and ends.

# Walking the Wash

We are like phantom
blood cells tumbling
through the arterial

spider webs that
intermittently cover
the land with a flash

flooding bleed of
water. Occasionally
a road crosses the

wash's path, threatening
its onward march like
a tourniquet stopping

the flow. We stand on
the edge, where wash
meets road, and see

the path of the vein
ooze to the other side.
No way to stanch this

flow when nature
asserts its right of
way and decides

a bloodletting is
is in order for the
health of the land.

*—25 July 2020*

Every summer in the desert we wait for the monsoons to bring heavy rains. That's when the washes, normally dry, fill up with water and become instant rivers.

On a map, the network of washes looks like the map of veins and arteries in a human body. Washes nourish the land in the same way that blood nourishes the body.

We often walk the washes when they are dry, which makes us kind of like blood cells traversing the vascular system. I started the poem with that image, then I brought in more blood imagery to make the metaphor as solid as possible. I made sure all the lines were short, to give the feeling of speed, like fast flowing blood.

# Alternate Worlds

In the light days before the Earth was round
we would sometimes sit on the rim and let

our legs dangle in the ethereal
muck surrounding our smooth and flat planet.

We reveled in the bold and curious
nature of the world, how it always sought

the new, its boundaries elastic and
brave, its footprint oozing into the void.

Then the expansive affect of our home
world grew fearful and turned in on itself.

Now what was once bountiful and freedom
loving has become a mere ball, what the

mathematicians call a sphere. Oh, how
the loss saddens us. No longer do we

sit with front row seats at the spectacle
of existence arrayed before our eyes.

We used to walk to the edge and meet the
cosmos. Now we traverse this curved surface,

endless path with nowhere to stop and the
only encounters are with our sad selves.

*—26 July 2020*

A metered poem this time. Each line is ten syllables long. I chose longer lines than I usually do to give it an expansive feel, which is counter to the sentiment expressed in the poem, that the world is not as expansive as when it was flat instead of round.

Of course I know that the world was never flat, but it is fair to say that in the past many people believed it to be flat. It is a fair poetic conceit to imagine that this false view of reality was once actual reality.

If, at one time, we could dangle our legs over the edge of the world, how would our view of things be different? Today's poem is my attempt at a possible answer to that question.

# 50 Things a Poet Should Know

1. The feel of the air at sunrise.
2. Where the line of ants leads.
3. The theoretical basis for astrology.
4. How to sweep the steps without raising a lot of dust.
5. How people express love.
6. What iambic and pentameter mean.
7. The scent of the ground after a rain.
8. How to draw stick figures with style.
9. The source of your water.
10. How empires rise and fall.
11. The feel of various tree barks on your palm.
12. The numbing effects of ice water.
13. How much salt is too much salt.
14. The view from a toddler's perspective.
15. The shape of a crow's wings.
16. When the first blossoms of the year bloom in your neighborhood.
17. The shape of the crack in the sidewalk.
18. Why revolutions persist.
19. The gripes of the privileged.
20. The joys of the poor.
21. The dread of getting lost.
22. What those blobs on a weather map mean.
23. Where the rare earth elements in your cell phone come from.
24. Who delivers your mail.
25. The buying power of a dollar in 1800, 1900, and today.
26. The benefits of remaining silent.
27. The benefits of expressing your opinion.
28. Your limits.
29. Sappho.
30. Rumi.
31. Emily.
32. The length of time it take for the leaves to fall from the deciduous tree closest to where you live.
33. The hiccup cure that works for you.
34. The crumbly texture of rust.
35. The life cycle of a scar.
36. The rhythm-breaking effects of walking on railroad ties.
37. How to hold a baby.

38. That grief passes.
39. The shape of an owl's eye.
40. Your neighborhood.
41. Your planet.
42. The feel of grass on your bare feet.
43. The pattern and color of phosphenes.
44. The rules of the game, any game.
45. The definition of free verse.
46. The definition of blank verse.
47. What a long afternoon of boredom feels like.
48. The lyrics of your favorite song.
49. The different types of clouds.
50. Why write poetry.

*—27 July 2020*

My morning routine includes a 45-minute fast walk around The Sanctuary. It is my main exercise. While I walk, I listen to podcasts on my cell phone. This morning it was Roman Mars's *99% Invisible*, which is about design. The episode included a tribute to Michael Sorkin, an architecture critic who died earlier this year. Mars suggested taking a look at a piece Sorkin wrote called "Two Hundred and Fifty Things an Architect Should Know."

As soon as I heard that title I rewrote it in my mind as "250 Things a Poet Should Know." When I got home, I looked up Sorkin's list on the internet and read through it. It was charming, baffling, intimidating, funny, ridiculous, and inspiring all at once.

I took the basic premise and wrote out some observations of my own about what I think would be useful for a poet to know. I didn't go all out and produce 250 lines. I stuck with a modest 50.

The basic idea here is that a poet should pay attention to the surrounding world. The specific things I mention in the poem aren't the point. Cultivating an attitude of curiosity and learning is.

# Sonic Encounter

Hummingbird, hummingbird,
why so close? Does my ear
resemble a flower?

Hummingbird, hummingbird,
gathering the wind. You
hover near me, but why?

Hummingbird, hummingbird,
your beak, thin and sharp, makes
me wary of your sting.

Hummingbird, hummingbird,
you strum the air; I hear
your purr and I hold still.

Hummingbird, hummingbird,
flying away. What did
I say? What did I do?

Hummingbird, hummingbird,
please hurry back. My ears
miss the sound of your wings.

—28 July 2020

This morning, while Kim and I were sitting outside, a hummingbird flew close to Kim, within inches of her hair. It hovered around her for about five seconds or so. It was amazing. A short time later, a hummingbird (perhaps the same one, perhaps not) came and hovered around my head, very close to my ear. I didn't see it, but I sure heard it. It was not more than about three inches from me. It remained for about five seconds, then flew away.

Well.

Encounters like that demand to have poems written about them.

I started each stanza with "Hummingbird, hummingbird," because I liked the sound of the repetition. That also suggested a form: lines of six syllables, which is what I did.

# Slow Light

We knew
the dark

days were
coming. So

we gathered
all the

light we
could with

our nets,
our traps,

and our
sweet seductive

voices and
stored all

the light
we captured

in big
rain barrels

in the
barn. When

the sun
took its

vacation, we
rolled the

barrels out
to the

grounds and
one by

one we
opened them.

The light
wouldn't come

out. We
shook the

barrels and
banged bats

on them
and kicked

them, and
cursed the

light. But
the light

would not
come out.

We sit
in the

dark now
and spend

our days
and nights

wondering what
went wrong.

—29 July 2020

I started out with some ideas about slow light. What would the world be like if the speed of light was much slower than it is now? For example, what it if was just a foot or two per second? We would no longer have more or less instantaneous images of the world imprinted on our retinas and brains. Sound, I suspect, would be much more important as a way of understanding the world around us, since it travels at over 700 miles per second. The observable universe would be much smaller. And so on. One could imagine lots of consequences. Which was the problem. So much would change in our world based on this one change that it was too much to put in a poem. Maybe the idea deserves a novel.

So I abandoned that approach and instead considered other aspects of light. What if it was kind of like a crop? You could harvest it and store it and take it out when you needed to. That notion got my attention. I jotted down some lines and kept going. I believe I ended up with a metaphor for abusing nature. But then, the author of a piece of writing is not always the best judge of that writing, so I will not insist on that interpretation.

Today's poem also had me thinking about aspects of form. What makes a poem a poem? What if, for example, today's poem was written out in paragraph form, like this:

> We knew the dark days were coming. So we gathered all the light we could with our nets, our traps, and our sweet seductive voices and stored all the light we captured in big rain barrels in the barn. When the sun took its vacation, we rolled the barrels out to the grounds and one by one we opened them. The light wouldn't come out. We shook the barrels and banged bats on them and kicked them, and cursed the light. But the light would not come out. We sit in the dark now and spend our days and nights wondering what went wrong.

Most people would not call this a poem, although there is such a thing as a prose poem, an oxymoron if ever there was one. The paragraph version has a different feel than the version presented in lines and verses. The more poem-like version, because it has more empty space, is filled with light, an appropriate property for a poem about light. It also has a lightness about it. It's kind of sprightly and moves me along quickly, at the speed of light, as it were, while the paragraph version is kind of plodding and slow.

I'm not trying to make a definitive statement on the difference between poetry and prose here, just making some observations about the differences in this particular case.

# Desert Pals

it's a mystic
scene when

the cottontail
rabbits

and gambel's quail
spend time

together in
the fenced

corral by the
cactus

*—30 July 2020*

We see this scene often, especially at dusk. The cottontails and the quail just hanging out, comfortable with each other, or moving together around the corral.

The form here is unrhymed two-line stanzas. Each first line has four syllables, the second line has two syllables. I consciously modeled it on William Carlos Williams's "The Red Wheelbarrow." He used a loose version of this form in that poem. "The Red Wheelbarrow" might be the most parodied poem ever. It is easy to make fun of. But it also has a quiet power that compels rereading. It evokes, for me, the feeling of the mystery of life and our place in it. Objects have power, and so do animals and the processes of nature.

I tried to bring out some of that mystery in today's poem.

# Buried Under Too Much Meaning at the Crash Site

Divide the good
from the bad

and the left
from the taken,

the old from
the young

and the right
from the wrong.

Now that you're
alone, it's easy

to see how
you veered

astray. No need
to find the

flight data
recorder: your

heart is the
true black box.

*—31 July 2020*

Although not exactly a diary or journal, these daily poems are, out of necessity, a reflection of what's going on in my life at the time of the writing. Today's poem came to me after watching an episode of *Air Disasters*, a show that examines the causes of airline crashes. Central to the investigations are the black boxes which fly with the planes and record flight data and cockpit conversations.

What if we have black boxes as well? The brain is an obvious example, but so is the heart. I took that conceit and tried to spin a poem out of it.

# August

# Reality Check

An expectation
is the
crack in
the sidewalk,

tripping you
up when
you least
expect it.

*—1 August 2020*

Short and simple today. We can expect many things in our lives, but life will throw you something you don't expect. All the time.

# My Reflection Switches Right and Left

The spider
most likely

does not
call its

web a
house or

a home.
That's not

the spider's
fault. We

see mirrors
every place

we choose
to look.

*—2 August 2020*

Today's offering is a reminder that just because we see something in a certain way, does not mean others see it the same way. This is a lesson I have to constantly relearn.

# Duration

A piece of time's cake cut
and slipped out of the sweet mesa

placed on the plate
the fork of division

pressed into action
to divide the slice

into more convenient spans
the crumbs dotting the table

like memories lost
along the way.

*—3 August 2020*

One of the essential qualities of poetry is an acknowledgment of the mystery of life. I believe there are no definitive answers to the questions that have persisted throughout history. Questions like "What is the meaning of life?" "Does God exist?" "What is the right thing to do?" These questions persist precisely because there can be no final answer for them. They are expressions of deep ignorance. Poetry of true power should wrestle with these questions in some way.

Today's poem is a mini examination of time. "What is the nature of time?" is one of the persistent questions that have no definitive answer. Nevertheless, thinking about time and what it means and how it works can be a fruitful inquiry. At least for me. Maybe for you as well.

# Every Recipe is a Formal Poem

The list of ingredients
A set of instructions
Some warnings
Friendly or stern advice
Several pro tips
Hope for the future
Blueprint for sustenance
Supplement to survival skills
Reaching for pleasure

*—4 August 2020*

Every time I look at a recipe, the layout and structure of it reminds me of a poem. I took that notion and put down the features of a recipe that feel like they coincide with the features of a poem.

# Hourglass Ambiguity

Past is on top, future is at the bottom.
But time is as fluid as fine-grained sand.
Flip the glass and past and present magically
exchange places. Do you remember the future?
Is the past a mystery? The sand in
the hourglass was washed down from
a mountain and into the ocean where it
churned for
years
and finally
tossed up on a beach where someone scooped
up piles of it and encased it in a glass
tube constricted at the middle. Narrow passage
for grains ticking off the seconds. Holding the
future captive for an instant at the narrowing
before letting it fall to its own heaping destiny
on the makeshift shore at the bottom of the glass.

—*5 August 2020*

I sometimes encounter hourglasses when I'm in a shop that sells such things. I usually flip them over, mesmerized by the flow of sand through the narrow crimp in the middle of the glass. The sand on top seems to be pushing down, telling the grains to hurry up, there are others waiting. But there is no hurrying. The sand moves at its own pace.

Below the crimp, the sand falls in plumes, spreading out as it falls through the gap, as though glad for the elbow room. Then it collects at the bottom in an ever growing heap. When the sand goes all the way through, I flip it over again. Just to see it go through in the opposite direction. It's very meditative to watch.

I remembered an occasion when I played around with hourglasses at a shop in Flagstaff and wondered about the sand and where it might have come from for today's poem. Also note that I tried to give the poem an hourglass shape.

# The Ocean Has Burdens Just Like You

It also has the wisdom
to let go. It releases
the sands of irritation,
the kelp of resentment,
the shells of guilt,
and the driftwood of grief
onto the accepting shore.

You can learn from
the sea. Just walk a
beach, any beach, and
drink in the lesson of
putting down your salty
worries. Then listen to the
soothing roar of troubles
released to the wind.

*—6 August 2020*

---

We used to live on the Oregon coast many years ago. Most days, weather permitting, we would walk the beach. The ocean would constantly toss up objects onto the sand. It was always interesting to see what we might find next.

I thought of the ocean today while sitting under the hot desert sun, and started wondering what the ocean was actually doing by ejecting those objects. Was it burdened by them? Probably not, but that shouldn't stop me from using the notion as the excuse for a poem. And it didn't.

# We Are Nothing But Bodies

How dragging your hand across unglazed clay
    scratches your fingertips with gentle roughness.
How the sharp irritation of the stone in your shoe
    can feel oddly comforting.
How a headache lodges in the back of your skull
    with a deadening effect that will not go away.
How the stab of a sudden bright light instinctively
    closes your eyelids in defense.
How a feather dragged along your arm raises goose-
    bumps in a pleasant manner.
How the wind through your hair after a haircut
    brings brief feelings of vulnerability.
How your new shoes require you to tread lightly in a
    world turned slightly more precarious.
How a cold wind makes you grab the lapels of your
    jacket and bring them together for shelter.
How the fragrance of a lilac bush shuffles the years
    of memory into a heady randomness.
How swimming in cold water gives you the shivers
    and feels more right than air.
How the taste of a competently cooked fish can close
    your eyes and make you sigh.
How applying floss to your teeth invites feelings of
    gratitude, hope, and pride.
How ice water coursing down your throat increases
    your pulse rate to pleasant effect.
How the sound of a fly buzzing against the window
    moves you to a modicum of pity.
How your eyes tracking across lines of small black
    marks on a page can make you cry.

*—7 August 2020*

---

The idea here is to play off the title and find experiences and sensations that reinforce the idea that we are nothing except our bodies. We sense the world through our bodies and are in the world through our bodies. We talk about having bodies but that seems to me something of a misconception. Having is owning. We don't own our bodies. Rather, we are our bodies.

At least that's what I believe today. Another day I might change my mind. And then I'd probably have a different poem.

# Snake Kin

your spine
like a

snake commands
your attention:

the shock
of recognition:

you are
like me:

but so
different I

choose fear
and send

a twisting
shiver slithering

down my
writhing back

*8 August 2020*

We saw quite a few snakes on the property last year but very few this year. I miss them. I like seeing snakes on the land. Remembering them made me remember the term "snake skin." I immediately twisted that into "snake kin."

Then I pursued that notion. Are we kin to snakes? Well, kind of. We both have spines and eyes and mouths and such. But after that, people and snakes are very different. So where is the kinship? I decided it rested mostly in the spine and wrote the poem accordingly.

# Someone Rendered My Poem Into Another Language

Translation wrung the words
of their music, then

placed them in a dictionary where
you can go look

them up if you are so inclined.
The melody is a

little deteriorated, and the
notes are somewhat

subdued. But if you press your
ear of understanding

to the page, a faint string
of notes, like the

song of a distant unfamiliar bird,
might find its way

to your heart, sent there on the
most modest of breezes.

*—9 August 2020*

As far as I know, no one has ever translated any of my poems. Nevertheless, any translation, however competent, must always lose something of the original, since the words of one language do not correspond directly with the words of another.

# Treading Delightedly

You slip into the day
like a foot slipping into a shoe.
Later, if you're not careful,
you might stub your toe on noon
or twist your ankle
stepping on the exposed root
of the afternoon. But
you might also find
the welcoming smooth path
of the morning,
or the delicious gravelly feel
of the early evening on your sole.
No matter. Sunset will bring
a cool relief as you slip
out of the day
like putting your feet up
and sighing as you
sip your drink.

*—10 August 2020*

Some days poems come easily. Some days they don't want to present themselves to me. Today was one of the latter days. I was about to dive into some reference books, maybe google "poetry prompts," or sit outside in nature, or read a favorite poet for some inspiration. Instead, as I was casting about for a subject, I sat down at my computer and kicked my slippers off. As soon as I did that this poem came to me.

You never know where inspiration will come from, obviously. It's always good to pay attention to everything around you, or enough of what's around you to get your creative juices flowing.

The title came last. It is a play on "treading lightly."

# Fish Tale

Lobe of cactus
in the desert dust
rotted to a startling
pale image of salmon skin
and fish shape
swimming against the wash's
ghostly flow,
always holding its place
in the current.

I travel against the rush
of dimming memories
to the spectacle
of salmon in a northwest creek
returning to the deep pool
beneath the dam.

How I made that pilgrimage
every fall,
witnessing their stubborn will
to make life
amidst their own death,
skin falling off at the end
like a rotted imitation
of desiccated cactus.

*—11 August 2020*

On my daily morning walk I usually notice this piece of a prickly pear cactus in the middle of the wash. It is fish-shaped and all its green has been drained from it so that it is this dull grayish-white, exactly like some of the salmon I used to see in the Pacific Northwest when they were near the end of their lives and their skin started to peel off of them.

    Today's poem tries to connect the two images into a coherent whole. The resemblance between the fish and the cactus is all in my head. The cactus knows nothing of the fish, and the salmon knows nothing of the prickly pear. But I, as poet and orchestrator of the senses, can bring them together on the page to, I hope, illuminate some of the connections in nature.

# Power

Oh, to drop pain as one
would put down a load

of firewood or deposit
a jug of water by the

side of the road. Take a
brief rest before

continuing on. Then
to realize there is no

need to take up the pain
again. The journey does

not need it, the final
destination complete without

the constant clamoring
of pain. You stand in the

sunlight, the shine more an
illumination than a glare.

The heat of ultraviolet rays
a cleansing of your skin.

*—12 August 2020*

---

I have had bouts of pain, as have most people. When I am in the midst of a bad attack of pain I always have this fantasy that I can take the pain and just put it down. Release it. It doesn't work, but that's what my mind wants. After all, what is pain? Just a sensation in the brain. It should not have the power over us that it does.

Sometimes it feels like the ultimate power would be to take pain away, hence the title of today's poem.

# Brief Visitor

The grasshopper jumps
with no thought to where
it's going to land,
whether there or here.

A grasshopper can,
from out of the sky,
drop in on your house
and crawl on your tie.

But grasshoppers won't
become your best friend.
They'll just hop away
again and again.

—13 August 2020

Every now and then I like to do a rhymed poem about insects and other tiny creatures. This one took a little time getting going. I decided on a grasshopper as the subject fairly quickly, and then began writing down lines that just didn't work. I did not give up. I decided that a grasshopper will never be a true friend because it is always hopping away.

Soon after that, I wrote out "The grasshopper jumps," which is a statement of its most obvious feature. That line suggested a form with five-syllable lines. I also decided each stanza should start with the word grasshopper in the first line. I settled on a 4-line stanza with rhyme scheme: xaxa.

It is meant to be light verse, frivolous fun, and illustrative of some aspects of its subject: that it arrives, stays briefly, then departs with flying abandon.

As I was editing this book prior to publication, I noticed that I had already written a grasshopper poem, "Jumper," on July 16. Less than a month ago and I had not remembered that when I wrote this one. Of the two I prefer today's. It has a better rhythm and does not over stay its welcome.

# The Mystery of Communication

The summer bees swarming on the pencil cholla
take the buzz of the cactus
back to their hives
leaving the thorny green joints
without a voice in the silent desert.

In winter's quiet months
the cholla bides its time
growing slowly
keeping its blossoms packed away
for explosive deployment in the new year.

And then the bees return in spring
bringing back the buzzing soothing voice
of the cholla
that they had borrowed for a time
to keep them company in the cold.

*—14 August 2020*

I did some pruning of cholla this morning. The bees were happily swarming over the cactus as I worked. I heard their buzzing. At first I was wary that I might antagonize them, but they didn't bother me as I methodically chopped away long branches of thorny green joints. As I worked I wondered what the bees found of interest in the cholla. There were no blossoms, so they were not collecting nectar. Or were they? Maybe the cholla has deposits of nectar, perhaps at the base of the thorns, or maybe in its green skin.

    I wasn't sure, but I liked the sound of them and I let my imagination come up with an unlikely but pleasing scenario about what was going on.

# I Used to Hold Hands With Strangers

They were clammy much of the time
and some people gripped harder than they should.
There was also a sense of forced camaraderie
since it always happened
in places reserved for spiritual practice.
We touched because the leader of the ritual

told us to and there was no way
to opt out of the practice
without feeling like a stick-in-the-mud.
Now in dreams I sometimes hold hands
with people I don't know.
A shivery sensation bordering on revulsion.

I want to pull away, but dream space
does not allow it. I feel their rough callused fingers
and our lifelines pressed one against the other
paths crossing then uncrossing
as we gratefully release our hold
in a ritual neither of us initiated.

*15 August 2020*

This is a more or less accurate account of times I held hands with real people and a time (last night) when I held hands in a dream.

# Perspective

Startling to witness
and a disturbing vision
that could evoke tales of loss

but the white rainbow
is not so much color choked off
from the world as it is

a thin blank parchment
awaiting your arching mural.

*—16 August 2020*

The other day Kim mentioned that she dreamed of a white rainbow. I was instantly intrigued by the image. What would a white rainbow signify, I asked? My first answer was loss. The loss of color. That seemed like a pretty drastic thing.

But then I tried turning it around and looking at it from another point of view. This is, of course, a good trick for writing a poem: take a received view of something and consider the opposite. Or take your first reaction to an object or an event, and consider the opposite reaction. So how would I present a white rainbow as something other than loss? Well, it could be seen as a blank canvas, something on which to add color.

I used some internal rhymes in this one: evoke/choked and parchment/arching. I didn't want them to be obvious by putting them all at the ends of lines, but I wanted them there to offer some sense of harmony in the words.

# Cooking From Scratch

The stove
painted green
like an overgrown plant
taking in light
and giving off heat.
The pans like blossoms
clustered into groups
with wooden spoons stirring
the contents
like the beaks of hummingbirds
searching for nectar.
We feel our own roots
sprouting from our soles
searching for the dirt
under our shoes.
But we live high above
the ground
on floors in houses
cooking our meals
on a rootless appliance.
No one told us
this was the way to be.
We took to it like bees
hovering over
nectar-laden flowers.

*—17 August 2020*

Compared to animals, my life is very artificial. Animals go their whole lives without clothing, wallets, bills, or mortgages. Not that they don't have worries. Prey, especially, must constantly be on guard lest they get eaten. But wild creatures, especially, live close to the earth.

Not that I would give up the life I have. I like shelter, electricity, running water, and all the other conveniences of modern life. It is still interesting to think about what life would be like if I didn't have those things. This poem isn't exactly that. It is more of a way of thinking about what I don't have in the midst of what I do have.

# Portrait

Like an artist holding a thumb up to her subject
we hold our lives up to the world
taking a measure of our presence.
Should I assert myself? Do I belong in this scene?
Will the likeness benefit from some shading
or perhaps an application of errant illumination
coming from beyond the edge of the canvas?
How much of myself is going to show?
Maybe it's best to acknowledge the perfection
of the original and let it stand as is.
No need to interpret it or let it guide our hand
to a facsimile of reality. Our eye is better off
taking in the pure true light streaming from above.
Stand in the flow. Accept the heat
as the welcoming embrace it is.

*—18 August 2020*

The point here is that many of us make a kind of portrait of ourselves by presenting a certain image to the world. I juxtaposed that notion with how an artist will use his or her thumb to measure the subject of their painting to get the proportions right. In some sense, many of us measure ourselves against the world to get the picture right, that is, to produce the image we want to project.

The poem considers these issues, then suggests that doing all that work might not always be a productive way to spend one's time. Sometimes it is best for one's soul to just observe, feel, and enjoy.

# Nature's Way

After the salmon died
her tiny pinkish-orange eggs
populated the bottom of the creek.

They proved irresistible
to the kingfisher
who dove into the water

and retrieved them for its lunch
trailing a cone of bubbles
like a comet's tail across the sky.

Salmon-colored jewels
winking out like stars
overwhelmed by dawn.

*—19 August 2020*

---

As I mentioned earlier, we used to make a pilgrimage every fall to a creek near where we lived in Washington state to see the salmon return to their spawning place near a dam. Their eggs were beautiful tiny spheres that populated the creek bottom. Very few of them hatched because most of them were eaten by other creatures, especially kingfishers. These birds were expert divers, going deep and snatching them up with abandon.

The final image, of a fading star field, came to me as I remembered how the kingfishers dove down with relentless speed and determination. They reminded me of a comet's unstoppable journey.

# Ice Age

Like a bug stuck in an ice cube
some memories are pests
following us our whole lives.
No way to be rid of them
without melting or breaking
its frozen package.
You recall that moment
when you hurt someone
or endured your own measure
of shame and embarrassment
and hope for the drip
of melting faculties
to release it back
to the wild.

*—20 August 2020*

---

This one took a while. I was not feeling any inspiration today. I wrote out a few words and lines in my notebook, but nothing was catching fire. I didn't feel that certainty that comes when you know you have something good.

So I asked Kim for some prompts to help me. She gave me four words: taco, love, ice, and fear. I played around with those for a while and finally settled on ice. I liked the idea of ringing changes on "ice age" and used that as a title and came up with today's poem.

After I wrote it, I told Kim that I wasn't sure I could finish my project of a poem a day for a year. I found that I was going over old tropes, falling into redoing poems and themes that I had already done before. She gave me some ideas for how to go on.

I've gone almost 10 months on this project, and there really isn't any chance that I'm going to abandon it now. But I wanted to say here that not every day is a day when something inspiring comes along. Sometimes you have to make your inspiration happen, which is, in a way, the point of doing a daily poem in the first place.

# Ill-Fitting

The shoes
the shirt
your skin.

Your thoughts
your steps
your hair.

The gloves
the laces
your voice.

The pain
the looks
your breath.

The apologies
the corrections
your regrets.

Your eyes
your feet
your will.

Your prayers
your hopes
your self.

*—21 August 2020*

---

This poem started out as a description of trying on clothes that don't fit. I wanted to use that as a metaphor for someone not fitting into the world. That quickly devolved into a tortured metaphor comparing a day to a shirt with such lines as "the shoulder of the sun." It was just as silly as it sounds.

So I abandoned that and considered stripping down the notion to its most basic. What are aspects of themselves that people feel don't fit in the world? There are many. Listen to conversations by ordinary folks and you will often hear a litany of features or characteristics that people feel don't fit well into their family, tribe, country, or world.

So I started writing some of those out, intending to gather them up and craft a poem out of them.

But as I wrote the list, I had this feeling that it didn't need any more elaboration. The list was the poem. I began with external things: shoes and an article of clothing but quickly moved to the internal and more personal, to the features which define us. As the list progressed, the external tried to assert itself once or twice, but the internal always took over.

# The Hawk's Gaze

Expect no trivial looks
from this hunter.
Each glance is an
appraisal and a threat,

measuring your congruence
to prey. And yet,
when it stares at you
for long heart beats

on a warm afternoon
primed with hunger,
it's easy to feel a kinship
as it tilts its head,

raises its yellow leg,
and examines your eyes
as you hold still
to keep from scaring it away

*—22 August 2020*

---

Driving home yesterday, we came to the carport and were surprised to find a hawk on the ground where we normally park our car. The hawk was working on a meal of a smaller bird, but it was taking its time. No frantic tearing and gulping of flesh, more a savoring of the tasty kill it had taken.

    We parked in the driveway and let it eat in peace, though Kim took pictures of it. It remained in its spot for some time. It would glance in many directions, including toward us. When it did look at us, I instinctively froze, not wanting to scare it away. It felt like we were connecting with the hawk. I tried to evoke that feeling of kinship in today's poem.

# Illumination

The sun shoots infinite darts
of swift light to the ground,
extinguishing the packets of dark
left over from the night before.

The plants, in their infinite wisdom,
intercept some of these missiles
and without fuss or fanfare
fashion cool green leaves from them.

The air, freshened by plant breath
and stained by the sun's light
slips into our welcoming lungs:
the benevolent spirit of the world.

*—23 August 2020*

---

One of the things I try to avoid in these poems is clichés, or, in other words, the usual way of expressing things. Why would I want to do that? Because new ways of expressing familiar events or processes can help us view those events and processes in different ways, which is one of the points of poetry in the first place. That's why here, in the opening line, I chose to refer to rays of sunlight as darts. I'm not sure if this is a successful attempt at expressing things differently, but it is an attempt to do so.

Avoiding clichés can be very difficult. After all, hackneyed ways of saying things have become common because they work so well. Later in the poem I use the phrase "infinite wisdom." That's a relatively common phrase, but I didn't find anything I liked better, so I left it in.

My point in this poem was to fuse the ideas of light and air. We take air into our lungs, but we also take light. How does that happen? The poem is an attempt at an explanation. Plants make themselves out of sunlight and they breathe out gas as a byproduct of that process. We breathe in that byproduct, so that means we, in a way, breathe sunlight. At least, that's the conceit of this poem. My hope is that you will look at air and light in a different way than you did before reading the poem.

# Trickster

Coyote eyes forge
their own lives.
Hanging like fine fruit
from high branches of trees,
They hold the long view
curving over the horizon,
bringing mysterious shores
back to the coyote.

Who paws the ground
for a returning sound,
calling the eyes
back to their sockets.
Loping then,
holding the visions
seeing the future
long before you.

*—24 August 2020*

Raven did the eye trick first, then Coyote copied Raven and really messed it up, which is what coyote usually does. Even so, even though Coyote had no idea how to do the eye trick properly, Coyote survived and went on. Tricksters usually do. They mess up, but don't let that stop them.

# F-Words

Fate has no favorites.
Fertility abounds.
Frontiers fool you.
Feelings play the field.
Freedom is personal.
Facts are final.
Fish don't know water.
Family holds you.
Favors obligate.
Fiddles bring joy.
Fear is information.
Feasts don't last.
Fainting is a poor escape.
Fences fall down.
Festivities can wound.
Futures arrive last.
Feuds hurt hearts.
Fevers seldom ignite.
Fun is an emerald.
Fields are often corn.
Ferocity begs for kindness.
Fights don't discriminate.
Fires cleanse.
Faith comforts.
Flesh is your suit.
Flying elevates.
Forks like roads.
Fantasy benefits reality.
Fortunes fade.
Friends disappoint.
Fiction is truth.
Fresh is an illusion.
Failure leads to success.
Frights wake you up.
Funerals break habits.

—*25 August 2020*

We all know the most famous F-word. I didn't use it here. I was looking for other F-words, ones that evoke strong feelings. I used the title as a cheap way to get people interested in the poem, then wrote quick observations on the F-words I chose to use. Most of these were very quick, a kind of snapshot of what all these words signify for me. Some are affirmations of the general meaning of the words, and others are contradictions of them. Some may not have much connection with the words at all.

    I chose the words by leafing through the F section of the dictionary and scanning the columns to harvest words that met my requirement of strong feeling. Then I shuffled the list so the poem did not end up in alphabetical order.

# Sea Creatures of the Desert

The ant hills
scattered across the field:
an archipelago of gills
taking in sustenance from
the roiling ocean
of the atmosphere.
Veins of yellow petals
networked on the ground
like the afterthoughts
of waves breaking
on a sandy shore.
Beneath it all,
in the murky depths:
schools of ants
swimming in harmony.

*—26 August 2020*

The desert, of course is dry and hot. Is it possible to plausibly entertain the notion that the ants that live there are like sea creatures? That was my idea in this poem.

# Ancient Story

Every generation
sees the wreck of the old
crash on the shore of the new.
High tide takes the remains
back to the sea where it churns
and bubbles and twists
until it acquires
a new skin and face.
That's when it comes back,
smiling and confident,
telling the world
it's the newest thing,
so shiny, so fresh.
It never lets on
that its true heart
was dredged up
from the depths
and reanimated
for the novelty-seekers
standing on the shore,
hungry for anything new.

*—27 August 2020*

All my life I've heard that there's nothing new under the sun. I never doubted it. Fashion comes and goes, ideas have their heyday, then recede, then return again. Novels and stories follow the structures of ancient myths and legends. Human behavior is remarkably consistent across epochs, countries, and tribes. We are always in a state of renewal, even when we believe we are being unique or original.

# Love Letter

*for Kim*

What is a love letter
but a promise
for the future?
Mine was posted
forty years ago,
and delivered to you
every day since.
No need for revision
in all that time:
the original sentiments
still as strong
as ever, still the
words that guide
me. They've never
been cancelled
or mis-delivered.
The heart in the
upper right hand corner
still the perfect stamp
to express my
eternal love for you.

*—28 August 2020*

---

An enormous number of love poems have been written over the centuries. Love is, of course, one of the major themes of life and literature. When I sat down to write one for Kim, I struggled to find something true and new. The term "love letter" came to me and I let it take me where it wanted to. Here is the result.

# Stealthy Visitor

The moth is a
random flyer,
sparking up like
embers from fire.

It will dodge right
through your doorway
and make a home
in your hallway.

Later you might
find it sleeping
right next to your
sneaker's shoestring.

Then it may move
to your pant cuff,
or your shirt sleeve
or your earmuff.

Really it could
be anywhere,
because moths find
comfort everywhere.

So if you see
one flutter out,
just let it flit
and fly about.

In time it will
find its way home
outdoors near your
garden's cute gnome.

Then have yourself
a jubilee
cuz your house will
mostly be moth-free.

*—29 August 2020*

I felt it was time for a bug poem, and I like to do those as rhymed poems. Bugs lend themselves to light verse. We have moths here on The Sanctuary. They are very good at getting into the house, even when we try to keep them out. It never seems like they *want* to fly into the house, but their random flight paths ensure that some of them will accidentally manage entry. Once they are inside, there is no telling where we might find them. They come fluttering up out of clothes, blankets, and remote corners.

I tried to capture their random nature in the poem. And I wanted a happy ending, so no killing of moths. They get to escape to the outdoors where they more or less belong anyway.

The rhyme scheme is xaxa for each stanza. I have mostly four-syllable lines except a couple where I couldn't make the line fit into four syllables.

Note that I had forgotten I had already written a moth poem this year. It was on March 5.

# Tooth

Member of the dentine tribe.
Sibling of fang, cousin to tusk.
Intimate with tongue, wary of decay.
Tasting nothing, chewing everything.
Living in harmony in its arced row.
Grinding out a life of service.
Basis of both smile and snarl.
Useful in fights, dirty and otherwise.
Formidable, even when false.
Bling for fairies, income for dentists,
source of aches, and canvas for whitening.
Not exactly bone, but close enough.
A bit of skeleton visible to the world.
Your inner being clutching at freedom.
Tearing through your soft gums
and into the world like a feral being
rising up from the dark interior.
Backing up hunger with ferocity.
Holding on tight for the wild ride.

*—30 August 2020*

---

I saw an illustration of a crocodile in the "Animals" issue of *Lapham's Quarterly* and really noticed the teeth. They were prominent and looked pretty lethal. I immediately decided I would write a poem about teeth.

I consulted the *OED* for a history of the word. It has been around a long time, as why wouldn't it be? It is a pretty important part of our anatomy.

I have always thought of teeth as the visible part of the skeleton, even though I know it's not bone. I associate teeth largely with smiles and also with the notion of falsity, since so many people have false teeth.

The poem ended up being a series of observations about teeth, though I tried to bring it to some kind of epiphany or conclusion. A lot of the lines got shuffled around from where they were first deployed.

# On the Antiquity of Microbe Eradication

Adam
may have had 'em

but Eve
made 'em her pet peeve
gave 'em the heave,
made 'em leave
brushed 'em off her sleeve
and caused 'em to grieve.

In other words,
she took care of those herds.

—*31 August 2020*

---

Strickland Gillilan, according to Wikipedia, is credited with what's often called the shortest poem ever written. It was composed about a hundred years ago. Here it is:

**Lines on the Antiquity of Microbes**

Adam
Had 'em.

It is also popularly known by a shorter title: "Fleas."
    I first heard this poem when I was in middle school. The class was assigned to write a poem. One of the students offered Gillilan's poem, purporting to have come up with it himself. I don't know if the teacher knew it was stolen. If she did know, she didn't let on. She praised the student for his humorous short verse.
    As I sat down to write today's poem, Gillilan's two lines came to mind. One of the best bits of writing advice I've ever heard comes from the late Theodore Sturgeon: "Ask the next question." I take this to mean that in any piece of writing you don't settle. You mine the depths of the concept by always asking what subsequent action or situation will arise from the present action or situation.

In the case of Gillilan's poem, the next question is: "What to do with all those fleas?" Well, Eve is there with Adam. She might have something to say about them. Or, more to the point, she might have something to do with them. Like, maybe, get rid of them.

So I took that concept and had Eve handle things. In a rhyming way, of course, as a salute to the original poem that gave me today's poem.

# September

# Some Random Entries From a Competition to Name the Sky

Blue Wonder
Broken Flood
Time's Mirror
Sun's Bath
High Expectations
Cloud Crib
Star Board
Air Head
Hope's Car
Air Born
Big Song
Body Blow
Sailor's Home
Plane Harbor
Sun Gap
Knitter's Yarn
Door Weight
Affectionate Object
Bone Break
Ceiling Fan
Contrail Closet
Keen Eye
Apple Skin
Big Bruise
Cousin Belle
Sea More
Aunty Ground
Artist's Paint
Floating Hearts
Vertigo Challenge
Eternal Flame
Apollo's Trail
Lunar Twitch
Smuggler's Haven
Modest Infinity
Frog's Jump

Close Up
Peacock Feather
Bound Less
Forty One
Wide Pink
Horizon Squatter
Alphabet Stew
Broken Fingernail
Petal Picker
Monkey Mind
Seashell Escape
Bird Home
Sewing Nook
Trumpet's Ear
Rest Ease
Studio Roof
Snake Tail
Tornado Avenue
Balloon Marrow
Rocket Juice
Egg Shell
Grape Skin
Berry Lane
Still There
Mountain Hat
Red Mind
Still Thought
Garden Weed
Private Loom
Earth's Wig

—1 September 2020

Woke up at 2 a.m. for some inexplicable reason. Could not get back to sleep, so I got out my notebook and began working on today's poem. I wanted to write something about the sky. I jotted down a few observations and then began playing around with them to see if any good lines presented themselves. After a while, I had a lot of short observations. What one might call quick descriptions. I looked at that short list and extended it. Half way through I came up with the title. Why not a competition to name the sky?

My hope for this piece is that as you read it you make some connection between the sky and the imagery in the line. Some of those connections will be obvious, others more obscure, and, for some lines, non-existent. By the time you get to the end, I would like you to have considered the sky in all kinds of new ways. By doing so, a very familiar part of nature may now be new and fresh to you.

This is a metered poem, since every line is exactly two words.

On the other hand, one wouldn't necessarily call this a poem at all. I suppose it's a matter of opinion.

# Birdbath

The finches
came fluttering
down to the

birdbath,
shuffled around
the edge,

and dipped
their beaks
into the water

just three times
each, taking up
enough moisture

to fuel
their flights
to the branch

in the tree
towering high
above them all.

*—2 September 2020*

My first try at this poem was to imagine the birds that come to a birdbath as a group of coworkers gathered around a water cooler on their break and discussing current events. I had lines like "Haven't seen the cat lately, have you?" and "How was your migration this year?" That try came to a dead end. It was a reasonably cute idea, but it didn't really go anywhere.

Then I decided to just watch the birds at our birdbaths and see what they offered me in the way of poetic vision or insights. One thing I noticed is that they take a long time to get to the birdbath. They will perch on a branch for a while, then descend to another branch that is a little closer to the birdbath, then descend again to a lower branch, remain there for a while, then, finally, decide to take the risk and perch on the edge of the birdbath.

I also noticed that many times the birds will take three drinks of water, no more and no less. Then they are off, flying at full speed to wherever, usually high in a nearby tree.

They also seldom use it for bathing. It is mostly for drinking.

# How We Grew

By instinct we made the world smaller.
Arranged to have our feet fit larger shoes.
Brought the sky closer to our heads.
Deflated the size of our home towns.
Let the trees shrink to shrubs.
Held the moon between thumb and forefinger.
Drew in the breath of giants.

*—3 September 2020*

Most of us forget just about everything that happened to us in our first few years. This has always seemed like a sad loss to me. It would be amazing to recall what it was like to take our first step, or how it came about that we understand an aspect of the world for the first time, or to be able to experience the construction of our first sentence all over again.

But, alas, we don't seem to have that capacity. In this poem I tried to convey what it is like to grow up. How it doesn't always feel like we are getting bigger, but, instead, that the world is getting smaller. We are nothing if not subjective beings, measuring everything against our corporeal selves.

# Sing For

the cardinal's bold red coat
the lizard's dour expression
the spine-livening rattle of the diamondback
the jagged dark path of the nighthawk
the grasshopper's arching jump
the bobcat's wide and curious eyes
the coyote's easy lope
the champion ears of the jackrabbit
the receptive oasis between your heart beats

*—4 September 2020*

I have some inspirational quotes on slips of paper at my desk. I flip through them periodically, and display different ones as I write. One of my favorites is by the artist Frederick Franck. It goes like this: "You shall not wait for inspiration, for it comes not while you wait but while you work." There's a lot of wisdom in those words. Often when I sit down to do my daily poem I have no idea what I'm going to write. I haven't the foggiest notion of subject, form, or approach. Nothing. If I let that bother me, I would be completely stymied and probably frustrated. It would most likely lead to some form of writer's block.

But putting Franck's words into action means that I just start writing. Something. Anything. It almost doesn't matter. Put down one word, then another. Construct a line. Is it any good? Who knows? Maybe it is, maybe it isn't. Then go on to the next line and the next. Don't worry about quality, not at first. Just put down words until something happens. Something called inspiration. This way of writing has never failed me, even though I sometimes have to remind myself of it, which is why I have Franck's words on that slip of paper.

Today's offering began with the word "forgave." Under that I wrote "cottony" and "elbow." Then I played around with those three words, seeing if they led to anything. Next I was struck by a rhyme: excess and express. So I wrote down "Express your excess." No inspiration yet, so I pressed on. "Hope will grow." What did that mean? I didn't know. I combined elbow and express to come up with "Elbow expressions." That had a certain something to it. Then: "bent elbow" and "elbow grease." Which felt like I was trying to say something about work. Maybe.

I pressed on. "So dangerous," came to me. No connections with what came before, as far as I can tell, but it sparked something. I went on: "So dangerous / to ascribe human attributes / to animals."

True enough, but not very poetic. There was no music to the lines and no imagery.

So I began writing down short lines about animals and tried to include images in the lines. Now I was getting somewhere. The lines soon started coming quickly. I was building up a picture of life on The Sanctuary, with all the animals we see here at various times during the day and year.

When I was done with lines about animals, I wanted a closing line that summed everything up. I chose to take things from the animal realm and move the reader deep into the heart of the poem: that is, the heart of the narrator. It is in stillness that we often see and hear things we would not otherwise notice.

The title came last.

# Free Climbing Eleven Lines

Start at the bottom, following gravity's laws,
because sudden heights can instill fear.
Use the uppercase *Y*
to hoist yourself to the penultimate line.
Admire the word *Stretch*.
Then keep climbing up the wall of words,
past *admire, hoist, uppercase,* and *fear.*
When you get to the top
stand on *bottom*'s double *t*.
Stretch your arms out.
You're a winner—you're a plus sign.

—5 September 2020

The idea here was to put the reader in the poem—literally. The poem describes a path from the bottom to the top, as though the reader is free climbing a wall of words.

I wanted to make the point that a poem is a physical object and that it could be thought of as something to traverse, the way a person in real life might traverse a rock cliff.

# Telling Time

Clocks on walls
arrayed like clouds
hanging in the sky

precipitating
misty seconds
rainy minutes

snowy hours
and when there's
nothing left

the hail of years falling
the sound of them
like ticks and tocks

dripping from clocks
collecting in piles
at your feet.

*—6 September 2020*

---

We have lots of clocks in our house on various walls. Also digital clocks on microwaves and our computers and the television. They do sometimes remind me of clouds hanging in the sky. I took that notion and extended it to make a rough comparison between different measures of time that clocks embody and the different types of precipitation that comes from clouds.

# Grand Canyon

Looped indentation in the skin
where I lassoed floss around my finger.
Something like a wound
but more a temporary valley
that will fill in over time.
My digit enacting a million years of erosion
in just a few minutes.
My skin mimicking
in sped up time
the skin of the earth.

*—7 September 2020*

I noticed how the floss I wind around my finger leaves an impression of itself, as though a noose had been cinched tight around it. I'd noticed this before, but never considered making it the subject of a poem. Today I did, trying to make the connection between my skin and the surface of the planet.

# Devotions

Let me flee the fires of autumn
the claws of unruly beasts
the tremors of calamity
and the vanity of celebrity.

Let me be the ink in my tattoo
the salt on my fries
the mist in the sky
and the hope in hearts everywhere.

Let me free the will to build
the soul trapped in pain
the snake in the swimming pool
and the yearning for illumination.

Let me plea for pristine air
the rewards of the wild
the buzz of exhilaration
and the abundance of justice.

Let me see the light of knowledge
the flight of nighthawks
the splendor of moonlight
and the dignity of teddy bears.

—8 September 2020

As is my custom, I began by writing down words and phrases that were floating around in my mind. I did this quickly, not editing or questioning anything, just letting the words pour out. I put down phrases about rainbows, raindrops, architects, deserts, prisms, and more. Unrelated items for the most part, they finally coalesced into what became today's second stanza.

I liked the form of that stanza so I produced a few more, then rearranged them to what seemed like a good progression. All the third words of each stanza's first line rhyme.

# Mushroom Field

Across the creek
houses springing up daily
the roofs like caps
on pale stucco stems.
The developer is not
a mycologist, cares little
for the aesthetics of
fungi, but has created
an inadvertent portrait
of considerable beauty.

—*9 September 2020*

When I was a young teen we moved to a part of town that was newly built and on the edge of undeveloped land. We would look out our back windows and see hills and fields. A few years later developers put up subdivisions on that wild land, the houses spreading across the fields and climbing up the hills. Those houses grew up quickly, seemingly overnight at times. My mother said that it was like watching mushrooms sprout up.

I remembered that image for many years and am always reminded of mushrooms whenever I see houses in the midst of their construction. That image returned to me this morning and I tried to give it justice in today's poem.

# Cold Front

The snow
expects nothing.
Even when
flakes land
on your
tongue, they
are grateful
for the
melting and
for offering
you a
taste of
freedom's sweetness.

—*10 September 2020*

I remember as a kid sticking my tongue out in a snowstorm to catch the flakes. I recall the sharp coldness and the taste: slightly sweet with a metallic undertone. I also recall wondering how the snowflake felt about its melting. Was it ready to go back to being liquid water? Or did it yearn to be steam, rising to sky again? OK, I was a weird kid. What I probably concluded, back then, was that the snowflake had no feelings about melting. It had no expectations.

# Love Eleven

Death cloaked not in black that day
but rather a billowing smoke-gray.
Scythe leaving cuts bleeding flame
in both towers. Then a cruel
mercy of time before the collapse

with death's hot breath prompting
cell phone calls streaming home,
expressing love, saying *I love you*
one last time, because, in the end
what else is there to say to the world?

—*11 September 2020*

Nineteen years ago I watched the towers burn and fall on television. Kim told me that now nothing was ever going to be the same for our country, and she was right.

This morning we watched some documentaries about that day. In one of them the producers interviewed people whose loved ones died in the towers. The survivors talked about the phone calls they received from their doomed spouses and relatives before they died. Every one of them included the words "I love you."

It was a very striking feature of all the conversations.

I wrote the above lines in response. The title came first. The words "nine eleven" were rattling around in my brain, and the documentary turned "nine" into "love." From there, the image of death tumbled out and the rest of the poem fell into place.

I hesitated to include this as one of my daily poems. I was going to just leave it in my notebook. After all, I wasn't there, I didn't have anyone I know die in the towers or on the planes that day. All I did was watch the disaster from afar.

But I decided I was not trying to co-opt emotions that weren't mine. I was observing the world and reporting on what I saw, which is, more or less, what I do in all my poems.

So I am including it here today.

# The Center of the Earth

All of us everywhere
on all the continents
and every ocean
have it directly under our feet.
Or in a straight line
through the tires of our wheel chairs
or telescoped down
from the legs of our beds.
You get the idea.
Even when we're flying
it's there under our seat.
Only the astronauts
who went to the moon lost it.
And they all came back to it.
It's our invisible comfort,
our shared vanishing point,
the one place
however remote and virtual
where we can all come together.

*—12 September 2020*

My first impulse this morning was to write about hummingbirds. I was going to do a perspective switch where the hummingbird, instead of flying in air, was going to thread the ocean of air around its wings. It is a powerful little thing, after all.

That didn't fly (so to speak) so I considered other forms of perspective. People are so different that there isn't much that everyone has in common. That led me to consider the possibility that some abstract point in space might be a commonality. What would that be? Well, the center of the Earth is directly under every single being that lives on planet Earth. Once I had that notion, the poem fell into place.

# Magic Trick

Pick a word, any word. You picked *it*.
Behold, I will now make *it* disappear:
Where did go? Do you see anywhere?
Here *it* is, silly, right behind your ear.

*—13 September 2020*

If a magician can make things disappear, why not a poet? Today's poem is, admittedly, a trifle, but maybe it gave you a laugh. I got the idea after watching a YouTube video in which a magician made an object disappear in front of a monkey. When the monkey saw what the magician had done, she fell over backwards and laughed and laughed and laughed.

In the poem I used the classic magician's trick of pulling objects from behind someone's ear. Also, lines two and four rhyme.

# The Risks of Knowledge

I met a moon savant once.
If you told her a date
she would know
the phase of the moon
on that day. It could be a date
thousands of years in the future
or hundreds of years in the past
or last week. It didn't matter.
Any date. She would know.

I asked her what the moon
meant to her.
She went wide-eyed,
the phase of her pupils
shifting from full to new.
I sensed confusion and
told her it didn't matter.
I shouldn't have asked.

Her pale face registered alarm
as though I had frightened her.
I have one skill, she whispered.
It's all I have. Don't make me
think about it or it might go away.

Then she looked up, past my face
to the wide and open sky above us.
I followed her gaze. The moon
was absent from the expanse.
Its benign light a peculiar
and distant memory
as though we needed a reminder
of its brilliance.

—14 September 2020

I am aware of savants who can tell you the day of the week for any date you care to name. There are also number savants that can do complex calculations quickly in their heads. I don't know of moon savants, but I like the idea and decided to use it here.

# Accept These Marvels

The dazzle of the cardinals.
The cold of the north wind.
The distress of embarrassment.
The sigh of the tall pines.
The sorrow of broken dreams.
The scratch of burlap.
The green of new leaves.
The hope of the heart.
The riddle of mystery.
The grumble of gravel.
The shelter of a fireplace.
The splendor of a spider.
The hush of hunger.
The light of the sparkling stars.
The call of the falcon.
The comfort of faith.
The clip of the lizard.
The appeal of a detour.
The chill of a pillow.

—*15 September 2020*

Some of the items in the poet's toolbox include *assonance* (the audible repetition of vowel sounds in words close to each other), *alliteration* (the audible repetition of consonant sounds at the beginning of words), and *consonance* (the audible repetition of consonant sounds in words whose vowel sounds differ). Careful use of these tools can make for very effective poems because they create patterns, and most people are pattern seekers, or, at least, pattern recognizers, even if the recognition may be unconscious or subliminal. I believe we are comforted and soothed by patterns.

Another tool in this vein is, of course, *rhyme*, perhaps the most well-known and obvious of all the poet's tools for making patterns. I have avoided it here to better highlight the other tools.

If a writer wants to distinguish their poems from prose, the above tools are excellent ways to accomplish this. In today's poem I consciously worked assonance, alliteration, and consonance in the lines.

The result is more pleasing and readable, more poetic than if I had simply made a list without using those tools.

# Dragon Bone

Found them
in the hills above my town.
Dragged them down
to the town square.
Showed them off
to my fellow citizens.
Sold them to a
traveling circus.
Now, at night,
I dream about them.
When I wake up
the floor is scorched black.
I touch the powder
and transfer my
fingerprints to the wall:
reminder of lost fire.

*—16 September 2020*

Dragons figure in myths from all over the world. A fire breathing creature. What strange twist in the human mind would make this a universal myth?

I don't know the answer to that question, but I am not immune to the lure of this particular myth.

# Super Power

When I was a kid
I would pluck rays from the sun
grab them like they were icicles of light
and stab the snow with them.
They would remain there
spires of brightness
for the rest of the season
melting only when spring came
and their light would flow to the creek
as sparkling fireflies on the water.

Since then some version
of kryptonite crept into me
relieving me of that ability
and now the sun's rays
are no longer within my grasp.
They wheel in the sky
like silent bicycle spokes
turning but going nowhere.

*—17 September 2020*

---

Imagination seemed stronger when I was younger. As I got older, it was more difficult to believe in magic, and more difficult to remember that once I could do magic: make the world bigger, discover new languages, ride my bicycle to the moon, close my eyes and transport myself to a different time and place.

Today's poem honors the kind of imagination that knew no limits.

# Leaf Song

Mostly a life of silence
except for wind passing
sighing over its surface
then the quiet turn
away from green
to a bold yellow
and the mute journey
to the forest floor
punctuated at ground level
by a surprising
and brittle final snap.

*—18 September 2020*

Kim and I went to Madera Canyon, a park south of Tucson up in the mountains. We walked trails, saw birds, lizards, squirrels, and a deer. We meandered along a dried creek bed populated with numerous rocks of all sizes and watched over by tall pale eucalyptus trees. It was a completely different ecology than the Sonoran desert surroundings we find here in the valley.

    One of the things I noticed as we walked was that some of the leaves in the trees were already turning color and falling. I watched one of those parachute down and land with an audible click on a creek rock. That image and that sound stuck with me. Later, after dinner, as I took out my notebook to write my daily poem, that moment came back to me and I turned it into today's poem. The title is a conscious play on the common phrase "swan song."

# Sky Glitter

The burning light of giants
made of mystery substance
installed at a dizzying altitude
distant gems of the night.

*—19 September 2020*

The method here was to first take a familiar poem and write it out with space between the lines.

I chose the well-known lullaby "Twinkle, Twinkle, Little Star." Its four lines are the first stanza of a longer poem called "The Star," written by the English poet Jane Taylor. It was first published in 1806.

You probably know it, but just to remind you, it goes like this:

Twinkle, twinkle, little star.
How I wonder what you are!
Up above the world so high,
Like a diamond in the sky.

Then I considered each line and wrote a response to it in the space below that line. When I was done, I removed the original lines and what was left were my lines. The hope is that they constitute a poem that is a response to and a meditation on the original, perhaps giving an insight into the substance of the lullaby.

I did this exercise with another poem on January 30.

# Trinkets

Cube of copper
next to the miniature rubber penguin.
Pyramid made of rock layers.

*The* OED *says the word* trinket
*is of obscure origin.*

Sphere of sandstone.
Eraser in the shape
of a carton of fried potatoes.

*No one knows for sure*
*where the word came from.*

Clay family of javelinas.
Glass globe filled with
sculptures of undersea creatures.

*All these items rest*
*on the table where I*
*am writing this poem.*

Lizard forged of iron.
Flat metal acorn, my father's
retirement watch, and
two stone arrowheads.

*Not obscure at all.*

—20 September 2020

Woke up with the word "trinket" in my head. Went to our trusty *Oxford English Dictionary* to research its origins, and found that no one knows where the word came from.
    Huh.
    That fact, I was sure, held the seed of a poem. I planted it and this is what grew.

# The Bite of the Deep

Salt from tears
hold the work
of the world.
Seasoning
emotions
with the tang
of brine, the
long slow rise
and fall of
ocean waves
revealing
the labor
of the moon
and the sun.
High tides and
low, all brought
together
in a crash
of feeling.
Step away
from the toil.
Wipe moisture
from your face.
Taste the salt
of the sea
on your hand.

*—21 September 2020*

Living in the desert, the ocean seems like a lifetime away. I remember the waves crashing on the shore with sometimes ferocious power. And the tides, how we kept track of them, knowing when to expect a wide stretch of revealed sand at low tide, and an abundance of water at high tide. I remember the salt on the seaweed, white powder as though from another world. What was this strange plant washed up on the sand, bulbous at one end and a clump of green streamers at the other?

Today's poem is a meditation on the sea. I made it a metered poem: each line is exactly three syllables.

# Draw

Draw out the hope in a desperate situation.
Draw a conclusion from scant evidence.
Draw a line in the sand but make it bold and expressive and wild.
Draw the cart down the slope slowly to prevent injury.
Draw your accomplice aside to impart crucial information.
Draw even with your adversary to make the race more interesting.
Draw the game if you cannot win the game.
Draw on your experience when confronting the unknown.
Draw smoke into your lungs to feel the pain of the world.
Draw your weapon before entering a danger zone.
Draw a hot bath at the end of the day even if you don't need it.
Draw your inspiration from ordinary objects in ordinary places.
Draw money from your account to support the cause.
Draw the look of surprise on the face of a child.
Draw in a breath and hold it before letting it go.
Draw an audience to your performance by employing charm.
Draw me into your argument if you dare.
Draw the campaign to a close when the results are settled.
Draw attention to what needs mending.
Draw a moral from the proceedings at your own peril.
Draw the shades when the world out there is too much.
Draw a clear distinction for yourself between truth and lies.
Draw straws if you must but try to force the short straw on the other.

Draw a blank and you lose any advantage you may
   have had.
Draw out the experience if it is pleasant.
Draw yourself up to full stature to feel your true
   power.

*—22 September 2020*

The idea here was to take a word—any word—and see if I could write a poem with that word as the first word of every line. I picked "draw" more or less at random and began composing lines. I soon found that "draw" has many meanings. It was a revelation. I got about 20 lines done before I started running out of meanings, but then I consulted a dictionary and found that there were a few I missed. I incorporated them into the poem and ended up with 26 lines illustrating 26 meanings of "draw."

    I suppose this poem might be thought of as a way to draw attention to the multitude of meanings that certain words have. Mostly we are unaware of them. Writing them out like this gives a new perspective on language, words, and meaning in general.

# Don't Stare at the Sun

She's shy.
Doesn't like the attention,
despite her dazzling presence.
Instead, just lift your arm
and wave at her as she passes by
on her colorless rainbow path.
She will appreciate
the gesture and shower you
with warmth and light
and greet you again
in the morning.
Because she may be bashful
but she's also loyal.

*—23 September 2020*

We're all told not to stare at the sun because it will damage our eyes. But maybe there might be another reason not to stare. It isn't polite, for one thing. There are other ways to make a connection. Here's one.

# The Numinous Heights

The top shelf
requires a long reach
and standing on tip toes
to retrieve the can of beans.
As you do so
the beans take on an elevated aspect
as though you are reaching
for the divine.
Don't fight the sensation.
Beans are divine
and, come to think of it,
so are you.

*—24 September 2020*

The divine lives in all of us, and all of us can express it. That expression need not be an obvious or a grand thing. Just reaching for the sky would be enough. Or even reaching for a can of beans.

# The Luminous Lows

The red leaf
on the forest floor
requires you to bend your knees
to retrieve it.
As you do so
you might experience a rush
of blood to your face.
This is the universe
working to match your color
to the leaf,
letting you know
you have a deep connection
to the wild.

*—25 September 2020*

A companion piece to yesterday's poem. If reaching high is an expression of the divine, then bending low should be as well.

# Generic Biography

Behold, if you will,
the new life
rising from its tiny sea
gulping from the ocean of air.
So much to get done, now.
The growing, the learning, the doing.
Later, looking back on it all,
some satisfactions,
a few regrets, surely,
uncountable highs and lows,
accomplishments and setbacks.
The final years a time for taking account,
but always pushing forward,
the life held tight
imprinting itself on the world,
making a ripple
in the waters of being.

*—26 September 2020*

I like reading about people's lives, but have to admit that I generally skip the first chapter of biographies. I am not so much interested in the person's parents and grandparents and where they grew up as children, and so on. Though such aspects are more or less unique to each individual, they still have, for me, a sense of sameness from person to person. That fact prompted today's title, which then led to today's poem.

# Before Regular Mail Service

Back then
social media was
a pigeon
with a slip of paper
wrapped around its leg.
I always wondered
what the pigeon
thought of the whole enterprise.
I could imagine
it shucking the message
off its limb
and letting the leaf flutter in the air
to some undetermined niche.
Then it would tweet its joy
at its newly found freedom.
Maybe arrive at its destination
years later
after numerous adventures
sans message
prompting the recipient to wonder
what went wrong
with the bandwidth.

*—27 September 2020*

I actually am not aware of when exactly pigeons were used for sending messages. I have some vague idea that it was during the middle ages, my notion made fuzzier, I suppose, by representations of the practice in popular culture, especially movies. It always seemed a little bit miraculous. First that the birds always returned to their homes, but second, that people were able to figure this out and use it to their advantage.

As with most things that intrigue me, I try to find an approach to the subject that is different from the obvious. I began to think about the pigeon, essentially used as a slave. If the pigeon had some choice in the matter, would it go along with the scheme? Probably not.

# Transformation

Going to retrieve my hat
from where the wind took it,
I noticed my head
felt lighter
like it had been drained
of thoughts.
It was as though
a meditation session
had achieved enlightenment
for me without me
even knowing it.
When I put the hat
back on
the world
receded a little
and crawled back
to a safe place
where I could not
make contact
until I bumped my head
on an unseen branch
stretching above me
across my path.

—28 September 2020

Putting on a hat changes my view of the world. I can't see above me as well as I normally do. I feel separated from my natural surroundings, and have a general feeling of artificiality. That sensation seemed like a good subject for a poem.

# Invaders

Shoes tied together
and hanging from a power line.
The birds stay away from them.
They know crazy when they see it.
Instead, they light
some distance away
and look sideways
at the incongruous sight.
They might wonder
as I do
what on Earth possessed someone
to throw those shoes
up there like that?
Whose feet are now
skating across the sky
looking for their shelter?

*—29 September 2020*

I haven't seen a pair of shoes hanging from a power line in some time, but I do recall when I was a kid that such a sight was relatively common. I'd see running shoes tied together by their laces draped over a black telephone wire in the neighborhood.

    I always wondered how they got there. Surely someone purposely tossed them up in such a way that they would get tangled up in the line, but why? What would make anyone do that? I never found out. Never knew anyone that did such a thing. I did think about birds. Power lines are their realm. They like to perch on them and gaze at the world. Seeing shoes in their territory could well have been at least a little bit surprising.

# Day of the Coat Hooks

Always ready
stalwart and solid
something to depend on
to hold your jacket
your hat
your feelings of home
as you walk through
the door

on rainy days
they will click
hook on hook
with your umbrella
team players
taking the moisture
without complaint
as you shake the drops
from your raincoat

lined up on the wall
they resemble
domestic gargoyles
hidden grins
awaiting your burdens
with pride
and a sense
of duty unbound.

—30 September 2020

As the old saying goes, home is where you hang your hat, or something like that. Most days when I come into the house, I hang my hat on one of the coat hooks on the wall next to the door. I took that notion and ran with it, writing an ode to coat hooks everywhere.

# October

# Everything's Different Now

After a hot summer
the prickly pears
look like wrinkled old folks.
They gather
in the dusty dirt
of their assisted living center
in the dry desert
and talk of old times
when the rains
were more abundant
and their complexions
were a deep dark green.
Now they wear
an uncertain shade of yellow
and they peer out at the world
through narrowed roots,
their thorns now more adornment
than sharp stabs at the world.

*—1 October 2020*

Here in the Sonoran desert we have had very little rain this past summer. No monsoon rains at all, which many of the desert plants rely on for their sustenance. We have noticed that a lot of the cacti looks very stressed, including the prickly pears, which usually have a robust appearance: bright green and pumped up with moisture. Not this year. All the cacti are having a hard time. We only hope they will get some rain soon that will put them right.

# Biography of a Rock

Born in heat or pressure,
maybe not even on this planet,
but here now.
Early years buried in dirt,
remembered later as the best time,
the sweetest days.
Unearthed by human
or geological forces,
laid bare on the surface
like emotion-stained sleeves.
Hungry for contact,
washed away in rain
and melting snow,
tumbling with cousins,
worn smooth by friction
and mounting years.
Later, in old age,
looking forward to a
quiet time of rest
contemplating the
might of the universe.
Finally, in some far future,
crumbling to dust,
cast on the wind,
looking for reincarnation
in the uncertain and shaky
circle of existence.

—2 October 2020

Many (if not most) of us divide the world into living and non-living. Plants and animals are living things. Lumps of copper, grains of sand, and concrete bridges, to name a few, are not living things. My idea in today's poem was to consider a traditionally non-living thing and treat it like a living thing and tell its life story in a poem. For those of you following along with me on this project, try the same thing: find something most people would consider non-living and write a biography of the thing in the form of a poem and as though it were a living thing.

# A Good Poem Should Be Like Your Best Friend

I remember the poem
that used to hop onto my lap
and ask to be rubbed
behind the ears.
Then it would stretch out
splay its paws
and curl up its stanzas
for a good long nap.
Years later I still remember
the shape of that poem
how it used to roam around the house
twisting its sinuous lines
down the hall
and into the living room.
It would hide there
waiting for the right moment
to come out and announce itself
to the world
with a measured line
and a slant rhyme.

—3 October 2020

Here's a quote from the poet Mary Oliver: "I learned from Whitman that the poem is a temple . . . a place to enter, and in which to feel. . . . I learned that the poem was made not just to exist, but to speak—to be company. It was everything that was needed, when everything was needed."

Oliver's quote reminded me of the cat we kept years ago. She was always a good friend. She would spend time with us and when things weren't going well, she would try to make us feel better just by being with us. Other times she demanded, in her feline way, to be rubbed or petted, fed or played with.

Taking that memory and combining it with Oliver's quote yielded today's poem.

# Thoughts While Pruning

After the cutting
with the lopped branches
dragged away

I imagine the tree
must hope for
perching birds

to come visit
and scratch the itch
on its phantom limbs.

—*4 October 2020*

I have read that amputees often report feeling itches on their missing limbs. It can be very frustrating because there is no way, obviously, to scratch the itch. As I was pruning some of the trees on our land I wondered how a tree would scratch an itch on its phantom limb? The answer came to me as I wrote the poem, which illustrates the core idea of this book: inspiration comes most reliably when one is doing the work, not before.

# An Ode to Oatmeal

Bountiful breakfast bowl.
Magnificent morning mash.
Oatmeal, you offer yourself
without reservation,
a nutritious assemblage
of grain for my gain.
I bow my head to your
unyielding mission.
I consume your awesome
granite strength with
gusto and gastronomic
gratitude. I adore your
simplicity and your
unyielding devotion
to my well-being.
You bring horse health
to start my day. I gallop
forward thanks to you.

*—5 October 2020*

Nearing the end of my year-long project, I have been thinking about what poetry means to me. I believe it is a way for me to make sense of the world. So much of life is chaotic. Writing and art brings order to that chaos by finding or highlighting patterns. Poetry does this with concise language, which is what I find especially attractive.

Today's poem began by thinking about something very ordinary and completely banal. Like a bowl of oatmeal. Could I find something interesting in such a mundane topic as a chaotic swirl of cooked grain? Today's poem is my try at doing just that.

# My Volcano

Ash and lava
doing their dance.
Hello Earth!
Thanks for supporting us
all these years.
I'll just step out
of your way now.
Let you release
all that energy.
Awesome spectacle,
I'll give you that.
Let me know
when you're
returning to sleep.
I can't wait
to go back home.

*—6 October 2020*

I saw the word "volcano." That is not a particularly remarkable thing. I've seen that word any number of times over the years. It's relatively common, even though a little bit exotic looking. This time the word stuck in my head. I used to live near Mount St. Helens. This was after its big eruption in 1980. Kim and I used to drive to its slopes. We were always amazed at how the trees had been knocked down like toothpicks, still there decades later. There were vast stretches of barren gray ash, but also lots of places where the forest had come back, green and lush.

    None of those memories or images sparked a poem in me until I began playing around with the title. I finally settled on "My Volcano" and the poem grew from there.

# Now O'Clock

You can kill time
or you can keep time.

Few of us want
to be short of time,
or have to admit
we lost time.

Some of us make time
and others do time.

Many of us would stop time
if we could,
others end up serving time,
that supposedly does them good.

We sometimes labor to save time
and often end up wasting time.

We tend to admire folks
who arrive ahead of time,
and are annoyed
with those behind the time.

We like a pleasant pastime
but express impatience with high time.

The great mystery of time
is that all of us are of our time
and no matter how we mind the time
in the end we will run out of time.

*—7 October 2020*

I've been reading the "Time" issue of *Lapham's Quarterly* and soon realized that the word "time" occurs in many expressions. I took some of those expressions and put them into this poem. I used "time" many times to give the feeling of a clock tick-tocking incessantly. Time has that quality for me: inexorable and never-ending. No way to stop it, it is relentless, unceasing. It can be a comfort because it is always there, giving room to our activities and emotions. Or it can be a torment, amplifying our fears and worries.

When I was done with today's poem, I considered deleting the first seven stanzas and leaving only the last one to stand alone as a small poem. Those final four lines have a rhythm and musicality all their own, somewhat removed and different in tone from the rest of the poem, which gives the piece a somewhat discordant feel. In the end, I chose to keep the whole thing. The first seven stanzas kind of stumble along, and then the final stanza draws everything together and makes the meaning of the poem crystal clear.

At least, that's what I see in the poem. Readers may have a different opinion.

# Vampire Trail

Greedy mountain
draining the strength
from my legs.
No wonder
it presents such power,
lifted up
on the energy
from the muscles
of hikers.
I've gone back
to the peak,
looking to retrieve
my might
from the serene rocks,
but here's a secret:
you can't do it.
The big rock
keeps it all
like it's some kind
of life blood
and won't ever
let go.

*—8 October 2020*

Climbing up steep hills is one of the most tiring things I do. I always feel it in my legs. Not just weariness, but as though a vital part of me has been taken away. If I let my imagination go, it feels like the hill is taking strength from my legs through my feet and hoarding it for itself. Of course I know this isn't true, but that's the way it feels.

# Slow Motion CPR

On the trail today I saw a dead oak
that had fallen years ago
resting at the base
of the vee formed by two branches
of a sturdy sycamore.

The older living tree
looks like it has been rescuing the oak
from crashing to the ground
for decades.

Lifting it inches toward the sky
every year as though righting it
after all that time
will bring it back to life.

—9 October 2020

I've mentioned Theodore Sturgeon's advice to "ask the next question" before. I applied that principle to the oak and the sycamore. I saw the oak resting on the sycamore where it had fallen a long time ago. I wondered what was going to happen next. Well, the sycamore was going to continue to grow, lifting the dead oak higher and higher all the time. What would happen after that? Maybe the oak would get to the point where it would right itself again. And what would happen then? Probably nothing, but what if the sycamore had other ideas? What if the sycamore was doing all this work to help the oak get back on its roots? Again, an unlikely scenario, but a compelling (at least for me) poetic image that came from asking the next question several times.

# Head Space

Snapping toes
and croaking crows;
seeing double
in the rubble.

I got visions
and indecisions;
lots of worries
and snow flurries.

Burrowing beetles
and lots of peoples:
full of brawn
and carrying on.

Bright blue sky
and annoying fly;
empire of air
their common lair.

Taste of metal
in the kettle;
reflective gleam
billowing steam.

All my revisions
lead to decisions;
all my thoughts
is all I gots.

Snapping toes
and croaking crows;
seeing double
in the rubble.

*—10 October 2020*

The most well known practitioners of nonsense poetry are probably Lewis Carroll and Edward Lear. Their verse revels in the sound of words, especially how they rhyme, and their poems often don't make a lot of sense. (Hence, I suppose, the name NONsense.) A somewhat more hoity-toity term for nonsense poetry is "light verse." Whatever they're called, what they do very well is provide a little bit of fun. It's hard to read Lear's "The Owl and the Pussycat" or Carroll's "Jabberwocky" without a smile on one's lips. At least I find it so. I hope today's offering causes a similar response.

# Loss

Closet full of their scent,
ghost presence at the table,
phantom slippered steps
triggering crushing grief.

Impossible to imagine,
more difficult to live through:
the world cannot have come
to this disaster. Could it?

Days marked
by a hollowed heart,
shaking knees, and
empty hands.

Anatomical reset
such a meager replacement
for the disruption
of this love story.

*—11 October 2020*

Most of us have to deal with losing someone we love at some point in our lives. In today's poem I tried to convey the sense of grief and world-changing perspective that accompanies any such loss.

# Scrabble Night

I see the letters
C A W
in my tiles
and make plans
to hook them onto
the free E on the board
when it's my turn again.
I savor the thought
of bringing a crow's voice
to the grid.
But Kim claims the E
with a word of her own
and my imaginary crow
falls silent

except for the
whoosh of air rushing
over black wings
as the crow flies overhead
following its own path
across the grid of land
spread out below it:
free of words or
letters or any hint
of human meaning.

*—12 October 2020*

The first stanza of this poem is a more or less accurate description of what happened during our Scrabble game last night. The second stanza is my flight of fancy, my attempt to extend the actual events into something poetic and meaningful. We were sitting outside this morning as I wrote this poem in my notebook. I then typed it into my laptop.

    Since Kim was mentioned in the poem I wanted her opinion. I don't normally solicit opinions of my poems, but in this case it felt right. When I read it to Kim I paused at the end of the first stanza and we both felt it came to an end at that point. I kept reading anyway, plowing through to the end of the second stanza. The original few lines of the second stanza went like this:

> except for the
> rush of air whooshing
> over its wings
> as it flies overhead

Note the absence of the word "crow" in those lines. Kim said the first stanza was solid, full of specific details that brought her into the poem. She liked that I brought a crow into the mundane world of a board game. That was the magic she saw in the situation and the poem. The second stanza did not have that quality for her. As I was reading the second stanza, her mind drifted and she did not find herself "in" the poem. For me, it was just the opposite: the first stanza felt like me being a reporter, telling what happened. The second stanza was the magic.

I then revised the first four lines of the second stanza to bring in more concrete words and detail: I mentioned crow, and stated the color of the wings. Kim then read it on the computer screen instead of hearing it, and she felt like it was fine. She saw connections between the stanzas (like the word "grid" in both) that she had not noticed when she heard it.

A good case can still be made for dropping the second stanza, but I'm keeping them both here for you to judge for yourself.

# Peaks

When mountains
by altitude or beauty
take your breath away

they turn it
into white snow
covering themselves

with your exhalations
in the color
of pure wonder.

*—13 October 2020*

The notion here was to examine the common phrase "takes my breath away." I considered things that do that: wondrous sights, beautiful visions, surprising turns of events, and so on. One of the big things that can take my breath away is a mountain. I think of the solid presence of Mount Saint Helens, the looming visage of Mount Adams, or the clean high lines of Mount Hood.

All of these mountains and many more can take my breath away figuratively by their majestic presence and they can do it literally by their altitude, drawing you up to the thin air at its lofty reaches.

# Before Blue

Bruises, drenched in red,
were much more alarming.

The sky constantly shifted
from yellow to green to violet
as though searching
for just the right color
but never finding it.

Robin eggs made
do with a pale and dull orange
verging on a camouflaging brown.

Blueberries were
mysteriously misnamed.

Picasso's famous early period
never materialized.

The most admired eyes
were hazel
and maybe they still should be.

Lakes were transparent
awaiting their ultimate hue.

And the deep crippling sadness
that overwhelms a soul
and pulls the world down
to your despairing core
was usually expressed
as having the grays.

—14 October 2020

I could have written this poem about any color (what color is an orange without the color orange?) but I picked blue because it seems particularly expressive, especially the idea of having the blues. My task in writing this one was to avoid repetition of the other colors I used in the poem. I made sure each one was used only once.

# Tornado Juniper

Twisted bark
turning the mosaic squares
of the alligator juniper
into a spiraled coat.
A whirlwind of rings
taking up the nutrients
of the soil
and swallowing down
the storm of solar heat.
Turning it all
into a sturdy cloud
of gray, as though
the air itself
was sculpting
this figure,
turning ephemeral wind
into the strongest
of woody bones.

*—15 October 2020*

While walking the trail at Madera Canyon this morning, I saw an alligator juniper all twisted with spiral lines that went around the trunk and gave the tree the look of a tornado ripping across the grass on the hill. As soon as I saw it I told Kim "Wooden Tornado" was going to be my poem for the day. It didn't quite turn out that way. "Wooden Tornado" was the original title, but after I wrote the poem I revised the title to what you see here.

# Visitor

You might think the light of other worlds
arrives as a brief guest when it lands here

in our world. But as it unpacks its luggage
of heat and illumination, you see it intends

to be more than an overnight visitor. It's
moving in, here to show you another way.

*—16 October 2020*

I began today by trying to write a poem about infinity. I was inspired by the first four lines of William Blake's "Auguries of Innocence:"

> To see a World in a Grain of Sand
> And a Heaven in a Wild Flower
> Hold Infinity in the palm of your hand
> And Eternity in an hour

My idea was to take off from that third line. I was going to confirm that infinity is in the palm of one's hand, then extend the notion to other aspects of the world, eventually making the point that infinity is everywhere, even in the smallest of objects, which is a nice paradox in its way, and something that a poem might express very well.

On my way to the poem, however, I lost my way. Or, at least, could not find the path to the lines. I filled up two pages of my notebook with false starts and rather uninteresting lines in an effort to find the heart of the subject. In the end infinity proved to be too big a topic for a poem, at least for me, today. Maybe another time.

So I started all over again, this time taking another big concept, light, and trying my hand at finding another way to look at it. Light is wild and unruly, relentless and bold. But it's also homey in it's own way. The soft light from a fire or the gentle illumination of a lamp next to a favorite reading chair are potent symbols of domesticity. Those contrasting aspects of light caught my interest and I tried to fit them both into today's poem.

# A New System of Pain

Close one eye and
if you see a green light behind your eyelid
everything is A-OK.
A yellow light means: Beware. Peril is close by.
Red indicates something is wrong:
your body is damaged and you have broken something
or you are bleeding and you must attend to it,
or the grief of loss is threatening to upend your world
with a crippling loss of power
and the abandonment of your will to go on.

Let's petition the universal regulator of pain
wherever that is
to at least consider such an approach.
If implemented, this scheme would be so much more pleasant
than the current method of causing extreme discomfort.
No one needs that particular universal,
truth or not. There are better ways
to connect with the life arrayed all around us.

*—17 October 2020*

---

Pain is considered one of those universals that all life seems to share, even though some people have a rare condition in which they feel no pain. Their lives, from what I have read, are in constant jeopardy because they have no good way of knowing if they are hurt unless they can see the wound or the site of the damage directly. Pain is an evolutionary adaptation, I suppose, designed to warn us and keep us alive. But why does it have to be so unpleasant?

In today's poem I speculate about the possibility of another conception of pain. It is a fantasy, obviously, but one I find attractive.

It is also my second take on pain in this book. The first one was on 12 August.

# Don't Ever Leave Me

The palm tree
and the sun
are in love.
How else
to explain how
they cavort
up there in the fronds?
Out of sight,
their private embraces
yield wild shivers
shaking and trembling
and raking the air.
Then at night,
pale moon lighting
the thin green
filaments fanned
out in the darkness,
no sound
comes from that
lofty perch,
as though the
palm is holding
its breath
awaiting its
one true love
peaking over
the eastern horizon
returning home.

—18 October 2020

Who knows what the private lives of plants are? Certainly not me. But it is fun to speculate. The palm tree in our back yard does get to shivering and shaking up at the top sometimes. Probably it's the wind that gets it going, but sometimes it might be the sun. The way the palm puts all it's greenery at the top of its trunk, as though yearning, reaching for the warm embrace of the sun.

# Things They Didn't Teach You in School

A pianist holds the keys to en-sound-enment;
remember the sea horse is a strangely shaped fish;
the dweller lives where it lives without shame;
instead of cyberspace live in fibrous space;
you must shrivel the past to enrich your future;
aiding a felon is not necessarily condoning crime;
the party begins only when the fiddler arrives;
homework usually gets in the way of learning;
mobilize the insects to liberate the world;
the root cellar holds the key to everything.

—*19 October 2020*

I believe randomness can be a boon to creativity so for today's poem I contrived an exercise in which I would accumulate a list of ten random words. I closed my eyes and fanned the pages of my spelling dictionary and put my finger on a page at random. It was pianist. I wrote that down. Then I repeated the exercise and got sea horse. I did this random word find ten times in total and came up with the following list:

pianist
sea horse
dweller
fibrous
shrivel
felon
fiddler
homework
mobilize
cellar

The idea was to try to get all these words into a poem. I played around with some connections: a shriveled sea horse, for example, or a fibrous fiddler. None of those connections proved fruitful.

Then I wondered if I could get all of these words into one sentence. I gave that a try, but it proved too unwieldy. Nothing much came of that approach. Finally, I gave each word its own line and tried to make something clever or imagistic out of it. I had fun with it.

Then I needed a title to bring it all together. As I read over my lines, they seemed like some kind of advice or lessons from a somewhat strange individual. They were things to learn. But they were things one would be unlikely to learn in school. Then I realized that was essentially my title.

# Hearing Aid

The planets strung out
on an unseen staff.

Notes struck high
in the heavens.

Music of the
spheres calling
down to your
ear drums:

the melody not
from this world,
but somehow of it:

redefining what
harmony denotes.

*—20 October 2020*

Today's poem started with the title. It came to mind as I sat down to compose today's poem and I typed it out immediately. It felt like a good poetic phrase: the name of an everyday object, but also a phrase full of potential meaning that had nothing to do with a physical hearing aid.

For example, the phrase could be saying something about listening to aid. What would aid sound like?

Or it could be asking the listener to help themselves to better hearing.

I took it to mean something like enhanced hearing, or hearing something that one wouldn't normally hear. In this case I remembered the phrase "music of the spheres" which I seem to recall was a thing in ancient astronomy, the notion that the heavenly bodies followed the harmony of musical scales. I took the meaning literally and gave the planets a song, of sorts, to lend more credence to the title. I had to look up what the five lines in musical notation was called, as I didn't know the term was "staff."

Then I tried to indicate how the music of the spheres, though foreign, is still a part of terrestrial hearing and therefore alters our perception of what music and sound is, and so voila!: hearing aid.

# Episode From an Unwritten Memoir

Sorting through the memories
I find an image
of a flat rock spinning
getting larger
looming like a humming spaceship
from a fifties movie
just before it hits me
half an inch
above my eye.
The thrower was clearly
an expert marksman.
Blood ensues
flowing like a red river
waterfalling over my eyebrow
into my eye
blinding me.
I'm maybe eight years old.
The kid who threw the rock
already long gone.
I walk home
maybe more of a stumble
than a walk
thinking how
the world looks different
tinged red
but also
how will I wash
all this blood
out of my white shirt.

*—21 October 2020*

I suppose lots of people have memories they return to again and again. This is one of mine. I was a kid in Northern Ontario playing near a pond that was at the base of a hill surmounted by railroad tracks. Another kid was walking along the tracks and saw me down below and began throwing rocks at me. I did not know he was doing this until I looked up just in time to get a rock in the face, exactly as I described it here in today's poem.

    I have used the incident in my short novel *Splitting*, and I recall that attack from long ago almost every time I cut myself or otherwise see my own blood.

# The Race

You don't have to run
if you don't want to.
Let the tape
wrap around someone else's chest
at the finish line,
trivial ribbon of victory.
Instead, look up
at the bark wrapped around
the tree, the green
pasted onto the leaves,
and the yearning
toward the sky
attached to the branches.

*—22 October 2020*

Today's poem began with the word "Medicine" as a title. I didn't know what I wanted to do with that word, but I liked the sound of it. I wrote down some rhymes for medicine that I might be able to use in a poem. This was my list: sin, fin, bin, kin, win, din, tin, pin, gin. Then I tried writing out some lines with these words. One of the lines was: We win the race when. I didn't know where to go from there, and it didn't feel like it had much potential. I let it sit on the page for a bit, and before long it suggested another line: The tape at the end of the race.

This second line felt like it could lead to something. I revised it a few times until it turned into the third, fourth, and fifth lines of today's poem. Then I fleshed that out with a few verses comparing a foot race to the reach of a tree racing up to the sky. I'm quite happy with the result.

## Good Eating

The termite exerts a sharp bite
on the ribs that keep houses upright.
No mere wood can dodge this dire plight
despite lumber's fabled strength and might.
All give way to termite appetite
as though it's the insect's birthright.
A ravaged house is a sorrowful sight,
collapsed from its once lofty height.
But do spare a thought for the termite,
and a grudging respect for its delight
in asserting its natural foresight
replacing sticks of dynamite
tearing structures down almost overnight.

—23 October 2020

Around here the saying goes that there are two kinds of houses: those that have termites and those that will have termites. I suspect some version of this saying is current in many parts of the country and the world. Today we saw a crawling insect on the floor. Our immediate thought: Is this a termite? Close inspection revealed that it was not. Whew.

With termites on my mind, I decided to use them as the subject for a poem. I've written a few poems about insects, some of them are in this book. Every time I do, I want it to be metered and rhymed, and often I like the rhyme scheme to feature the name of the insect if possible. Fortunately, the word termite ends in a common rhyming syllable and I was able to compose a light verse in which every line rhymes with termite. This was very satisfying to write.

I did not keep a consistent meter in the lines. I have a mix of eight-, nine-, and ten-syllable lines. I let my ear guide me in choosing line length, opting for a smooth and flowing rhythm when the verse is read out loud.

# Nothing Doing

Knife slices
through vacuum
separating voids.

The invisible cut
closes in on itself
a seam with no place to go.

Zero expectations
when there isn't anything
to see.

Like Utopia: ideal
imaginary country
awaiting ghost inhabitants.

Everything unseen
unheard unfelt and
infinitely remote.

*—24 October 2020*

I was considering some of the sayings involving the word nothing: Better than nothing; nothing of the kind; nothing doing; nothing matters; nothing to do with; nothing to lose; and so on.

Nothing is a strange concept in itself. What is nothing? The word is a noun, but a noun generally denotes something and nothing isn't something, so what is it? The absence of substance? Maybe the absence of everything? Nothing, in a pure form, may not even be possible. Space is nothing, but not really. Physics tells us it is filled with potential energy, which is certainly something, since we can name it.

I liked "Nothing Doing" for a title, so I wrote that down and then began to make observations about nothing.

I made today's poem short because I fear too much musing about nothing could get pretty tiresome pretty quickly. That's nothing I want to do to any reader.

# Theft

if you leave an object
on the beach

like a key, maybe
or your hat
a flip-flop
the coin from your pocket,
whatever

the sea will come in the night
like a sinewy pack rat
and steal it for its lair

*—25 October 2020*

A relatively simple image here: the ocean waves as thieves, grabbing up anything that isn't tied down on the beach and pulling it into the sea. I brought in the pack rat because some of that animal's characteristics are congruent with oceans and ocean waves. For example, pack rat societies are long-lived: some of their nests have been shown to be many thousands of years old, and, of course, the ocean is very old. Pack rats also move in a fluid motion, like waves undulating on the ground, mimicking to some extent the waves of the sea. Pack rats also like to grab up things that aren't tied down—especially shiny things—and take them to their nests, exactly as the ocean takes down things that are not properly moored and/or secured. So maybe this poem is as much about pack rats as it is about the ocean.

# Identity Gift

doesn't come
in a box with wrapping paper
and a bow

instead it arrives with your birth
attached to every cell
determining who you are

before anyone
tells you otherwise and
begins to dissect

you looking for
what they want to see
in your one true face

—26 October 2020


Here is an example of taking a common phrase—in this case "identity theft"—and turning it on its head by writing down its opposite and seeing where it leads.

# Benign Stain

Meaning seeps
into things
without you
noticing and
then no
amount of
scrubbing will
get the
memories out
of the
object or
out of
your mind.

*—27 October 2020*

I began writing a poem a day on 28 October 2019, so this is the end of my project: one full year of daily poems.

    The impulse was strong to try to do something grand as a culmination. Only thing is, the muses were not forthcoming with something grand. So, instead, I did as I have been doing for the past year: writing about what was readily at hand in my heart, my mind, or my life.

    Today's offering began with the concept of stain. The word has a mostly negative connotation, but it can also mean something more agreeable, as when a piece of wood is stained with a pleasing color. I liked the idea of making stain a good thing.

# Further Reading

Here is a list of books I either read or consulted during my year-long enterprise. Some are poetry collections, some are poetry anthologies, and some are books about poetry or about how to write poetry. All of them aided me in my project and I believe most of them would be useful to any poet.

Agodon, Kelli Russell and Martha Silano. *The Daily Poet.* Two Sylvias Press: 2013.

Akbar, Kaveh, *Calling a Wolf a Wolf.* Alice James Books: 2017.

Basho, Matsuo. *Basho: The Complete Haiku.* Jane Reichhold, trans. Kodansha International: 2008.

Behn, Robin and Chase Twichell, ed. *The Practice of Poetry.* HarperCollins: 1992.

Borzutzky, Daniel. *The Performance of Becoming Human.* Brooklyn Arts Press: 2016.

Boyer, Anne. *Garments Against Women.* Ahsahta Press: 2015.

Brehm, John, ed. *The Poetry of Impermanence, Mindfulness, and Joy.* Wisdom Publications: 2017.

Burt, Stephanie and David Mikics. *The Art of the Sonnet.* The Belknap Press of Harvard University Press: 2010.

Carey, John. *A Little History of Poetry.* Yale University Press: 2020.

Dante. *The Divine Comedy.* Clive James, trans. Picador: 2013.

Diaz, Natalie. *When My Brother Was an Aztec.* Copper Canyon Press: 2012.

Erdrich, Heid E., ed. *New Poets of Native Nations.* Graywolf Press: 2018.

Espada, Martín. *The Republic of Poetry.* W. W. Norton & Company: 2008.

Forché, Carolyn. *Blue Hour.* HarperCollins: 2003.

Harrison, Michael and Christopher Stuart-Clark, eds. *The Oxford Treasury of Time Poems.* Oxford University Press: 1999.

Hass, Robert. *A Little Book on Form.* Ecco: 2017.

Heaney, Seamus and Ted Hughes, eds. *The Rattle Bag.* Faber and Faber: 1982.

Helal, Marwa. *Invasive Species.* Nightboat Books: 2019.

Hirsch, Edward. *A Poet's Glossary.* Houghton Mifflin Harcourt: 2014.

Jackson, Major and David Lehman, eds. *The Best American Poetry 2019.* Scribner Poetry: 2019.

Kaminsky, Ilya. *Deaf Republic.* Graywolf Press: 2019.

Kaur, Rupi. *Milk and Honey.* Andrews McMeel Publishing: 2015.

Kaur, Rupi. *The Sun and Her Flowers.* Andrews McMeel Publishing: 2017.

Kay, Sarah. *No Matter the Wreckage.* Write Bloody Publishing: 2014.

Kinzie, Mary. *A Poet's Guide to Poetry, Second Edition.* The University of Chicago Press: 2013.

Kooser, Ted. *The Poetry Home Repair Manual.* University of Nebraska Press: 2005.

Kowit, Steve. *In the Palm of Your Hand: the Poet's Portable Workshop.* Tilbury House: 1995.

Lerner, Ben. *Angle of Yaw.* Copper Canyon Press: 2006.

Lerner, Ben. *The Hatred of Poetry.* Farrar, Straus and Giroux: 2016.

Lewis, Robin Coste. *Voyage of the Sable Venus and Other Poems.* Alfred A. Knopf: 2015.

Limón, Ada. *The Carrying.* Milkweed Editions: 2018.

Lockward, Diane, ed. *The Practicing Poet.* Terrapin Books: 2018.

Lovelance, Amanda. *The Princess Saves Herself in This One*. Andrews McMeel Publishing: 2017.

Mateer, Trista. *Aphrodite Made Me Do It*. Central Avenue Publishing: 2019.

Olivarez, José. *Citizen Illegal*. Haymarket Books: 2018.

Oliver, Mary. *Blue Horses*. The Penguin Press: 2014.

Pastan, Linda. *Traveling Light*. W. W. Norton & Company: 2011.

Perillo, Lucia. *On the Spectrum of Possible Deaths*. Copper Canyon Press: 2013.

Petrosino, Kiki. *Witch Wife*. Sarabande Books: 2017.

Rossetti, Christina. *Gobling Market and Other Poems*. Dover Publications, Inc.: 1994.

Ryan, Kay. *Elephant Rocks*. Grove Press: 1996.

Ryan, Kay. *The Niagara River*. Grove Press: 2005.

Silverstein, Shel. *Falling Up, Special Edition*. HarperCollins: 2015.

Smith, Carmen Giménez. *Be Recorder*. Graywolf Press: 2019.

Smith, Tracy K. *Wade in the Water*. Graywolf Press: 2018.

Strand, Mark, ed. *100 Great Poems of the Twentieth Century*. W. W. Norton and Company: 2005.

Turco, Lewis Putnam. *The Book of Forms: a Handbook of Poetics: Including Odd and Invented Forms, Revised and Expanded Edition*. Dartmouth College Press: 2012.

Trethewey, Natasha and David Lehman, eds. *The Best American Poetry 2017*. Scribner Poetry: 2017.

Vecchione, Patrice, ed. *Revenge and Forgiveness: An Anthology of Poems*. Henry Holt: 2004.

Vecchione, Patrice, ed. *Whisper and Shout: Poems to Memorize*. Cricket Books: 2002.

Videlock, Wendy. *The Dark Gnu and Other Poems*. Able Muse Press: 2013.

Videlock, Wendy. *Nevertheless*. Able Muse Press: 2011.

Videlock, Wendy. *Slingshots and Love Plums*. Able Muse Press: 2015.

Weinberger, Eliot. *19 Ways of Looking at Wang Wei (with more ways)*. New Directions: 2016.

Zollo, Paul. *More Songwriters on Songwriting*. Da Capo Press: 2016.

Zollo, Paul. *Songwriters on Songwriting*. Da Capo Press: 2003.

# About the Author

Mario Milosevic's distinctive byline
has graced anthos and mags both numerous and fine.
His collections and novels are some of the best,
but he won't agree since his demeanor's modest.
He's won some awards, but that fact's secondary
to his wordsmithing skills: he's so good it's scary.
Like most modern authors he maintains a website.
Browse mariowrites.com for further delight.

www.ingramcontent.com/pod-product-compliance
Lightning Source LLC
Chambersburg PA
CBHW081738100526
44592CB00015B/2222